BREWING BRITAIN

The quest for the perfect pint

www.transworldbooks.co.uk

Also by Andy Hamilton

Booze for Free

For more information on Andy Hamilton and his work, see his website at
www.theotherandyhamilton.com

BREWING BRITAIN

The quest for the perfect pint

Andy Hamilton

BANTAM PRESS

LONDON · TORONTO · SYDNEY · AUCKLAND · JOHANNESBURG

TRANSWORLD PUBLISHERS
61–63 Uxbridge Road, London W5 5SA
A Random House Group Company
www.transworldbooks.co.uk

First published in Great Britain
in 2013 by Bantam Press
an imprint of Transworld Publishers

A CIP catalogue record for this book
is available from the British Library.

ISBN 9780593072400

Addresses for Random House Group Ltd companies outside the UK
can be found at: www.randomhouse.co.uk
The Random House Group Ltd Reg. No. 954009

The Random House Group Limited supports the Forest Stewardship Council® (FSC®), the
leading international forest-certification organisation. Our books carrying the FSC label are
printed on FSC®-certified paper. FSC is the only forest-certification scheme supported by the
leading environmental organisations, including Greenpeace. Our paper procurement policy
can be found at www.randomhouse.co.uk/environment

Typeset in 11/15pt Fairfeld Light by
Falcon Oast Graphic Art Ltd.
Printed and bound in Great Britain by
CPI Group (UK) Ltd, Croydon, CR0 4YY

2 4 6 8 10 9 7 5 3 1

To my son Loki: I'll be proud of you whatever you do, unless you become a cider-drinker (and even then I might forgive you).

CONTENTS

Part Five: The Beers

Part Six: Directory

INTRODUCTION

Food in Britain has improved dramatically since the 1970s and the main reason for this is that our access to quality ingredients has increased greatly. Demand for such foods was fuelled after the Second World War by people like food writer Elizabeth David and chef/restaurateur George Perry-Smith, founder of the legendary Hole in the Wall restaurant in Bath (one of the first decent restaurants in the UK), both of whom helped to educate the masses about such exotic foods as avocados and bell peppers. During the 1970s these once rare ingredients gradually became commonplace and since those pioneering days chefs have been able to flourish, until now we have food that doesn't just equal that of our continental neighbours but surpasses it.

The same has happened with beer in the UK: a few changed a lot. In 1971 a group of fellas in Ireland who were not happy with the crap beer that was taking over started one of the most successful consumer lobby groups this country has ever known. We have Graham Lees, Bill Mellor, Michael Hardman and Jim Makin, the men who started the Campaign for Real Ale (CAMRA), to thank not just for saving our beer from bland, mass-produced mediocrity but for the vast array of beers available to today's discerning drinker. Home-brewers should also be grateful to writers such as David Line and Graham Wheeler, who in the 1970s were releasing books to help the home-brewer move away from making kit beers with bread yeast. They may not have had the sophistication of today's home-brew books but, combined with a love of our Ales, they were enough to influence a generation of brewers over in the USA.

As our cousins over the pond got a taste for our Real Ale, so the demand for home brew increased – the Americans, after all, had a much direr crisis with their commercial beer than we had with ours. First Charlie Papazian, founder of the Association of Brewers and the Great American Beer Festival, and in later years home-brew writer John J. Palmer have both fuelled a demand for better ingredients for all brewers. Many American home-brewers started microbreweries and are now flooding the world with (arguably) some of the best beer it has ever seen.

As this wave of beer from the USA influences home-brewers and commercial brewers alike all over the world, so ingredients are improving year by year. New strains of hops are being developed, malts and malt extract are of a consistently high quality and teams of yeast scientists are developing new strains that help reliably produce great-quality beer. This is indeed a brave new world for beer – but what does it mean for beer in our country?

When I set out to write this book I asked myself two questions: what does this country have to offer and what is the perfect pint? The title *Brewing Britain – the Quest for the Perfect Pint* then fell into place. Having completed the book I now feel that the perfect pint is something of a dichotomy: it can never be found and yet you always have it. The perfect pint is always going to be the one that you are enjoying right now – perhaps a sneaky lunchtime half of Mild, a mind-blowingly powerful IPA to start an evening, an Imperial Stout to finish one off, a Best Bitter amongst friends to celebrate a promotion, a Wee Heavy to warm the cockles after a trek through the snow, a refreshing Saison to quench a summer thirst, a crisp Lager after a hard day's graft, or even a few pints of Golden Ale at a beer festival with friends; each and every one is the perfect pint because they are all perfect for whichever moment you choose to have them.

But for this very reason the perfect pint can never be found, as your mood and situation will always change, new beers will come and go and tempt you, each being perfect at the right time. This means the quest for the perfect pint can never have an end – and it is this fact that makes it the most enjoyable quest possible.

This book will help you along that never-ending journey. It will take you on the same path of discovery that I took, looking at the bare bones of beers, taking them apart so you can really get to know what you are supping and, of course, learning how to make them. But it is also about trying other people's beer. Just as a good chef, chocolatier or wine producer will sample the produce of others in order to perfect their own, so any good brewer should try as much great beer as possible in order to influence their own style positively. There would be no use trying to create a Porter, Stout or Brown Ale had you never tried what they can taste like at their best.

ABOUT THIS BOOK

Think of the pages of this book as a brewery tour. Granted, it will be an in-depth tour, covering many aspects of brewing; and granted too, if you wanted to drink every beer you might have to put a year or so aside, give up your job and have a huge stack of cash. But this book is a brewery tour none the less and I invite anyone with any interest in beer to continue their personal quest for that elusive perfect pint as they follow it. Drinkers, kit brewers, all-grain brewers, brewers who want to garden, aficionados, and even self-proclaimed pub bores will all get something different from the pages that lie ahead.

As you may have gathered, you don't have to brew to enjoy this book; indeed, drinkers are invited to find out more about the ingredients just by drinking beers that contain them. If you do brew, then it should help you find out more about what ingredients you have been brewing with, and perhaps along the way also learn a thing or two about the beers you have been making.

The beers I mention may not be the best examples of the styles I have chosen to represent British beer, but they have been the tastiest I have found – my favourites, the ones that are now my main staples, the beers I'd happily serve to anyone. My desert-island beers, if you like.

The book has been split up into six parts, each giving you the extra layers of beer knowledge that will make drinking that next pint a full sensory experience. But before you begin, there is a very useful section called Understanding Beer Terminology that I'd highly recommend book-marking so that you can easily refer back to it. It will help you not only better understand what lies ahead but will also vastly improve your nuts-and-bolts beer knowledge.

Part One is written with the drinker firmly in mind and will help you really appreciate your favourite tipple, offering advice on tasting, pouring, storing, shapes of glass, buying beer and dealing with a hangover.

Part Two guides you through the brewing process and, as most people will start with a kit, so does this section, leading on to brewing using raw ingredients.

Part Three should interest anyone with a garden, an allotment or even access to a wild space. It strips back brewing beer even further, right down to the seed. This is the section for the gardening brewer, showing you how to grow and prepare the ingredients to make beer in their rawest form.

Part Four carries on naturally from this to cover the ingredients once they have been grown and prepared. Both brewer and drinker are guided through a range of flavours, with examples of the different hops and malts used in brewing and suggestions of beers that have used them.

Part Five forms the hub of the book: the main styles of beer available in Britain today. The history and origin of each style is covered, along with some examples of beers for you to try yourself. The drinker may only wish to sample each beer – but trying the beer whilst also trying to work out what has gone into making it really does, I think, improve the enjoyment of what already is one of the greatest pastimes on our planet. The brewer will find this section a useful source, too, as after each description there are recipes and tips on making your own, from kit suggestions to some amazing all-grain recipes. Using this together with the general instructions in Part Two provides an excellent toolkit for would-be brewers to get started.

The book rounds off with enough information to keep the drinker and brewer (or even the drunk brewer) busy for a long time, as it gives a springboard of information about beer festivals, websites, books and bottle shops to help you start on your own quest for the perfect pint.

Cheers and enjoy!

Andy Hamilton, 2013

UNDERSTANDING BEER TERMINOLOGY

As with any subject, the more you get into it the more jargon and terminology you meet. We brewers and beer geeks tend to forget that we are sometimes talking a different language, so instead of a glossary going at the back of the book as is normally the case, here it is at the start to help you understand the nuts and bolts of brewing terminology, and to help you get to grips with some of the trickier aspects of the humble pint of beer and of brewing. It is also worth a quick glance through to refresh your memory from time to time and then you'll be armed to tackle even the geekiest beer conversations you will come across in pubs, breweries, brew clubs, festivals and online forums.

ABV Alcohol by volume – very simply, the percentage of alcohol present in the beer. Most UK beers fall between around 2.5% and 10% ABV. There are beers brewed to a pointless 0%, but I'd rather not give them too much of a mention. At the other end of the scale, the Brewmeister brewery in Westhall, Scotland, produces a beer called Armageddon that is 65% and by all accounts is rather tasty!

Acetic acid It is acetic acid that is formed when beer exposed to the air goes all vinegary. Also carried by vinegar flies.

Acetification What happens when some or all of the alcohol oxidizes to acetic acid (see above).

Acidity The sourness, pH or total acid content of beer. It is measured by its hydrogen ion concentration. A pH reading of between 3 and 3.4 is the desirable level for typically British ales.

Adjunct Any fermentable sugar that isn't malted barley (see Malt, page 27). This can mean oats, wheat, maize, rye, corn, and sugars such as candi, brown and even granulated sugar, but it isn't limited to them.

Aerobic fermentation Also known as the 'first ferment', this is the quick, intense ferment in brewing when the yeast multiplies like mad. 'Aerobic' means 'with air' and this ferment occurs at the stages when the wort (see below) is covered loosely, allowing air to get in. See also 'Anaerobic fermentation'.

Aftertaste The taste that develops on the uvula at the back of the throat after you have swallowed your drink. It is also known as the 'finish'. See also 'Farewell'.

Alcohol The oldest manufactured psychoactive drug known to humankind, with the chemical formula CH_3CH_2OH. There are, of course, different types of alcohol, but the one us brewers are interested in is ethyl alcohol.

Ale In the past, 'Ale' meant any beer that wasn't hopped. It is now synonymous with 'Real Ale' and CAMRA. Broadly speaking, it is any beer made with top-fermenting yeast strains rather than bottom-fermenting yeast (see below).

All-grain brewing Brewing with just grain and no malt extract.

Alpha acids Often abbreviated to AA, these are acids present in hops that impart bitterness. When your hands get a yellow sticky substance on them after handling hop cones (flowers) it is because of a resin in the hop called lupulin. Alpha acids are found in this resin and they therefore make up a certain percentage of what's in the hop, hence the AA% on the side of the hop packets bought from reputable sources.

These alpha acids are made up of other chemicals, each of which imparts a different type of bitterness to the beer. The two most important are humulone, which in high levels is thought to give beer a 'clean' bitterness, and cohumulone, which in high levels is thought to give it a harsher bitterness. It has to be noted that the bad reputation of cohumulone is down to one suspect study in 1956; subsequent studies have suggested there is no harsher bitterness from hops that are high in cohumulone. This apparent myth unfortunately, for some hop growers, still prevails.

Ammonium phosphate Yeast nutrient.

Anaerobic fermentation Also known as the 'second ferment'. Slower than the initial stages and with the exclusion of air. See also 'Aerobic fermentation'.

Aroma Often when I walk into a pub the smell of beer will send me back to what turned out to be my well-spent youth. The sense of smell is powerful and primitive; it needs to be – it has kept humans alive for many generations. If you have ever smelt rancid meat and nearly gagged, then that is your sense of smell keeping you safe.

When we drink (beer), the aroma will trigger our olfactory system long before our sense of taste is triggered. But the aroma will also be the last thing we sense, as the residues of the compounds we first smell feed back into the nose on the farewell (see below).

Fruit, floral and alcohol aromas are some of the easiest to smell from a beer. Aroma is the smell of beer, but it can be so much more than that.

Aroma hops Hops used late in the boil or during dry-hopping (see below) which add to the aroma (see above) rather than the bitterness of the beer. Essentially the terms 'aroma hops' and 'bittering hops' are over-simplifications, but they work as a shortcut and brewers will know what you are talking about.

Attenuation Yeast is a sugar fungus and it consumes sugar. Generally it will consume between 65% and 80% of the sugar, depending on the strain (type) of yeast and gravity (strength) of the wort (unfermented beer). Different beers need a different balance of sugars against the other ingredients in order for them to taste true to style. A Mild, for example, needs some residual sweetness and so is considered properly attenuated when 65% of the sugars have been consumed, whereas a Lager is closer to the style when more sugars have been consumed and so is drier. A Lager yeast strain might therefore consume up to 90% of the sugars before it has reached an attenuation considered true to the style.

Balanced A beer is said to be balanced when the level of hops and the level of sugars (from the malt) are in perfect harmony. The opposite might be called 'jagged' or 'disjointed'.

Balling A scale used to measure the density of a liquid in comparison with water.

Barm The now antiquated term used to mean the scum on the top of wort when fermenting (see below). Once used to make bread, and ancestor to many yeast cultures – which is perhaps why it was also once used in place of the word 'yeast'. Used as a verb it can also mean to add yeast or to 'pitch' (see below).

Barrel During the war people used to roll out barrels in order to have a barrel of fun. The modern equivalent would be 136.274824 litres (of fun).

Batch A batch of beer simply means the amount of beer that you make in one sitting. A batch could mean a 1-pint batch or a 10,000-litre batch, or more, as there is no specific measurement. In this case a cigar is just a cigar.

Bead The bubbles in beer.

Beer God's greatest gift to man and, according to the great Homer (Simpson), the cause and the solution to all of life's problems. Less emphatically described as any alcoholic beverage made from the fermentation of sugars that have derived from grain.

Beta acids Bitter acid found in hops.

Bitter wort Wort (see below) with bittering agents such as, but not exclusively, hops.

Bittering hops Hops that are added at the start of the boil and will add more in the way of bitterness than aroma to the final beer.

Bladdered To be drunk after drinking too much alcohol.

Body The body is related to how dense the beer feels when you drink it. It can be an element of the 'mouthfeel'. An example of a full-bodied beer might be a Stout, as it can feel thick and creamy as you drink, whereas often Lagers can feel light or thin-bodied in the mouth. This is partly due to carbonation and higher levels of attenuation (see above). Or in plain English: there are more unfermented sugars left in a beer with a fuller body.

Boil (the) This is simply the stage where you boil your wort (see below). Most beers are boiled, although in the specific brewing period known as 'the days of yore' beer was heated with hot stones as they didn't have metal to boil the wort in. Nowadays most beer, or rather wort, needs to be boiled before it is fermented in order to sterilize it and isomerize the alpha acids (see above) from the hops. Put very simply, this means that in order to get the compound from hops that makes beer bitter, you need to boil them in the pre-fermented beer.

Amongst other things, boiling also concentrates the wort, removes unwanted volatile chemicals that can mess up your beer and sterilizes your wort, making it less prone to infection.

Bottom-fermenting The process of fermenting, normally – but not exclusively – by a Lager yeast that ferments on the bottom rather than producing a beer cap. Bottom-fermenting usually occurs at lower temperatures.

Bottoms Arses, or in brewing terms the deposits of yeast and other solids formed during fermentation.

Brew Another word for 'ferment' when used to describe beer fermentation. Also used to mean the final product, as in 'I'll have a brew.'

Calcium sulphate One of the chemicals that gives water permanent hardness. Commonly called gypsum or plaster of Paris.

Campden tablet A tablet about the size of an aspirin that contains about 7g of potassium metabisulphite. When dissolved it releases sulphur dioxide. It is used to sterilize and as an antioxidant.

Cap The lid used to seal a beer, such as a crown cap.

Caramel Sugar syrup darkened by heat and used as a colouring for dark beers.

Carbon dioxide It is said that during the fermentation process the yeast pisses alcohol and farts carbon dioxide. It is the gas that is formed when fermenting, and it is trapped in or added to the bottles or cask in champagnes and some beers and ciders. It is what gives beer its head and champagne its fizz.

Carboy A 20–60-litre (35–105-pint) glass or plastic container with a narrow opening at the top. Also known as a demijohn and usually fitted with a rubber bung and airlock. Comes from the Persian word *qarabah*, meaning 'big jug'.

Cask Traditionally, a small oak barrel used to store beer or wine. These days casks are made from stainless steel, aluminium or plastic and are predominantly used for Ale. The most common size of cask in use in the UK holds 40.9 litres (72 pints/9 gallons) of liquid and is known as a firkin.

Cask ale Also known as cask-conditioned beer. Unfiltered, unpasteurized beer conditioned and served from a cask without adding carbon dioxide or nitrogen pressure. This is the type of Ale for which the Campaign for Real Ale (CAMRA) have very successfully campaigned.

Cellar A cool, dark place used to store beer or wine. It does not have to be under a house just as long as it keeps an even temperature and has no light entering it.

Chambré At room temperature.

Clarify To make beer/wine/any drink clear of any nasty bits floating around in it, such as hazes caused by excessive pectin, or cloudy beers. A clarified beer can also be called a 'bright beer'.

Conditioning The act of leaving a beer to stand in order to allow it to develop its optimum temperature and carbonation level. Ales are warm-conditioned, which helps further develop the complex of flavours. Lagers are cold-conditioned or 'Lagered', which helps to impart a clean, crisp taste. Conditioning happens in three steps: maturation, clarification and, finally, stabilization, and can happen in the cask or bottle.

Copper The copper is the vessel in which the brewer will boil wort (see below). So named as they always used to be made of copper. Also known as the kettle or hot liquor tank (HLT).

Crown cap The metal stopper used on beers with edges crimped over the mouth of the bottle.

Cutting Stopping fermentation.

Decant To pour liquid from one container to another without disturbing the sediment.

Demijohn A glass or plastic container used for the secondary fermentation of wine or beer. In the UK they are usually a standard 4.5 litres (1 gallon) and are clear glass or plastic. In the USA a 4.5-litre 'carboy' (see above) is known as a jug.

Dextrin A short starch molecule produced during malting and mashing. It is residual dextrins that contribute to the body of a beer.

Dextrose See Glucose.

Diastase A complex of Malt extract (see below).

DMS Diastatic malt syrup. Malt extract containing some diastase (see above), used to convert the starch in the adjuncts (see above) to sugar.

Draught Spelt 'draft' in the USA, this is seemly beer that is served from a cask or keg rather than a bottle or can.

Drop clear To clarify spontaneously.

Dry The taste of beer when very little or no sweetness can be detected.

Dry-hopping Adding hops after vigorous fermentation or conditioning (see above) to give the beer extra aroma or hop character. Dry-hopping normally occurs during the last five days in the fermentation vessel. Not to be confused with teabagging, which is something altogether different.

EBU European Bittering Units – see 'International Bittering Units' below.

End point When mashing grains, this is the moment when all the starch has been converted into maltose and dextrins.

Enzyme A protein that helps cause a complex molecule to change into a simpler one. Enzymes are essential in the fermentation process.

Esters Flavour compounds in alcoholic beverages that give fruit and fruity flavours. There are a few different esters in beers: isoamyl acetate, which gives a banana-like flavour; ethyl acetate, which can give a range of flavours, from good ones such as fruity to flavours akin to nail-polish remover; ethyl caprylate and caproate for apple flavours, the latter also giving notes of aniseed; and phenethyl acetate, which adds rose and honey flavours. Esters are produced during fermentation and brewers will pick specific yeast strains in order to produce particular flavours.

Farewell This is really a wine term used to mean 'aftertaste' (see above) but can also be used to describe beer aftertaste by big ponces like myself.

Final gravity (FG) The stage after all fermentation has ceased. FG is deduced when the hydrometer (see below) gives consistent consecutive readings over a period of time (normally a couple of days), even when moved to a warmer spot.

Finings Any substance mixed to the wort (see below) or must that clarifies.

Finishing hops Hops added during the final moments of boiling to impart flavour or aroma to beer.

Flat A bubble-free, lifeless beer.

Floater What's left in the toilet that won't flush down. Alternatively (and equally unwanted), a minute particle of debris floating in beer.

Flocculation When yeast nears the end of fermentation the cells will form clumps containing thousands of yeast cells. This will then fall to the bottom of the fermenting vessel forming sediment and leaving the beer nice and clear. If this clumping happens too early the beer will be sweet, and if it doesn't happen – or doesn't happen sufficiently – the beer will be 'yeasty' and cloudy. Yeast strains are often classified as low-, medium- or high-flocculent strains. Most yeasts used in British Ales are high-flocculent strains.

Fobbing When a lively beer foams continuously out of a bottle after being over-primed (see 'Priming' below) or kept too warm.

Fret To re-ferment in the bottle, cask or barrel.

Fructose Fruit sugar.

Gelatine Also known as 'gelatin'. A translucent, colourless, brittle (when dry) solid derived from the collagen found in animal skin and bones. Used as a fining agent (see above).

Gelatinization The process of making starch soluble during mashing (see below). Normally used in reference to boiling adjuncts (see above).

Glucose A fermentable grape sugar also known as dextrose.

Glycerol Also known as 'glycerine'. Produced during fermentation and often used as an additive to dessert wines to make them richer and smoother.

Goddesgoode Meaning 'God's gift' – an antiquated name for yeast.

Goods The porridge-like mix of grist (see below) and hot liquor.

Gravity Abbreviated version of 'specific gravity' (see below).

Grist Ground malt and other adjuncts (see above).

Gyle Unfermented wort (see below) that is put aside to be added later to finished beer in order to condition it (see above).

Hard water Water with a high mineral content, much sought-after for brewing certain Ales.

Haze A lack of clarity in beer due to tiny particles of matter that remain in suspension. Often caused by pectin, starch or protein.

Head The foam on top of a beer.

Headroom The space between the top of the wine or beer and the cork, bung or cap. Sometimes referred to as the 'ullage'. Also, surname of the first computer-generated TV personality, first name Max.

HLT The abbreviation for 'hot liquor tank' – the tank your wort (see below) is boiled in.

Hop-forward This is a relatively new phrase that helps to reflect some of the recent changes happening in available ingredients, namely, hops. It helps to describe beers that make heavy use of high alpha acid (see above) New World hops, typified by breweries like BrewDog, Summer Wine Brewery or, to give one random beer example, Durham Brewery's Magnus Bitter. Of course in all these breweries there is more going on than just hops, but it's a useful phrase to pop into a beer conversation instead of just saying 'hoppy'. As the alpha acids (the stuff that makes the beers bitter) degrade over time, hop-forward beers will lose their character unless they are of Imperial strength (9% and above).

Hops Cones or flowers of the hop (*Humulus lupulus*) bine used to add bitterness and to preserve beer.

Hydrometer Could also be called a 'sacchrometer', as it is an instrument used to measure the sugar content of a liquid.

Hydrometer jar A narrow jar made of plastic or glass perfectly designed to float the aforementioned hydrometer.

Helles German for 'light', as in colour.

Home brew That which is brewed at home and, according to the great Charlie Papazian, something with which you should relax, not worry and have fun (I agree, and you will too).

Home-brewer You (let's hope).

Inhibit A fermentation is inhibited when the action of the yeast is prevented.

International Bittering Units (IBU) A system for measuring bitterness devised by brewing scientists and used as an accepted standard across the planet, with 1 IBU equal to 1mg of iso-alpha acid in 1 litre (1¾ pints) of beer or wort.

Invert sugar A mixture of the two mono-saccharides glucose and fructose. It is obtained by splitting sucrose and it ferments immediately, so is often used for priming (see below) or the final stages of brewing.

Irish moss A seaweed used to clear beer.

Isinglass A substance taken from the swim bladders of fish used as a fining (see above) in beer and wine.

Isomerized This is the chemical process through which one molecule is transformed into another with the same atoms. In brewing, the alpha acids (see above) in hops are isomerized (to become iso-alpha acids) when boiled and this happens through a series of chemical reactions. The iso-alpha acids present are minute, at up to around 100ppm (parts per million), but they have a huge effect on flavour.

The reason we get more IBUs (bitterness – see above) when we boil hops for longer is that more alpha acids get isomerized.

Kiln A building used to dry malt after germination, or to dry hops.

Krausen The foamy head that develops on the surface of the wort (see below) in the open days of fermentation.

Krausening Priming (see below) beer using unfermented wort (see below) instead of sugar.

Lactose Milk sugar. Unfermentable sugar used to sweeten wine and beer.

Laevulose Fructose (see above) .

Lager Derived from the German *lagern*, meaning 'to store'. Taken to mean a bottom-fermented beer brewed at comparatively (to Ale) cold temperature and stored for a period of time.

Lagering Ageing a beer.

Lager yeast *Saccharomyces uvarum*. A specific strain of beer yeast that ferments best at 0.5–10°C (32.5–50°F) and does not flocculate (see above).

Lambic A Belgian style of beer infected with a bacteria that gives it a sour taste.

Lautering The process of removing spent grains or hops from the wort (see below). It is done by sparging (see below) and straining.

Lees Sediment.

Liquor Brewers' term for water.

Lupulin The yellow powder found at the base of the hop flower (or cone) that contains the oils and resins that give hops their bitterness.

Magnesium sulphate Also known as Epsom salts, this is added to water to improve the quality and increase the acidity of the liquor. Also used in recipes where fermentation can be a challenge. Not a great nutrient on its own, but when combined with other yeast nutrients it can enhance their rate of fermentation.

Malt Also known as malted barley. Partially sprouted and then dried barley. In this process its starch has been changed to maltose by diastase (see above).

Malt-forward This is just a progression of terminology and should be fairly self-explanatory if you understand the term 'hop-forward' (see above). Malt-forward beers are beers in which the malts are the predominant characteristic. Milds are a classic example, as are Wee Heavies such as Traquair House Jacobite. If you want to drop 'malt-forward' into a beer conversation, make sure that you are describing a beer which has strong tastes, such as biscuit or roast flavours, coming from the malt to save you looking a bit daft.

Maltase An enzyme that changes maltose to fermentable glucose.

Maltese Someone from Malta.

Maltose A sugar produced from starch by the action of diastase (see above).

Malt extract A syrup or dry form of concentrated maltose and dextrin. It is derived from mashing barley and dissolving evolved sugars in water. Both are made by evaporating water from mashed barley.

Malted barley See 'Malt'.

Mashing The process of converting grain starches to fermentable sugars by mixing grains with hot liquor, then keeping the liquor at a set temperature between 60°C and 71°C (140°F and 158°F) for a set time.

Mash tun Also known as a 'mashing bin'. The vessel in which mashing takes place.

Maturation The perfection of wine or beer through ageing.

Mulled Heated but not boiled wine, cider or Ale with added spices. Often drunk during the winter months in the northern hemisphere.

Muselet The wire cage that fits around a cork and keeps it in place on a champagne, cider or sometimes strong beer bottle.

Musty The off taste caused by mould in cask or bottle.

Nose All that can be learnt from a drink by smelling it.

Nutrients Mineral salts, vitamins and trace elements needed by yeast for most favourable fermentation. Also known as yeast nutrients or, at the most simplified, yeast food.

Original gravity The specific gravity of wort prior to pitching the yeast.

Osmotic shock Exposing yeast to too much sugar, often with fatal effects.

Oxidation Exposure of beer to the air, causing discoloration and sometimes off and/or stale flavours. The high alcohol level in some Barley Wines and strong beers can make oxidation a characteristic rather than a problem, though in lower-alcohol pale beers it is almost always a fault.

pH   Stands for 'power of hydrogen'. A measure of alkalinity or acidity on a scale of 1 to 14, where 7 is neutral. The pH balance in water (liquor) is managed by brewers to enhance yeast performance.

Pitch   To add yeast to the wort (see below) so that it can get to work turning it into beer.

Plato   A more exact version of specific gravity (see below) used by commercial brewers.

Polishing   A very suspect old style of filtering beer using asbestos.

Potassium metabisulphite   An additive (see 'Campden tablet') used in beer and wine to inhibit the growth of wild yeasts, bacteria and fungi.

Potassium sorbate   Used with potassium metabisulphite to stop fermentation.

Primary fermentation   The initial fermentation where between 60% and 75% of the sugar content is turned into alcohol.

Primary fermenter   Vessel in which primary fermentation happens.

Primer   Sugar or sugar solution that re-starts fermentation in the bottle or keg just enough to carbonate.

Priming   The process of adding sugar or sugar solution to a wine or beer in order to carbonate it.

Proof   The measure of alcohol in wine or spirits. 100% proof = 57.06% ABV (see above).

Quart   Quarter of a gallon, or roughly 1 litre.

Rack(ing) The process of moving partially fermented wort (see below) or must from one fermentation vessel to another by siphon so that it is not fermenting on yeast sediment.

Reinheitsgebot Pronounced *Rine-Hites-gaBoat* and translating as 'purity law', Reinheitsgebot is a law that originated in 1487 in Augsburg, Bavaria (and by 1516, at the decree of Duke Wilhelm IV, applied to the whole of Bavaria), stating that beer should be made out of just three ingredients: barley, hops and water. It was still thought that fermentation was a spontaneous process and therefore yeast was not recognized as an ingredient. Many German brewers still abide by the law and every beer geek should at least know how to pronounce it.

Respiration Metabolic and aerobic cycle performed by yeast before its fermentation cycle, during which oxygen is stored for later use.

Ropiness An oily appearance in beer or wine caused by lactic acid bacteria. Thankfully, fairly rare.

Rouse Stirring to mix thoroughly in order to bring air to the wort (see below) or must, normally to wake up sluggish yeast.

Saccharomyces Literally, 'sugar fungi' – the family name for yeast.

Sacchrometer An antiquated term for hydrometer (see above).

Saint Arnold of Metz Saint who said, 'Don't drink the water, drink beer.'

Saint Patrick Patron saint of home brew. Seriously!

Secondary fermentation The stage that precedes bottling, when the last 25–40% of fermentation happens. It is much less active and therefore does not create a protective layer of carbon dioxide, meaning the wort (see below) or must is vulnerable to airborne contaminates and so is generally kept airtight.

Sediment Insoluble substances that settle at the bottom of the wort (see below) or must, or even beer or wine, during fermentation and storage. It is made up of dead yeast cells and decomposing ingredients. Also known as 'trub'.

Session The short description of a 'session beer' is simply a beer that can be drunk, in quantity, over a drinking session without the drinker becoming too hammered. In other words, low in ABV (see above) and with pleasant yet not too strong flavours so that the drinker can consume one after another.

For the longer explanation, a drinking 'session' has to be defined. When I first started going to the pub there were two drinking sessions, between 11am and 3pm, and then from 7pm to 11pm. This was a hangover from the First World War, when pubs were only open from 12 noon to 2.40pm and 6.30 to 9.30pm. So a drinking session would never be more than around four hours. Most drinkers will consume, on average, a pint every half an hour. This means that around 8 pints can be drunk in the average session, so any beer over around 4% is going to get anyone but the most hardened of drinkers hammered.

In 1988 some pubs could apply to open for longer and this was the end of the four-hour drinking session and the start of the twelve-hour one. My local at the time, the Racehorse Inn in Northampton, didn't open all day until 1993 and when this happened we celebrated the event by going on our first all-day session. See Hangovers and Hangover Cures (page 57).

Sessionable A beer with an ABV of 4% or below (5% for Northerners, as they are a little bit harder) is said to be of a 'sessionable' strength, meaning that many can be drunk during a drinking session.

Siphon A plastic tube used to remove wine or beer off the sediment. As a verb it means the action of siphoning.

Sparging A hot-water rinse at the end of the mash (see above) in order to remove all the maltose.

Specific gravity (SG) The weight of the must or wort (see below) compared specifically with water.

Star-bright A most brilliantly clear beer.

Starter A batch of already fermenting yeast added to wort (see below) to initiate fermentation. See page 209 for how to make a yeast starter.

Sterilize A process of cleaning that rids equipment of as many bacteria, wild yeast and other contaminants as possible.

Straining Using a sieve, muslin cloth or both to remove solids.

Stuck fermentation A fermentation that stops before it has finished.

Sucrose Ordinary cane sugar.

Sulphite See 'Potassium metabisulphite' and 'Campden tablet'.

Sweet Term used to describe a beer that contains some residual sugars; the opposite of dry.

Sweet wort Wort (see below) without bittering agents.

Tannin Astringent polyphenolic compounds (substances) from the skins, pips and stalks of grapes that act as a preservative and gives a slight bitterness.

Tartaric acid The acid of grapes and bananas which helps in the maturation process.

Thin A watery beer that lacks body.

Top-fermenting Fermenting on the surface of the wort (see below).

Trub Proteins precipitated from the wort (see below) during boiling. See also 'Sediment'.

Ullage See 'Headroom'.

Vinegar fly *Drosophila melanogaster* – little bastard flies also known as fruit flies that are often the source of acetic infection.

Wort The mixture of malt and herb or hop essences in liquor prior to fermentation – in other words, unfermented beer.

Zymase The name given to apo-zymase, a complex of enzymes secreted by yeast that are responsible for turning sugar into alcohol (fermentation).

Zymurgy The science of yeast fermentation.

PART ONE

The Drinker's Guide to Beer

1

TASTING BEER

'AN AUTHOR SITTING sharing a beer with a couple of builders . . . beer is a great leveller,' mused a builder with whom I shared a pint in a pub in Cambridge. He was right, as undeniably one of the greatest things about beer is that it cuts right through the silly class divide that exists in our country. Pubs have always been places where rich builders can share in the enjoyment of beer-drinking with poor authors or where gentry can have a pint of the usual with the workers after a hard day. But when we start creating parallels with wine by doing things like having tastings, then are we not in danger of at the very least a *poncification* of beer – creating a divide between different beers and therefore a divide between different beer drinkers? Are we in danger of the gentrification of this drink of barbarians and thereby of turning some beers into a drink for snobs and elitists?

Well, no, not at all. For a start beers are generally not as expensive as wines and most will fit into a similar price bracket. A beer is best drunk within a few months, or in some cases a few years, but never a few decades like wine. This means that beer can never be a long-term investment and therefore should always be accessible to everyone. Beer-tasting, in my experience, is much more about mutual enjoyment than about one-upmanship. Or at least it should be. Learning to taste the subtle and not so subtle flavours in each hop, the sweetness of the malts and the interplay between the two just adds to the enjoyment of beer. Learning to taste rather than drink a beer is a great skill, and is available to anyone who can afford a beer and has a working tongue and olfactory system rather than a big bank balance.

According to Jane Peyton from the School of Booze, 'The nose and palate can be trained to recognize aroma and flavour so lots of practice is required! But some people have a condition called "onosmia" (smell blindness) and unless a person can smell properly then they will not taste properly so should not try being a professional taster.'

HOW TO TASTE BEER

The first step into the beer-tasting world is very easy: just sit back and really think about what you have in the glass, bottle or even can in front of you. Pause and give your beer some of the true reverence it deserves. Take the time to work out what you are smelling, what you are tasting and how it feels in your mouth. It really is that simple; it's just a different approach. You can even do it with food to get you started. Swap your knife and fork from your usual hands; you'll eat more slowly and will taste the food more. The reason is that you have to think about what you are doing, and it's the same with tasting instead of just drinking beer.

Improve your skills further by starting to think about the glassware you serve it in. If you only have pint glasses, don't worry, but do consider how clean they are. My friend and fellow beer writer Zak Avery suggests in his book *500 Beers* that 'dishwasher clean isn't good enough, as the residues on the glass will at least spoil the head on the beer, and at worst will interfere with the aroma and flavour of the beer itself'. Putting this to the test and serving the same beer in identical glasses, one dishwasher clean and the other cleaned with washing-up liquid, thoroughly rinsed and polished with a crisp cloth, I found that there was more than a noticeable difference.

If you are tasting at home with your own or shop-bought beer, then you can choose the type of glass you serve it in. Any glass that is tulip-shaped will do the job – but you could also ensure you have the right glass for each beer (see pages 44–48).

At a professional tasting or when judging beers, you'll also swirl it around in the glass and give it a good look. Take notes on the colour, whether it is clear or not, how dark or light it is, whether there are any other colours. Also, this is a chance to get your nose right in there. If trying a bottled beer, I like to sniff straight from the bottle, putting a nostril over the neck after removing the cap. This gives me a little edge before really working the aromas in the glass.

Keep swirling, as this helps to release aromas, and keep sniffing. Don't be afraid if the beer doesn't really smell of anything – some Lagers really don't, and even some Ales are so delicate that it takes a bit of practice before you really do smell anything. Remember, though, that other smells, especially strong ones like tobacco smoke, also affect what we taste – so although the smoking ban might be considered the biggest culprit behind pub closures (along with successive idiot chancellors), it might actually be helping to fuel our demand for better beer. Because pubs are no longer filled with smoke, we can now taste our beer. If you don't believe me, hold your nose and take a sip of beer. What did you taste? Nothing? So look around wherever you are tasting and ensure that there are not any overpowering smells. I remember once smelling wet dog on a beer in a country pub, only to look down and see one staring right back at me from under the table. Keep smells from barbecues, aftershaves and perfumes at bay. Further advice from Zak Avery is always to taste beers indoors, away from any rogue smells.

Jane Peyton also suggests you 'Take a sip and let it sit on the tongue for a few seconds. This will warm the drink/beer and release aromas which then travel from the mouth into the olfactory glands in the nose. A few seconds later the brain will register the flavours.' Tom Spencer, an Aussie friend who works in the wine trade, also taught me to bring air over the beer. Hold the beer in your mouth and suck a little air over it. Close your eyes if you have to; although you may well get mercilessly teased if you are doing this in your local, get all Zen on the beer if you can. Be just you and the beer. The tastes will come dancing out.

If you are still not really getting it (or even if you are), try drinking with friends, as everyone picks out different flavours and this will further what you are tasting. Some of the comments I've written about the beers in this book come from a selection of drinking partners who helped me to select the beers for this book and they picked out the subtlest of flavours I may otherwise have missed. You'll be surprised at what people notice and point out (I was). Even my next-door neighbour, who mixes orangeade with cheap cider as his drink of choice, was picking out flavours that existed only as tiny details of beers. What is really interesting, too, is just how collective beer-tasting can be. If someone says, 'Er . . . mango, I think I can taste mango,' often everyone else tasting the same beer will agree (as long as it is evident). Try it next time you are in the pub.

It may also help to have a list of flavours and aromas that you might be able to pick out to help you get started. Beer-taster, author and aficionado Melissa Cole rightly bemoans the phrases 'hoppy' and 'malty' when applied to a beer, as they don't really mean anything ,and I'd add the word 'bitter' too, yet you'll see these descriptions everywhere, from beer blogs to the sides of bottles and in beer-festival programmes. What kind of malt or hops and what sort of bitterness can you taste? Is it a piney hop, a marmalade bitterness, a caramel malt? Otherwise it's similar to describing music as 'notey'. Can you imagine being down the pub and hearing, 'Went to a great opera at the weekend. It was very notey,' or picking up the music press to read 'Chvrches, the Glaswegian electro three-piece, have been wowing audiences across the world on their latest tour with lyrics using words and full-on electro-notiness through their music-playing from the keyboards'. You just wouldn't, and nor should you hear or read such lazy descriptions of beer.

As each of us experiences things in a different way, it can be difficult to tell people what they might be tasting. For a start, each taste needs to relate to the foods you know. For some a flavour might resemble a ripe mango picked fresh whilst on holiday in West Bengal; for others the same flavour would be like an Um Bungo drunk in the pouring rain at Stockport bus station.

Not only are our experiences of flavour different from everybody else's, but there is even a theory that our own tastebuds change depending on what our body needs. For instance, an account from a dehydrated and starving Steve Callahan, who was stranded at sea for seventy-six days after his 21-foot sailing boat capsized, suggested that he found a taste for fish eyes. To him these slimy bits of fish offal took on a delectable quality and he craved them as his food of choice. There isn't a fish-eye-equivalent beer, but bitter receptors can become more acute depending on diet.

There are still some aroma/flavour descriptions that tend to be fairly universal and hopefully, if nothing else, these will get you started. You might also want to cross-reference the hops in the hops chapter with single-hopped varieties of Ales in order give yourself a crash course.

- Aromas/flavours from hops: herbal, floral, spicy, tropical fruit, piney and blackcurrant.

- Aroma/flavours from malts: chocolate, nutty, biscuit, caramel.

- Bitterness: marmalade, dandelion, astringent.

Occasionally, you'll be experiencing flavours and aromas that the brewer didn't intend. I had many whilst writing this book! The most memorable was one that tasted so strongly of nail-polish remover that I had to chuck it after one sip. It would pay to familiarize yourself with some of the off flavours that can manifest in beer – turn to Detecting and Dealing with Faults and Off Flavours, page 101.

Do remember, though, that a little knowledge can be a dangerous thing. I recall one fella at a beer-tasting evening dismissing a beer out of hand for being off; he even offered some advice on how to rectify the problem, involving more hygienic brewing conditions. The beer in question was a Belgian Lambic which has been deliberately infected. He kept quiet after that, a little too embarrassed to speak. To make sure you are not that person, there are guidelines available online covering every style of beer. The Beer Judge Certification Program (BJCP) is the one used by most home-brewers and descriptions can be found on their website, bjcp.org. However, this is biased towards American beers and SIBA (Society of Independent Brewers Association) is a more British-centric organization that also offers beer descriptions on its site.

The final thing you really need is experience. It can take time to hone your tastebuds. I have to admit it took me quite a few beers until something clicked and it all dropped into place. But at least you can use the excuse that you are becoming a beer-taster when you have to argue the need for that one last pint.

THE COLOUR OF BEER

If someone handed you a pint of Lager and it was black, or a pint of Stout and it was pale, even close to white, then you might well hand it back to them (although both do exist). Over the years we have grown accustomed to specific beers being specific colours, ranging from a pale straw yellow (which has the standard reference 4 EBC) for a pale Lager to a Stasi brown (24 EBC) for a bitter, right up to almost jet black (138 EBC) for an Imperial Stout.

EBC stands for European Brewery Convention and is the accepted beer colour-measuring scale across Europe. It replaced the Lovibond scale created by J. W. Lovibond in 1883, which involved holding a series of coloured glass slides up to the beer and comparing the colour. This was, of course, liable to subjective observations by whoever was holding the glass slides, especially if they were too stubborn to admit they had colour blindness.

Lovibond wasn't replaced completely, however, and it is still sometimes used today when measuring the colour of grain. To confuse matters further, the Americans measure to a different scale – the Standard Reference Method (SRM) scale. This mirrors Lovibond, in that if a beer is 10 Lovibond it is also 10 on the SRM scale. EBC is approximately double that of SRM/Lovibond (it's actually 1.97). So a pale Lager is 2 SRM and 4 EBC and a very dark Stout 40 SRM and 79 EBC.

HOW AND WHY BEERS TASTE DIFFERENT IN DIFFERENT GLASSES

Most of the bestselling beers have their own specially shaped glasses. Think Guinness and you think of that almost vase-shaped pint glass, thinner at the bottom and rounder at the top. Kölsch Lagers from Köln (Cologne) come in small, beaker-like glasses; Stella use a posh-looking oversized wine glass that some clever marketing bod has named 'a chalice'; and who can forget their first taste of the Belgian beer Pauwel Kwak, served in a glass with a rounded bottom supported on a wooden stand? They all create an experience, an engagement with the beer that goes beyond taste, and all create a look, a recognizable brand.

During the time of the Black Death in the fourteenth century, beer mugs were fitted with a lid, examples of which can still be found in the tourist shops of Bavaria. These lids kept out flies (and presumably plague-carrying fleas too) and so the drinking vessel you used was a matter of life and death. These days cynics suggest that branding and marketing are the only reasons for choosing different glasses and in some cases this is of course true. But it goes beyond that. The right glass can actually enhance the beer you are drinking. Some even suggest that drinkers should be demanding the right glasses, as we are being short-changed on the taste front if we don't get the proper ones.

THE STANDARD NONIC PINT GLASS

Near cylindrical, with a slight bulge near the wide mouth. Cheap to make and easy to collect and store in stacks, it's little wonder this is the landlords' glass of choice. The bulge serves a few purposes, none of which affects the taste: the grip is improved, it prevents the glasses from sticking when stacked, and it stops the rim from being nicked – think 'no nick', or 'nonic'.

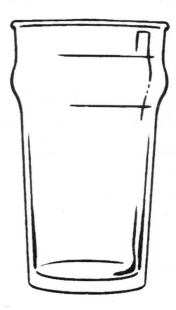

Suitable for most classic Ale styles.

BEER MUG

Invented in the 1960s, the classic beer mug had fallen seriously out of fashion by the time I was drinking pints in a pub in the late 1980s/early 1990s and was nowhere to be seen. Which is perhaps why I now get rather excited if I'm offered a pint out of one. The heaviness of the glass, the big handle, the array of dimples all add up to enhance my drinking experience. They don't do anything fancy and won't really improve the beer, but that is no reason to shun them completely.

Suitable for most classic Ale styles.

WHEAT BEER GLASS/ WEIZEN GLASS

Whilst in Romania I was served a Wheat Beer. The barmaid poured a head twice the size of the beer and seemed to be very proud of it. It was served in a beer mug and so I had to wait about half an hour before I could tackle my drink without fear of looking like Father Christmas. If it had been served instead in a long, cylindrical Wheat Beer glass, I could have got at my beer and stayed foamy-beard-free. So the shape of this glass has a very practical purpose: long and cylindrical offers the head space to move whilst allowing the drinker to pour the beer down their gullet.

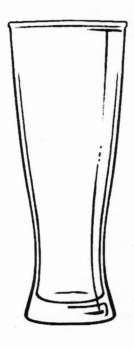

You may also see bar staff rinsing the glasses before pouring gently at an angle, as both these things help to control the head, which should be large but not excessively so. Unlike many other beers, the yeast sediment in a Wheat Beer will actually add to the flavour and keeping a head on the beer will ensure the yeast fills the glass with aromas without actually entering the beer. The flaring sides of the traditional glass will also funnel any aromas up to the drinker's nose.

It is also true to say that the shape of the glass helps to accentuate the clove and banana aromas that are indicative of the style. You could even add a grain of rice to your beer, just like any good Bavarian would, as this will help it keep its head!

Suitable for Wheat Beers.

SNIFTER

Whilst these are great for swirling an expensive brandy around, they can also be used to capture and enhance the volatiles of strong Ales. The volatile aroma compounds will stay trapped in the glass rather than evaporating out as they would in a straight glass.

Suitable for Barley Wines, Imperial Stouts, Imperial IPAs, Old Ales and Wee Heavies.

PILSNER GLASS

Tapered inward from top to bottom, Pilsner glasses are designed to help the beer keep its head, thus enhancing the hop aroma and extenuating the bitterness. The long glass will showcase the clarity of the beer too. As bubbles form due to dust particles trapped on the nicks in the glass, often Pilsner glasses will have marks etched into the bottom of the glass.

Suitable for Blondes, Saisons, Pilsners.

TULIP GLASS

These are starting to become fashionable in some of the Craft Ales bars and pubs, where often all beer will be served in them. The curved edge helps to keep the rich aromas inside the glass, releasing them almost in a puff as you sip. This makes it an ideal shape for beers that are full of complexity. Something like Magic Rock's Imperial Stout or Bearded Lady, or Harviestoun Ola Dubh 30 with all

their rich aromas and flavours will taste significantly better if drunk from a tulip.

The tulip shape also helps when swirling the beer, as the aromas will get activated and will stay trapped in the glass due to the smaller opening at the top.

A slight variation of the tulip glass can also be found in Scotland, and that is the thistle-shaped glass. It works in a similar fashion and is great for capturing the richer complexities of Scottish beers.

Suitable for Imperial Stouts, Imperial IPAs and barrel-aged Ales.

SERVING BEER

The glass will make a difference to the taste of your beer, but not as much as the temperature at which you serve it. Remember that the next time someone serves you a Stout or Porter from the fridge, as many of the subtle flavours and nuances of aromas will be muted at colder temperatures.

To ensure you get it right, here is a guide to correct temperatures and some suggestions about how to obtain them in the British climate. (If you live in a warmer or colder country, you may wish to adapt this accordingly.)

4–7°C (fridge): Lagers

8–12°C (fridge, then taken out whilst drinking another beer): Bitters, Golden Ales, Blondes, IPAs and Pale Ales

12–14°C (kitchen cupboard): Porters, Stouts, Milds and Tripels

14–16°C (room temperature) Barely Wines, Imperial Stouts, Old Ales

STORING BOTTLED BEER

There would be little use spending your hard-earned cash (or even your ill-gotten gains) on a very special beer only to ruin it by storing it improperly or for too long. Some of the better bottled beers are now starting to have a 'born on' date and you should try to drink them within three months of that. Unfortunately, these are few and far between. Where there is no guideline, think about what is in the bottle. A beer full of hop character will need to be drunk within a few months or it will start to change. That said – and hopefully without complicating things – you might want a subdued hop character, in which case let it sit for longer; but remember this is unlikely to be how the brewer intended it to be drunk. Weaker pale beers also need to be drunk within a few months.

But not all beers are equal. Some will not only keep better than others but will improve the longer you keep them. Old Ale, for example, is meant to be aged. As a good rule of thumb, anything above 7% ABV can and probably should be aged for a while. Generally speaking, over a year will be too long. However, there are always exceptions that break this rule. Check with the brewery if you are not sure.

Different beers will also benefit from being kept at different temperatures, all within a range of a steady 10–13°C (50–55.4°F). As a rule, the higher the ABV of your beer, the higher the temperature at which you can keep it. However, that doesn't mean you should ever keep beer at too high a temperature: try not to let it get above 25°C (77°F), whatever type it is.

If you have a cellar or a cool larder, then either will be ideal. For everyone else, it can be difficult, so aim for the closest thing possible and keep the following two suggestions in mind:

Keep your beer away from any fluctuating heat sources – so not near a draught, oven or at the back of a fridge.

Keep the bottles upright and away from any bright light. Beers in anything but brown glass should be kept away from any sunlight and/or indoor lighting to save them from skunking (see page 106) – though, again, this is all a matter of taste, as it has been reported that many people actually like a beer that has skunked.

2

DISCOVERING NEW BEERS

YOU MIGHT THINK it is very easy to find beer – you've no doubt been finding it for a few years. It's everywhere, and you can just walk into any corner shop with an off-licence or into a pub and ask for a beer. However, if you want to try something different then the task can become a little more difficult, as more often than not you'll just see the same few beers from the same few massive breweries. I'm not saying there is anything wrong with these, but to be on your own quest for the perfect pint you'll need to know where the rarer beers are hiding. So really we are talking about finding new beers from smaller and artisan brewers, and by their very nature these are not to be found everywhere.

Once you do find a pub or shop with a suitable array of beers that are new to you, the variety can be bewildering. How do you choose? How do you know that you are coming home with something worthy of your hard-earned money? Luckily, there are some simple and straightforward ways of searching that can help turn the simple act of buying a beer into an adventure involving new tastes, aromas, experiences and styles.

Of course this book is one place to start. After each of the beers I recommend I've also suggested where you might be able to buy them; in some cases this includes specific pubs. This is meant just as a guide, as beers are not always kept on tap and some will even, in time, go out of production.

SPECIALIST HIGH-STREET BOTTLE SHOPS

These places are often out of the central areas of towns and cities and therefore need to be hunted out; the Directory at the back of the book will help (see pages 374–80), and with luck you'll find a bottle shop near you. If there isn't one in your area, then perhaps ask your local wine merchant, as many are starting to sell a select range of beers. If they don't, suggest that they do!

When you do find your bottle shop, I'd strongly suggest going on a weekday afternoon if you have the chance, or failing that then as soon as they open on a Saturday or Sunday morning. This is because these are generally quiet times and you'll have a chance to talk to the people who work there. They will know their stuff, and what's more they are generally more than happy to talk beer until the cows come home or until another customer demands their attention.

If you don't see what you like, or you don't really know what you're looking for (or at), then describe some of your favourite beers to whoever is working and get them to make suggestions of similar beers, or ask them to recommend what they like. If you don't want to spend a fortune then make sure you tell them so; a good bottle shop will have some beers at eye-wateringly high prices. That said, if you pay more there is more chance that you will get an extraordinary beer: oak-aged limited-edition runs don't come cheap. But these sorts of beers are often best put on a Christmas or birthday list.

Lastly, sample some of the suggestions throughout this book if your bottle shop stocks them. A good idea might be to try one beer of each of the styles I recommend, invite some friends round and a share a bit of each one. I'll often do this when researching a brewery or area and you can whittle through a lot of beer that way (depending on how many friends you have). It can be a very enjoyable evening. You can always go back and buy more of the favourites.

OFF-LICENCES/CORNER SHOPS

Conventional off-licences or corner shops will stock a limited range, often the same few beers from the same predictable breweries. However, if you notice that your shop displays tins of macaroni cheese next to organic baked beans and has rice milk sitting next to Polish sauerkraut, then the chances are it will be run by the sort of forward-thinking owners who will happily buy in stock for their customers and, as long as it sells, will continue to do so. You could give them a list of your favourite breweries and the number of a good wholesaler (see Directory, page 379) to make life easier for them and up your chances of getting beer at your local shop.

PUBS AND BARS

Still the most enjoyable place (in my opinion) to drink beer is a pub or bar with friends. You'll no doubt have your favourites, but if you are new to an area, just visiting or want to explore something different, then pick up your local CAMRA magazine and look for suggestions. The magazine is distributed around CAMRA pubs and many issues are available online as pdf files. The ones I've read will always have details of a local pub crawl that a member has been on, along with an account of what they drank.

If you join CAMRA yourself, often good pubs will give you a discount when buying their beer. Look out too for *What's Brewing*, CAMRA's monthly newsletter, which is available online from the CAMRA website and is also delivered free to CAMRA members. Turn to the back pages for details of beer festivals, pub crawls and other beer-related events.

Websites like perfectpint.co.uk allow you to search for places that serve your favourite beer. beerintheevening.com is one of the better pub-review sites, but do ensure that you are looking at up-to-date reviews as changes in management can turn a bad pub good and vice versa.

Lastly, just ask the punters themselves. A seat at the bar can be a great place to be if you need information. Ask whoever is serving and other drinkers will join in. Or even just ask on the street . When the Beer on the Wye Festival got flooded out in 2012 we found ourselves in need of an alternative. We stopped people on the street and asked for a 'Real Ale pub' and had a great mini pub crawl around Hereford.

BREWERIES

Over in America many breweries will have a bar attached. They welcome visitors and often offer tours that end with a few drinks. Some brewers over here do the same and others are starting to catch on and offer a few beers on their own taps, but as yet these are few and far between. Still, it is worth searching online to see if your favourite brewer does have a bar, as there is nothing like drinking a beer with the brewer.

If your brewery doesn't allow piss-ups, then check their website. Some will offer bottles or polypins (small, pressurized barrels, the modern equivalent of the Party Seven can) direct from their site, or they will at least link to a website that does sell their beer.

BEER FESTIVALS

See The Year in Beer Festivals, page 361.

ONLINE

The online world has revolutionized how we buy beer and should not be ignored. Finding out about beers and buying them can both be done without leaving your seat.

BLOGGERS, TWITTER AND FACEBOOK

In the Further Reading section I have mentioned some of my favourite bloggers. They can be great for filtering out beers that might not do it for you, or for finding true gems. I'd suggest picking out bloggers that live in your area, as not only will they blog about local breweries but they will often mention beer festivals, special events and limited-edition runs from some of the breweries nearby. They can be your eyes and ears in the beer world. A well-run blog will have an RSS feed, the option to sign up to a newsletter, and/or an attached Twitter feed that will tell you when the blog is updated so you don't physically have to check their pages every day. When you do find a good blog it can be worth trawling their archives, as there are bound to be some beers you'll want to hunt out.

Then there are the breweries themselves. They don't just embrace new ingredients, but new technology too and, as Twitter can be a relatively cheap marketing tool, most breweries will have a feed. Pubs and bottle shops too will often tweet guest Ales and new arrivals.

As many good pubs and bottle shops are always looking for new beers and brewers want to sell their beer, it is even worth mentioning them both with the @ sign in a tweet to get them talking. I've successfully arranged for a barrel or two of my favourite beers to come to me by doing this! (In case this is nonsense to you, the @ symbol is placed before a name, in my case @Andyrhamilton, and if that person is mentioned in a tweet it means that they will see you have mentioned them and can respond.)

Facebook is another option and often the very small breweries will maintain a Facebook page rather than have any other web presence. Just search Facebook to find them and make sure you 'like' a brewery page in order to get updates.

ONLINE BOTTLE SHOPS

Many good bottle shops and pubs will have an online presence – see the Directory, pages 374–80. The downside compared with your own local shop is that you don't get chance to chat, but the upside can often be a wider range. Always ensure that they deliver to your area before spending your time carefully choosing your favourite beers. I've abandoned many carts after reading the small print! You might also want to check postage costs before you finish your order – every bottle shop seems to operate a different system, from cost per twelve bottles/case to a flat fee. A few offer free delivery but will reflect that 'saving' in the cost of the beer.

3

HANGOVERS AND HANGOVER CURES

'I can't drink like I used to' is the morning-after cry of many a beer drinker as he or she grows older. Other drinkers report that the more often they drink the less severe their hangovers. Far from being idle observations, both these statements are rooted in fact and both are due to the same chemical enzyme called alcohol dehydrogenase.

Alcohol dehydrogenase is released from various locations around the body as we drink, including the stomach lining and liver, helping to break down the alcohol in beer before it enters the bloodstream. Young people and regular drinkers produce more of it and so their bodies are dealing with less alcohol the next day, therefore their hangovers are not so bad.

There is one little ray of hope for rest of us, and that is that hangover headaches will get less severe as we get older. The reason, however, is less than hopeful: it is because our brains are getting smaller as we age. Alcohol makes the brain swell and bang against the skull causing a headache; less brain means less of it will hit the skull.

The best natural hangover cure should really start the night before. Over in the States they have the right idea and many bars also sell food. Food helps to soak up the booze, and fatty foods are ideal because they take longer to digest and so will help protect your stomach against the irritating effects of alcohol for longer.

Whilst drinking, try to have a glass of water for every unit of alcohol consumed as a preventative, anti-hangover measure; fizzy drinks are not advisable as they actually increase the amount of alcohol heading into your bloodstream. Alcohol acts as a diuretic, increasing the flow of urine from the kidneys, and so leads to dehydration. It's this dehydration that causes some of the tell-tale signs of a hangover, such as dizziness, dry mouth and nausea. Increased bladder flow can deplete valuable vitamins and minerals like potassium, vitamin C and various B vitamins. What's more, due to a change in brain chemistry there is an increase in REM (rapid eye movement/dream) sleep which means your brain has been falsely excited and this can lead to depression and anxiety.

The depleted vitamins and minerals have to be replaced in order for you to start feeling human again. Potassium can be reintroduced by eating bananas, potatoes, spinach or mushrooms. Vitamin C can be found in chillies and bell peppers, strawberries, oranges and kiwi fruits.

The loss of vitamin B12 when drinking can bring on feelings of guilt which sometimes plays a part in the psychological side of a hangover. B12 can be found in eggs, bacon and black pudding, which is why, if you can get it down you, a fry-up always helps. Eggs are doubly a good idea as they contain Cysteine and evidence is emerging that suggests this chemical will counteract the poisonous effects of acetaldehyde, a by-product of alcohol metabolism that is responsible for many of the long-term adverse effects of excessive intake of alcohol. Or if you want to try an ancient Greek hangover cure, how about fried sheep's lungs?

If even the thought of sheep's lungs is causing your stomach to churn, then a dose of ginger and cardamom tea will help. If you can't get even that down you, then pour the tea on to a flannel, let it cool and place it directly on to your stomach.

Food cures are much better combined in a breakfast and I often make friends a 'full Andy' after a night of beer-tasting gets out of hand. This consists of bacon, sausage and black pudding for the B12, all fried in dripping (more B12 and some fatty acids) with bell peppers, mushrooms and spinach. Then I crack two eggs on the top and finish off under the grill.

Alongside the breakfast I make the following tea, which can be drunk freely throughout the day. Normal tea and coffee are not advised as the caffeine in both will dehydrate you further.

Andy's Hangover Tea

INGREDIENTS
thumb-sized piece of bruised root ginger
10g (¼oz) rosemary
10g (¼oz) nettle leaves
handful of pine needles
3 green cardamom pods
500ml (17 fl. oz) hot water

1. Boil the kettle. Put all the ingredients into a teapot and cover with hot water. Allow to infuse for 5 minutes. Meanwhile, hold head and say, 'Never, ever again.'
2. Pour through a strainer into a cup. Allow to cool then sip. This will make two cups and you can also keep topping up the teapot and drinking it all day until you start to feel a bit more human. Couple it with drinking plenty of water.

If nothing seems to work then go back to bed for a bit and try to get some normal sleep. Also take some good-quality vitamin B-complex tablets.

Of course if any of my sensible suggestions don't sound like your bag, you could always try a hair-of-the-dog method. My favourite is a Roman one which consists of 5 litres of wine infused with 16 bulbs of garlic.

PART TWO

The Brewer's Guide

4

USEFUL METHODS AND TECHNIQUES FOR BREWERS

T HERE ARE A few methods and techniques in brewing that, if you are an experienced brewer, you'll be able to do in your sleep as they are the same for each batch of beer. These are some of the fundamentals of brewing, but as a novice brewer you may, at first, struggle with them. But don't despair – brewing really is pretty straightforward and once you get your head around just a few simple techniques you'll be making perfect pints every time.

CLEANING AND STERILIZING

Brewing is, of course, a science, which means it's not always exact; which is possibly why, depending on which brewer you talk to, you will hear that good brewing is all about anything from 50% to 90% cleaning. It's true: cleanliness – or, rather, good hygiene – is fundamental to producing a good pint. Get this wrong and you will never make good beer.

The reason for this is that wild yeasts and bacteria, which are not just all around us but in us too, are happily waiting to infect our pint unless we prevent them from doing so. It does perhaps sound a little paranoid, but I'm afraid it's true; and if you don't want all your hard work and ingredients to deteriorate into something at which even a dog in a desert might turn up his nose, then you'd better adopt some good cleaning and sterilizing practices.

WHAT TO CLEAN AND WHAT TO STERILIZE

Throughout its history beer has been a source of disease-free liquid. The simple fact is that when liquids are boiled it helps kill off any pathogens. In the past, this has meant beer drinkers avoided cholera by drinking beer instead of water. For brewers it means that you don't have to be too OCD about anything pre-boil. It makes sense to break up the cleaning regime into two camps: items that need to be clean and items that need to be sterile. That is not to say that everything won't benefit from a good thrashing with a sterilizing solution now and then – it's simply good practice.

Clean: Mash tun, paddle, boiler, thermometer (in the mash).

Sterile: Fermenting vessel(s), lids and airlocks, siphon, thermometer (chill onwards), hydrometer and jar, yeast starter jar (if using) and any measuring equipment, wort-chiller, bottles, barrels, caps, bottling bucket and bottling wand.

HOW TO CLEAN

I tend to clean using either hot soapy water for bigger items or the dishwasher for smaller items. Normal washing-up liquid is fine to use. **Everything** should be cleaned of all visible deposits.

When cleaning use a nylon brush for bottles and a cloth for everything else. Don't be tempted to use anything abrasive, as scratches can harbour bacteria and wild yeasts. Also, make sure you rinse very, very well after using soap, as soapy-tasting beer is not the best beer in the world.

HOW TO STERILIZE

Having wasted plenty of beer due to improper sanitary conditions, I adopt the belt-and-braces technique. After I finish a brew I rinse everything I have used to be sure it is clean of all traces of anything. Before I use anything I make sure it is clean and I also spray it with Star San (see below). On top of that, after every fourth brew day I soak everything in a bleach solution. When not in use everything is covered with a plastic sheet.

Star San

This is an acid-based, no-rinse sanitizer. It is made from food-grade phosphoric acid (E338), which is used in some soft drinks. 'No-rinse' means you can spray a diluted solution on to your equipment without having to rinse it off.

To use Star San, I dilute as directed on the bottle and pour some into a spray gun. This is then squirted over whatever I am using, making sure that every bit that comes into contact with the wort/beer is covered. It can be used on all equipment.

Bleach

The bleach solution I use is VWP. I dilute it, fill a fermentation vessel with solution and soak whatever needs sanitizing in it.

WHAT DOES 'SPARGING' MEAN?

When you mash your grains there are some sugars left on the husks, so you'd be throwing money away if you didn't 'sparge' or rinse them off so that they end up in your wort ready to make beer. Around 1½ times the amount of water you used for mashing is normally used to sparge, and this needs to be heated to 74–77°C (165–170°F).

There are two different ways of sparging. The technique I have mentioned above is known as 'batch sparging'; the other method is 'fly sparging'. In some cases beer is made without sparging at all, though this is an expensive business as you won't get as much sugar from the grain, but the resulting beer is richer and smoother and can feel like velvet on the tongue. All the breweries I have visited use fly sparging – that is to say, a rotating arm gently sprays the heated sparge water over the grains and the brewers run this water off, allowing continuous movement. When the gravity of the runnings reaches between 1.010 and 1.005 then stop. (Home-brewers tend to sparge to 1.010.) This technique is open to home-brewers too, but it involves either creating your own fly-sparge arm or buying in more equipment. However, since fly sparging is more efficient than batch sparging, if you are brewing a lot of beer you'll soon make up the cost difference.

WHY CHILL?

Chilling your wort is very important. In days of yore brewers didn't bother, and in days of yore beer was often slightly funky due to infection. Wort that is boiling, wort that is fermenting and, to a lesser degree, wort that has become beer are all less prone to infection. But until your yeast gets started, your wort is open to whichever wild yeast or bacteria might be passing by, so it is imperative to create the right conditions for the yeast to survive as soon as is humanly possible. Fast chilling also causes a 'cold break' which will help reduce chill haze and increase your beer's shelf life.

There are three different types of chiller available: immersion chillers, counter-flow chillers and plate chillers (which are essentially very small, very efficient counter-flow chillers).

An immersion wort chiller

Immersion chillers are made of long metal pipes, normally copper, which is coiled. The coil is dunked into the boiling wort and cold water passes through the metal tubing; since it has a large surface area, the pipe rapidly cools. Heat is taken out of the wort and warm water will run from the other end as the heat is sucked from the beer. It is like having cold feet put on your leg in the middle of the night!

A counter-flow chiller is also a coil but with some silicone, or just hose-pipe piping, covering it. Cold water is pumped through the silicone and the wort is siphoned through the inner piping in the opposite direction. This cools the wort very quickly.

Plate chillers are awesome bits of kit and work using the same counter-flow principle, but instead they do it on a micro-scale and will chill from 100°C to 18°C (212°F to 64°F) in the blink of an eye.

Immersion and counter-flow chillers can both be made at home, and I'd suggest looking for online videos for ideas on how to make yours.

YEAST STARTER

A yeast starter is made 12–24 hours before fermentation and it helps the wort to ferment quickly, thus avoiding it being open to infection.

The day before you brew, mix 200g (7oz) of dried malt extract into 2 litres (3½ pints) of water. Bring this to the boil and keep it boiling for 15 minutes. Cool it rapidly in a sink full of iced water, then pour it into a sterilized container – a half-size demijohn is ideal. Pitch your yeast and attach an airlock. You now have a yeast starter ready to pitch on your cooled wort.

For a more comprehensive guide to making a yeast starter, see page 209.

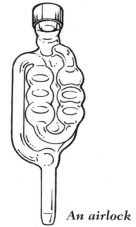

An airlock

PITCHING YEAST AND FERMENTING

You will need to pitch your yeast at as close to 21°C (70°F) as possible for an Ale and at around 16°C (61°F) for a Lager.

After you pitch, it will go through various stages before fermentation is finished. First is the 'lag' phase, which can last up to 15 hours after initial pitching; this leads into the 'exponential growth' phase and finally the 'stationary' phase.

I've gone into more detail on the lag phase in the yeast chapter (see page 205), but essentially it is the period when the yeast cells will absorb what they need to grow more cells. It is very important to ensure that the yeast cells have enough oxygen at this point – you will need to aerate the wort, getting oxygen into it. This can be done by shaking, stirring or using an aquarium pump. I have gone into more detail in the yeast chapter (page 211).

After the lag phase, the yeast cells start to consume the sugars in the solution, creating CO_2 and other compounds: this is what causes the layer of foam on top of the beer, and it has also been known to blow the tops off fermenting buckets! This is the exponential growth phase, during which the cells actually 'bud', creating daughter copies of the original cells. Ideally you should keep the fermenting vessel at around 20–22°C (68–72°F) for an Ale and 7–13°C (45–55°F) for a Lager, with closer to 10°C being ideal. This process lasts for about four days for an Ale and up to three weeks for a Lager. It is essential to try to keep both at constant temperatures. In practice, this means keeping a regular eye on your thermometer and using a duvet wrapped around your bucket or, in the case of a Lager, adapting a fridge.

The stationary phase follows on as the yeast growth starts to slow down. This phase is sometimes referred to as the 'conditioning' phase, since it is when the yeast slowly consumes some of the flavours associated with young beer. Different yeasts will ferment at different speeds and every brewer will ferment at slightly different temperatures, but to ensure that your beer has conditioned properly wait until there is no yeast activity and the gravity has stabilized (when you have identical hydrometer readings over two consecutive days), then give your Ale a two-day rest before bottling or kegging. Lagers will benefit from a 'diacetyl rest', which you can provide by raising the fermentation temperature to 20°C (68°F) for two days. Diacetyl is a compound produced during fermentation, a by-product of the yeast. If you don't give your Lager this rest you might suffer from buttery flavours. The fermentation temperature for Lager should then also be reduced at a rate of 1°C (1.8°F) per day until it reaches 4°C (39°F). If possible, Lagers should be kept at this temperature for a month or more.

For more on pitching yeast, see page 208.

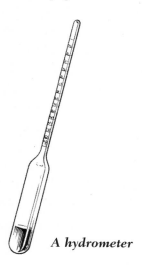

A hydrometer

PRIMING

When your beer is ready, the final step before putting it into bottles or kegs is 'priming' – which is basically adding just enough sugar to reactivate the yeast and allow a little more fermentation in the bottle or keg. With nowhere to go, the small amount of carbon dioxide produced from fermentation stays in the beer and carbonates it.

Older books (including my own, *Booze for Free*) will suggest that you add sugar to each of the bottles – a process that takes ages! It is far easier to boil 250ml (8 fl. oz) of water and dissolve the sugar in that, allow it to cool, then add the sugar solution to your bottling bucket before pouring over your wort. Or, if bottling straight from your fermenting vessel, gently stir the sugar solution in, trying not to disturb the trub (crap on the bottom).

Any sugar will do the job: granulated, honey, molasses, malt extract or brown sugar. Stronger-tasting sugars, such as honey and molasses, will impart a flavour to your beer – great if that is what you are after and a bit of a pain if not. Honey can contain varying amounts of sugars, but a good rule of thumb is to use about 1 tablespoon per litre (1¾ pints). Dried malt extract (DME) will be around 75% as efficient as sugar, meaning you have to use more – about half as much again. This means for every 1 teaspoon of sugar you'll need to use 1½ teaspoons of DME.

Alternatively, you could use carbonation drops, which are essentially sugar lumps made with priming sugar. Use 1 drop per 500ml (17 fl. oz) bottle, or 1½ drops per bottle of Lager.

When you carbonate, the bubbles help to accentuate some flavours and carry some of the delicate aromatics that emanate from the hops. As this is not always appropriate to the beer style, different beers require different carbonation levels. Below is a simple guide to help you carbonate some of the beers in this book. The amounts are per 500ml/1 pint.

Barley Wine, Old Ale: 2.4g (0.09oz)
Best Bitter: 0.5g (0.02oz)
Brown Ale, Mild, Porter, Stout, Pale Ale, IPA: 4.3g (0.15oz)

AN ALTERNATIVE WAY TO PRIME

Vince Croker from the Ashley Down Brewery passed on this little trick. After making a wort, at the stage after he has pitched the yeast he fills 1.5-litre pop bottles with unfermented wort, then refrigerates them. The refrigerated wort is then poured back into his casks before they are sent out. The wort re-starts just enough fermentation to give some carbonation to the beer. The same principle could of course be applied to home-brewing – I've just not got round to doing it yet!

BOTTLING OR KEGGING

Once your beer has been brewed you have to think about how it's going to be served: bottles, keg or Cornelius (see below).

What you choose to keep your beer in will largely depend on what you intend to do with it and on personal preference. There are a few things to consider when deciding.

If, like me, you like to give friends beers as presents, then unless you are so generous that you give away a whole keg, bottles are the way forward. Also, most brewing competitions will ask for two (or more) bottles from participants.

If ageing a beer, then a keg will work better than a bottle as the larger size reduces temperature fluctuations and there is no light absorption. However, if space is an issue it is much easier to squirrel bottles away all over the place than it is to store a big old keg.

If you are short on time, then using a keg is much, much quicker. It can take over an hour to bottle a batch of beer and, especially if you use an auto-siphon, kegging can take no time at all.

BOTTLES

The cheapest option in terms of initial layout is bottling. For this all you need is a keen eye and some crown caps (bottle tops). To obtain free beer bottles, you have a few options. You could strike up a good relationship with a local pub, café or bar and ask them for any empties they might have; nip out the evening before recycling day and raid your neighbours' bins; ask all your friends to keep theirs; drink loads and keep the bottles; or throw a bring-a-bottle (or ten) party. You will soon develop an extra sense that alerts you to the proximity of empty beer bottles.

Ideally you need to obtain the standard 500ml (17 fl. oz) brown beer bottle, but some breweries – such as Hobgoblin and Badger – have a slightly different bottle which is a right pain in the arse to cap. Also avoid any colour of glass other than brown. Brown glass helps to filter ultraviolet light from the sun or fluorescent lighting that can react with the hops and cause 'skunking'. 'Skunking' means that your beer has created the same chemical as a skunk uses for its defence mechanism. So any colour of bottle other than brown means that the marketing department has more say than the brewer and they are happy for their consumers to be drinking skunk piss.

I'd also rule out re-using swing-top bottles. Whilst these seem attractive at first, as you don't need to buy any extra equipment and they are very easy to use, the rubber seal is not the easiest to keep bacteria free.

Many home-brewers get into the habit of swilling out their bottles immediately after use, which is really good practice and cuts down the need to do them all in one go. This works well if you have only one or two beers of an evening, but problems can arise if you have more, as beer isn't really a drink that is conducive to such good behaviour – in which case, or if you're using bottles that someone else has drunk from, you will need to clean thoroughly. This can be done in a number of ways. Some people pour in full-strength bleach and leave the bottles to stand – a practice that will rid you of even the strongest of stains but requires thorough rinsing. Others use a nylon brush and hot, soapy water. I've even seen brewers attach their brush to a cordless drill for extra efficiency. Do ensure you rinse thoroughly afterwards, as soap can really wreck a beer. As a cautionary note, don't bother with a dishwasher, as the jets of water don't go right inside the bottles and can often give you results like Piers Morgan's sense of humour: gleaming on the outside and filthy on the inside.

The bottles will then need to be sanitized. I used to fill my bath with sterilizing solution, submerge all the bottles and then rinse them using the shower – a method that can take some time, and there are easier ways.

Firstly, a device known as a 'sulfiter' or Avvinatore can be bought from home-brew shops or online. This is a plastic bowl with a squirting mechanism. Bottles are placed on to the squirting bit and it fires in sterilizing solution which is placed in the bottom bowl area of the Avvinatore. If you are using a no-rinse solution like Star San, the whole process takes no time at all. Alternatively, get a spray gun, fill it with solution and spray the inside of the bottles. With a bleach-based solution, ensure that you rinse thoroughly.

Another little trick is to sterilize the bottles the day before you need them, so that you are not doing too much in one day. Place small circles of sterile tinfoil over the mouths of the bottles to keep them sterile.

Bottling Up

Bottling is another of those jobs that you might as well learn to enjoy, or perhaps teach your children to learn to enjoy (if you trust them not to drink your beer). Make sure you get comfortable and are warm enough/not too cold, put the radio on or catch up on podcasts and zone in.

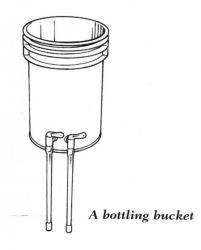

A bottling bucket

Once you are settled there are two ways to bottle from your primary or secondary fermenting vessels. Either siphon directly into the bottles, or use a bottling bucket and a bottling wand (see Equipment, page 80). The latter makes life infinitely easier. The wand is an ingenious invention. It is a long tube that attaches to the tap on your bottling bucket (a fermenting vessel with a tap) and when you turn your tap on it fills with beer. Then you place the wand inside a beer bottle and press a small 'button' on the end of the wand. This releases the beer into the bottle.

Don't forget, whichever way you bottle up you will have to prime your beer first – see page 70. If bottling without a bottling bucket, pour your priming solution into your FV and give it a very gentle stir. Leave it to settle for 30 minutes, then siphon into your bottles one at a time. If using a bottling bucket, pour your solution into that, then siphon your beer off the trub into your sterilized bottling bucket. Then fill the bottles one at a time using the wand. Remember to leave a gap of around 3cm/1 inch in the neck of your beer bottle. This airspace is called the 'ullage' and is needed so that the beer can carbonate correctly.

Finally, you will need to cap your beer. You will need a crown capper (see Equipment, page 80) and some crown caps. Make sure you have sterilized the caps too before putting them on. A two-handed crown capper will have a magnet that secures the cap; you then place the cap on the bottle and pull down the two handles. Make sure all the caps have been secured correctly: I once embarrassed myself at a home-brew club meet by bringing in a stale beer as the cap hadn't been properly secured. Turn the bottle upside down and try turning the cap; if it turns or any beer comes out, then you are going to get stale beer too.

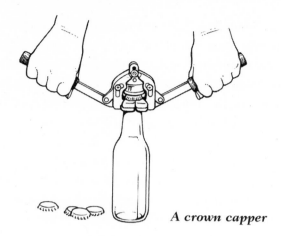

A crown capper

KEGGING

Kegs can be bought from your local home-brew shop or online. If buying second-hand, have a smell. I found one in a loft that had had cider left in it for over a year and whatever I did I couldn't seem to get it clean.

To keg straight from your fermenting vessel, simply pour your sugar solution into the bottom of your clean and sterile keg and siphon in your beer, ensuring that you leave the trub (crap at the bottom) behind.

A keg

You can also buy attachments for kegs that inject CO_2 right into the beer, in which case there is no need to prime with sugar. Also the level of CO_2 protects your beer and means that it can be kept fresher for longer. I find that if not using CO_2 kegged beer is past its best within three days – which is no good really, unless you are throwing a party or can sink an unhealthy amount of beer in one go!

Cornelius Kegs

If you have tons of money, are sleeping with a home-brew stockist or have started to get a little obsessed with beer-making, then you might consider getting a Cornelius keg. These are pressurized containers originally designed for American sodas. Or indeed if you just want to serve your beer professionally, they are great pieces of kit. If the idea appeals, then Chapter 18 of *Home-brewing for Dummies* by Marty Nachel gives you a lot of good all-round information.

STORING YOUR HOME BREW

Your home brew should be stored in the same way as shop-bought beer – see page 49.

COLOUR: EBC, SRM AND LOVIBOND

For notes on the different colours of beer, see page 42.

To work out the EBC of your home-brew (that is, where it sits on the standard European colour-measuring scale), by far the easiest way of doing it is to use brewing software like BeerSmith, but if you are intent on understanding every little micron of beer-brewing mystique, then over the page is an equation you can use:

Weight of all grains and adjuncts x colour in EBC

Each grain should have its EBC written on the label. Apply this equation separately for each grain/adjunct then add the results together to get N.

N x 10 x mash efficiency as a decimal (e.g. 72% efficiency = 0.72) ÷ volume brewed

Add these numbers together. So for example:

5kg pale malt (5 EBC) = 5 x 5 = 25

0.3kg Crystal (140 EBC) = 0.3 x 140 = 42

Total (N) = 67

Mash efficiency 72% (0.72), thus: 67 x 10 x 0.72 = 482.4

Divided by the volume of 25 litres = 460.8 ÷ 25 = 19.296

If you are boiling any other ingredients that add colour, these will also need to be added using the same equation, but as you are not mashing them you don't have to adjust for efficiency.

5

FIRST STEPS TO MAKING THE PERFECT PINT

THE TRUTH IS, making beer really isn't that hard. It's rather like the game of backgammon: it takes a moment to learn and a lifetime to master. Speaking to many want-to-be-brewers, I've noticed the first hurdle can be confidence – or, rather, lack of it. Perhaps if we all had a motivational expert on hand at all times, reminding us that anything is possible, telling us that 'we can do it' and whooping in our ear, then we might become the best we possibly can be (or a needy narcissist, or even a murderer of motivational coaches). Likewise, if we had a master brewer helping us every step of the way then we might be able to make the perfect beer right from the first brew.

Luckily, with brewing you can take one step at a time and really get to know the craft. As long as you keep your wort (unfermented beer) from getting infected (by wild yeasts and bacteria) at every stage of the process, then you should avoid any major catastrophes. I'd strongly suggest reading the Cleaning and Sterilizing section (page 63) before starting your brew. Do this and there is nothing to say that you won't get perfectly good, drinkable beer, or even award-winning beer, on your first go. Indeed, I've been to home-brew meetings where some of the best beer of the evening has come from someone who has brewed all grain for the first time (see page 93), which means they brewed with just the bare ingredients and not from a kit or with malt extract. I'd even go as far as to say that some of the best beer I've ever tasted was brewed by a first-time all-grain brewer.

But let's not jump the gun. I want to take things slowly here, because we are all different and so we all learn in different ways. Some people learn best by reading, so this book and some of the others in the Further Reading section (page 405) will help. Others learn better by being hands-on, so joining your local brew circle (see page 410), going to an organized brewing workshop, watching videos online or just getting stuck in will help. Most will learn through a mixture of both. But, whoever you are and however you learn, you are more than capable of making remarkable beer. The important message is: don't worry if this doesn't all go in the first time. I've tried throughout to make things as simple as possible, but it won't hurt to buy other brewing books and to look across the internet too. People who are great at anything are so because they work at it.

This chapter has been broken up into three parts: kit, extract, partial-extract and all-grain brewing.

KIT BREWING

Brewing using a kit is a great introduction to making beer as it's relatively easy, you don't need much equipment and as long as you get a decent kit you'll make decent enough beer.

EQUIPMENT

I'd suggest completely disregarding any all-in-one complete beer systems. They might seem attractive at first, but they have their limitations, not least of which is that they lock you into buying products made by that company every time you want to make a beer. On top of that, you can't use the equipment to make kits from different companies, the choice is limited, they are overpriced and, more importantly, in my experience the beer produced can be more than a little bit, well, shite.

Don't confuse these complete beer systems with kits containing equipment from different companies that have been put together for your convenience. Some of the better online and high-street home-brew shops will do just that, so don't be afraid to ask.

The beauty of putting together your own brew kit means that you can shop around and buy the best kit at the best prices, or even use second-hand and borrowed equipment. What's more, it can all still be used should you decide to progress with your brewing.

Equipment needed:

Can-opener	Bottles/keg or barrel
Saucepan or kettle	Crown caps and capper (if using bottles)
Fermentation vessel	Siphon
Hydrometer	Large spoon or paddle
Measuring jug	Airlock
Sanitizer	Measuring spoons or scales
Thermometer	Best part of an evening

Optional but useful: bottling bucket

Kit brewing used to mean one tin of malt extract with hops already in it, a sachet containing a dried Ale yeast and instructions printed on a bit of paper that you needed a magnifying glass to read telling you to add granulated sugar. The resulting beer was drinkable but not of a particularly high standard and it gave home-brewing a bad name. Kit manufacturers have since cottoned on that if a brewer makes bad beer with a kit they will do it only once and won't return to their product, and as a result kits have vastly improved and, of course, sales are increasing. There are still some pretty ropy kits out there, but if you follow a few simple suggestions then your beer will be perfectly good.

1. Buy a decent kit. In Part Five I've outlined a kit for each beer style to get you started and each one should give you a great result.

2. Don't be tempted to buy a liquid malt extract kit that is being sold off cheaply because it's out of date. Out-of-date kits will taste soapy and stale and, as your beer could at worst be undrinkable, please consider that your time is worth more than whatever the bargain price is.

3. Consider swapping the yeast. Yeast can make a huge difference to the final taste of the beer. If the packaging just says 'Ale yeast' and there is no mention of it being any particular strain, try using a yeast that will benefit the style. There are suggestions under each beer category in this book, or if you go to the yeast manufacturers' websites you will find some very good suggestions too.

4. Don't use granulated (table) sugar for more than a small percentage of the brew as it tends to make beer thinner. Using a good dried malt extract or spray malt instead will result in a fuller-flavoured beer.

5. Consider boiling your extract for at least half an hour before making your beer. This helps to sanitize it, reducing the chance of infection, and if you are throwing in hops it helps to isomerize the alpha acids (or in English: it will make your beer bitter).

6. Have patience. Leave your beer in the fermentation bin/primary fermenting vessel for a little longer than suggested. A week to ten days is a good amount of time to ensure that the beer has completely finished fermenting (leave Lager for four weeks or more). Once bottled or kegged, don't touch the beer at all: leave it to condition at room temperature for at least three weeks. Both these measures will give the beer a little longer to develop and can make the difference between a drinkable beer and a great beer.

7. Don't be afraid to experiment. Adding your own hops, changing the yeast, even perhaps adding speciality grains (see below) doesn't take much more effort and can really aid a brew.

8. Make sure you sterilize everything you use. If you are not cleaning and sterilizing like a Stepford wife by the time you have finished, then you will risk the chance of infection. See Cleaning and Sterilizing, page 63.

9. When your beer is fermenting, try not to let the temperature fluctuate too much. Around 20–22°C (68–72°F) is the right level for an Ale and 7–13°C (45–55°F) for a Lager.

10. Brew something you like. Sounds obvious, but there is no use brewing a beer that won't get drunk.

HOW TO MAKE BEER WITH A KIT

Once you have all that equipment, you can get brewing. Sometimes the kit instructions are worth following, sometimes less so; it tends to be the case that the more expensive the kit the better the instructions (unless someone is ripping you off). However, the guidelines below should help with all but concentrated wort kits. Kit brewers can 'turbo-charge' with an array of extras just like extract brewers – see the advice on using steeped grains on page 89 and dry-hopping on page 128.

Hopped Liquid Extract Kits

These tend to be at the cheaper end of the range of kits and contain just yeast, perhaps some finings, and one or two tins of malt extract. When the extract is made, the hops (or hop extract) are infused into the malt extract by boiling so you don't have to add them separately.

So if there are no hops, hop extracts or hop 'teabags' to add, the chances are the malt extract in your kit is pre-hopped, but unfortunately manufacturers don't always make this clear. If you are not certain, then assume that your kit is hopped and make sure you don't boil the extract; instead just dissolve it in boiling water as described below. (The reasons for boiling are to impart bitterness to the hops and in some cases to kill off any bacteria or wild yeasts that might be lurking in the extract or water, but as kits are sterile at the point of packing and the bitterness is already added in hopped kits, then boiling is not necessary.)

1. Pour boiling water into a cup, allow it to cool to below 35°C (95°F), then sprinkle in the yeast.

2. Meanwhile remove the labels from the can(s) and submerge them in warm (not boiling) water for 10 minutes. This softens the sticky extract, making it easier to pour.

3. Sanitize your fermentation vessels (see page 63).

4. Boil 3.5 litres (6 pints) of water and open the can(s).

5. Pour the extract straight into the fermentation vessel. You may need to use a little boiling water to get the last bit of extract out of the tins; if you do, remember to wear oven gloves when picking the tins up as your hands can get badly scorched!

6. Pour the boiling water over the extract.

7. If a recipe calls for sugar it is an excellent idea to add spray malt/dried malt extract instead. To add, stir your spray malt/DMA into enough cold water to allow it to dissolve fully. It's much easier to mix when the water is cold, otherwise the DME can stick together. Mix with a whisk.

7a. If making a lighter beer or a pale (not black) lager, do consider that spray malt will darken the final result. If directed to use sugar, in this instance it might be advisable, in which case at this point stir it into the boiling water in your fermentation vessel.

8. Top up to 19 litres (33½ pints) or as directed. Adding less water will make for a fuller-bodied beer – it's up to you if you wish to experiment here.

9. Take a hydrometer reading (ensuring that your hydrometer has been sterilized) and make a note of it. (If you don't have a hydrometer don't worry too much, but they are pretty cheap.) Then wait until your wort has cooled down to 19°C–22°C (66.2–72°F) and pitch (add) the yeast.

10. Cover with the lid, add a nip of vodka to the airlock and leave to ferment in a room that keeps a steady temperature of around 19–22°C (66.2–72°F) for an Ale, 7–13°C (45–55°F) for Lager for a week to ten days.

11. After ten days keep checking your hydrometer. For a normal Ale, if it reads around 1.010 (+/– .004) for three days then your beer should be done. It could still be worth moving it to a slightly warmer place for a day, especially during our many colder months, just to see if any extra fermentation occurs. A general rule is that consecutive readings indicate that the beer is done, but, depending on the yeast, it can sometimes stall and get started again.

12. For a standard 23-litre (40-pint) kit, boil 500ml (17 fl. oz) of water and stir in 100g (3½oz) of sugar until it has fully dissolved. The amount of priming sugar needed differs according to the type of beer and the temperature, but to save getting too technical at this point 100g (3½oz) should keep you explosion-free and give you just the right amount.

13. Let the sugar and water solution cool down to 21°C (70°F), then pour it into your fermentation vessel.

14. Siphon the beer from your fermentation vessel into bottles (or better still, into a bottling bucket first and then into bottles – see page 75). Ensure that you don't disturb the sediment (trub) at the bottom of the vessel.

15. Seal the bottles.

16. Leave for at least two weeks – or even longer if you can manage it. Beers with a high ABV will need up to six weeks.

Unhopped Liquid Extract Kits

If your kit is 'unhopped', it may well contain hops, hop extracts or hop 'teabags' to add and you will have to boil the extract, as described below, as this will impart bitterness to the hops.

1. Follow the instructions for hopped liquid extact, but if you are adding your own hops or speciality grains bring half the water you will be using to the boil. For a typical 23-litre (40-pint) kit this will mean 12 litres (21 pints) of water. Remember that some liquid will evaporate. Once boiling, add your extract, speciality grains (see Turbo-boosting Your Kit, below) and whichever hops you are using to impart bitterness. Boil for 30 minutes.

2. Add your aroma hops at some point during the last 5 minutes of the boil.

3. Remove from the heat. Best practice is to bring the heat down as quickly as possible (see Chilling, page 66), but using half the amount of water then dumping in the remainder as ice-cold water will work too. In other words, if you are using a 12-litre (21-pint) recipe, use 6 litres for the boil, then add 6 litres (10½ pints) of ice-cold water. I've never had any problems using tap water, but some people suggest buying bottled water or using water that has been pre-boiled and cooled.

Follow steps 9–16 on page 85.

Turbo-Boosting Your Kit

It is so easy to turn a kit into something a little more special. Techniques such as dry-hopping (adding hops to partially fermented wort – see page 128), adding steeped grains (see page 89) and adding herbs and spices either during the last 10 minutes of the boil or in the same manner as you would dry-hop are all very easy techniques for the would-be master brewer.

Remember you are not restricted to the hops supplied in your beer. Many brewers will actually use kits so they can really get to know some new ingredients. So perhaps you could introduce a new aroma hop to your kit – check out the hops chapter (page 147) to get an idea of some of the great flavours out there.

EXTRACT BREWING

Malt extract is basically concentrated wort that has been evaporated at temperatures below 50°C (122°F) in a controlled environment. It is the next step in brewing from kit brewing and is the type favoured by most home-brewers over in the States – and with good reason, as it is relatively easy and means you have more control over your ingredients than you would if you were using a kit. Great beer can be made with extracts and it takes a fraction of the time that it takes to brew all grain.

EQUIPMENT

See list for kit brewing (page 81), but in addition you will need:

Boiler or saucepan big enough to boil 21 litres (37 pints) of water

Muslin cloth or jelly bag

Wort-chiller (optional but advisable)

A whole evening

YOUR FIRST BEER

The recipe over the page is a useful and easy step away from kits. Please note that it makes a smaller amount than many of the standard recipes in this book.

The recipe below simply works and is the first beer recipe I devised. I've really oversimplified the ingredients, stating just 'hops', 'Ale yeast' and 'liquid malt extract'. Read the hops and yeast chapters (pages 147 and 202), or at least glance through them, if you want to use specific strains of yeast or varieties of hops; as long as you are using unhopped extract you can really take your pick of what your home-brew shop has to offer. You can even use the malt extract that comes with a kit beer. But if this is your first beer, don't worry too much about this sort of thing. I'm sure you just want something that tastes OK!

INGREDIENTS
13 litres (23 pints) water
55g (2oz) dried hops
1kg (2lb 3oz) barley liquid malt extract
1kg (2lb 3oz) granulated sugar or 1kg (2lb 3oz) dried malt extract
1 packet dried Ale yeast – I suggest Danstar Nottingham

1. Before you start, don't forget the golden rule: everything that touches the wort/beer needs to be sterilized beforehand. Failure to do this will result in infected beer that will taste rank.
2. Get a really big pan/cauldron, or if you don't have that then two pretty big saucepans will do. Bring 7 litres (12 pints) of water to the boil then throw in the hops, malt extract and sugar and stir. Keep boiling for 30 minutes, stirring until fully dissolved.
3. Meanwhile sterilize the fermentation vessel and rehydrate your yeast.
4. Strain the hop liquid through the muslin/jelly bag.
5. Pour over enough cold water to bring the total volume up to 13 litres (23 pints), ensuring the temperature is below about 18°C (64°F), then pitch (add) your yeast. The gravity (if using a hydrometer) should be roughly 1030.

6. Put the top on the fermentation vessel. If it has an airlock, seal it; if not, then loosely fit the lid and leave it for a week or until fermentation stops.

7. Bring 100ml (3½ fl. oz) of water to the boil in a pan. Add 20g (¾oz) sugar, stir until fully dissolved, then take off the heat and allow to cool. Now add this to the beer in the fermentation vessel – yes, you can now call it beer! Gently stir it in with a big spoon, trying not to disturb the sediment. Leave it to settle down a little anyway – go and have a cup of tea or a beer.

8. Now siphon the beer into sterilized bottles and seal them with sterilized caps, leaving about the same amount of room between the top of the beer and the top of the bottle as you normally see in a shop-bought beer. (For more information on bottling and kegging, see pages 72–77).

9. Leave the bottles for two weeks, or more if you can handle it, then they will be ready to drink. The beer should be about 4.5% ABV.

10. Drink your beer and raise a glass to the newest brewer in town – yourself.

EXTRACT BREWING USING STEEPED GRAINS

It might at first seem like a big step to move from making a very simple beer to using grains, but really it's like adding extra toppings on a frozen pizza – a simple process that will turn the everyday into something a little more personal and special. Since steeping grains doesn't add much in the way of fermentable sugars to your beer, just flavours and colour, the rest of the process is as in the recipe on page 88 plus one simple step: steeping the grains.

Put the grains you wish to steep into a muslin bag or bit of muslin cloth that you can tie up. Heat 4 litres (7 pints) of water in a pan to 65–75°C (149–167°F). Place the grains in the pan, dipping them in and out until you are satisfied that the colour and flavour of the water has changed; this will take about 30 minutes. Don't worry too much about the temperature. Granted, boiling the grain won't do you much good and you should make sure you don't heat to over 77°C (170°F) – if you suspect you have, take it off the heat for a minute, especially if you're using a slow-to-react electric hob – but as long as you keep it roughly within the 65–75°C (149–167°F) range you should be fine.

After 30 minutes, remove the grains from the pan and allow the water to drip out. You now have some wort to add to the rest of your recipe.

Consider steeping 200g (7oz) of crystal malt and adding it to the above recipe, or adding 200g (7oz) of steeped chocolate malt or other roasted malts to make a darker beer from a pale recipe; or jump right in and follow one of the recipes further on in the book.

UNDERSTANDING A PARTIAL-GRAIN RECIPE

Partial-grain brewing could be described as the midway point between extract and all grain, a sort of intermediate level of brewing.

Since many recipes across the internet and in books are presented in the same fashion, below is a breakdown of a typical partial-grain recipe. This one is a recipe for Mild from Dave Taylor of Cheshire, aka Orfy (see page 295 for recipe), and I'll go through what each bit means.

Batch size: 19 litres (33½ pints) – the volume of beer this recipe will make.

Boil size: 25.7 litres (45.2 pints) – the volume of the beer when boiling.

2.2kg (4lb 13oz) light extract (16 EBC) 75.0% – good malt extracts should tell you their colour. There are various colours available, ranging from light to dark and the EBC is the scale by which European beer colour is measured; see page 43 for more information. The percentage is the amount of grain or extract used in the recipe; this helps if you wish to make larger or smaller batches of beer than the batch sizes given in a recipe.

400g (14oz) crystal malt (60L) – to add sweet, caramel flavours. Note that in this case malt is sold using a Lovibond number; 120 EBC would be the equivalent.

125g (4oz) chocolate malt (1,000 EBC) – to add colour (note the high EBC number) and also flavour.

25g (1oz) Fuggles hops (4.50%) @ 45 minutes (15.1 IBU) – the weight and type of hop. The percentage is the alpha acid level (see page 15 for a description of alpha acids). Interestingly, in most recipes you could use half the quantity of a hop with twice the amount of alpha acids. The time is the time for which the hops will be boiled – so this particular addition will be in the boiler for 45 minutes. Often brewers will use the @ (at) sign as a shortcut. So if you see '@ 45 mins' it means with 45 minutes left of the boil, '@ 10 mins' means with 10 minutes left, and '@ 0 mins' means at the very end of the boil (but this is sometimes referred to as 'at flame out').

Hops used in the first part of the boil are known as bittering hops. Since the hops are being boiled for longer, more bitterness is isomerized from them. Note that the IBU (International Bittering Unit) is higher. (See page 25 for an explanation of bittering units – essentially they are a measurement of how bitter a beer is.)

25g (1oz) Fuggles hops (4.50%) @ 15 minutes (8.2 IBU) – hops added during the last 15 minutes or so of the boil are known as aroma hops. Note that despite using the same quantity of hops here as in the first part of the boil (see above), the bittering units are now reduced to almost half of the earlier addition.

1 packet Danstar Nottingham Ale Yeast – the suggested type of yeast for this recipe. Note that if a recipe simply says 'Ale yeast' you should try to match up the type of yeast with the selected style of beer. Many English Ales can be made with Nottingham, which is one of the yeasts used most widely by home and commercial brewers.

Original gravity (or OG): 1.034 – this is the amount of potential alcohol in the beer. It is a measurement of the sugar level.

Final gravity (or FG): 1.010–1.016 – and this is the acceptable range measured after fermentation.

Some tips:

- Always use crushed grains. Most grain comes pre-crushed here in the UK anyway, but it doesn't hurt to ask your supplier if you are not sure.

- Use only fresh grains.

- Don't leave the grains in for too long. The steeped water will become astringent and will ruin a perfectly good beer.

- Get your water right. Hard water is great for extraction rates with darker grains, and soft water for lighter grains.

FOLLOWING ORFY'S RECIPE

1. Measure out your grains.
2. Bring 4 litres (7 pints) of water to 75°C (167°F).
3. Put the 400g (14oz) crystal malt and the 125g (4oz) chocolate malt into a muslin bag and dunk it in and out of the water from time to time.
4. Keep an eye on the temperature: this can mean taking the pan off an electric hob, or turning off a gas or induction hob now and then.
5. Remove the grains after 30 minutes.
6. Stir in the 2.2kg (4lb 13oz) of extract and add the whole mixture to the brew pot/boiler/copper.
7. Top up the water to a volume of 25.7 litres (45.2 pints). In order to get this right, it is a good idea to pour 1 litre (1¾ pints) of water into your pot, insert a piece of wood and mark off the 1-litre (1¾-pint) level, then repeat going up

the wood so that you have an accurate measuring rod for your quantities.

8. Bring to the boil.
9. When boiling, add 25g (1oz) Fuggles.
10. After 30 minutes add another 25g (1oz) Fuggles.
11. Boil for another 15 minutes.
12. Cool to 18°C (64°F).
13. Transfer to your fermentation vessel.
14. Pitch the yeast.
15. Ferment and bottle as usual (see pages 68 and 72).
16. Pour yourself a beer and put your feet up.

ALL-GRAIN BREWING

Many of the beer recipes that you find on the internet, in brewing books and in brewing circles will be for all-grain beer. This is how most commercial brewers will brew and it's how beer has been made since we humans first started to make it. As brewing archaeologist Merryn Dineley puts it: 'Basically, making Ale from the grain is a process that has not changed across the millennia. You take crushed malted grain, you heat it with water to make a sweet mash. Next, lauter and sparge to extract a clear wort, then boil it up with herbs.'

EQUIPMENT

As kit brewing and partial-grain brewing (see pages 81 and 90), but in addition you will need:

Mash tun

Wort-chiller (essential)

A spare afternoon **and** evening, or a whole day

STEP-BY-STEP ALL GRAIN

This is a very simple guide to making an all-grain batch. I'll go into more detail below.

1. Find a recipe you like, or design one yourself.
2. If the recipe asks for a yeast starter, make it the day before if possible (see page 209).
3. Assemble and clean equipment (see page 63).
4. Weigh out your grain and hops.
5. Bring some water up to 71–75°C (160–167°F). This is known as your 'strike water'. The temperature depends on how hot your chosen recipe requires the water to be; remember you'll lose about 4–5°C (39–41°F) on transfer, so for a typical 67°C mash temperature your water will need to be 71–72°C (160–162°F). You'll need 1 litre (1¾ pints) of water for every 450g (1lb) of grain in your recipe, so a 4.5kg (9lb 14oz) recipe will need 10 litres (17½ pints).
6. Meanwhile, boil a kettle of water and pour this into your mash tun; it helps to have it a bit warm before starting. Boil another kettle – hot water is always useful!
7. Now 'mash in' – that is, add layers of water and grain until you have exhausted both, stirring carefully in order to mix without adding any air; in other words, don't be really vigorous. Ensure that you have met your mash temperature (usually 65–68°C/149–154°F) – you might need to add more hot or cold water to get it right. Make sure there are no dry clumps of grain and that all are sufficiently wetted.
8. Once you have the required mash temperature it's time to mash. Set your timer for your mash, which will normally be 60, 90 or 120 minutes. You will need to keep the temperature as constant as possible, so stir and check every 15 minutes and if it dips add boiling water until the correct temperature is reached again.

9. Meanwhile, heat about 19 litres (33½ pints) of water to 73–77°C (163–171°F). This will be for sparging the grains.

10. Turn the tap on your mash tun and allow it to drain into your brew pot/copper. Let 2 litres (3½ pints) out and then pour it back over your grains. Repeat until the liquid starts to clear.

11. Drain carefully into your brew pot/copper; if you turn the tap on very quickly it will clog, so open it gradually. Don't expect this to be a fast process: depending on your set-up it can take quite some time. Some silicon tubing attached to the tap and placed inside your brew pot will ensure your wort doesn't oxidize (see page 28).

12. Once your mash tun has drained, turn the tap off and slowly pour your sparge water over the grain bed using a jug.

13. Gently stir the grains.

14. Put the lid back on and leave for 15 minutes.

15. Repeat steps 10 and 11.

16. Using a hydrometer, measure the gravity of your wort and take a note of the volume too.

17. Boil, adding the hops as directed in the recipe.

18. Chill to 18°C (64°F) using a wort-chiller (see page 66). If you don't have one, use an ice bath.

19. Transfer the wort into your fermentation vessel.

20. Pitch your yeast.

21. Ferment and bottle as directed.

22. Have a well-deserved beer or two.

ALL-GRAIN BREW-IN-THE-BAG METHOD (BIAB)

The brew-in-the-bag method originated in Australia as a method of brewing that reduced water consumption. It is often considered an interim method between extract and all-grain brewing, but is slowly gathering momentum as a method all on its own. The beauty of it is that everything (post-fermentation) happens in one vessel and a bag.

Equipment

As kit and extract brewing (pages 81 and 87), but you will also need the following:

Bag (obviously) – this can be any bag with a fine mesh and strong weave capable of holding 15kg (33lb). Bags labelled as 'mashing and sparging bags' from your home-brew stockist are good for smaller batches, but many brewers will make their own using voile.

Large brew pot/copper – in reality, this means up to 40 litres.

Bulldog clips – to attach the bag to the brew pot.

Gas burner – unless you have a large, fancy hob with a massive burner in the middle, you will need something bigger than a usual hob to heat a container of this size. Of course you could just brew with smaller batches.

Thermometer – a digital probe type is ideal.

Some people also use a pulley system to take the bag out of the brew pot, as lifting out a dripping bag full of scalding-hot water can be a bit of a nightmare!

Step-by-Step

1. Prepare your grains. Often boil-in-the-bag brewers will get less efficiency, so increasing the base malt by 8% might be a wise move.
2. Put your bag into the brew pot/copper and fill with 29 litres (51 pints) of water.
3. Heat water up to 72°C (162°F).
4. When this temperature is reached, turn off the heat and start adding your grains, stirring as you do so.

5. Adding the grains will lower the temperature of the liquor, so take a temperature reading and adjust to match the required mash temperature by adding hot or cold water.

6. Cover with a lid and towel and try to maintain the mash temperature.

7. After your 60-minute mash, increase the wort temperature to 77°C (171°F) and maintain it for 10 minutes. This is called the 'mash out'.

8. Lift out the bag and let it drip. You might want to push down gently on the grain bed with a saucepan lid.

9. You now have your wort. Boil, add hops and ferment as directed by the recipe.

From Home-brewer to Commercial Brewer
by Michael Hopart of Top Out Brewery

'That's really good, mate, you should become a proper brewer and sell your beers!' How many times have you heard this from the friends you're sharing your home brew with? Well, are you brewing full mash at home? This basically means brewing from scratch using malts and hops rather than malt extracts or brew kits. And have people who tasted your beer nodded approvingly rather than run away screaming? If that's two answers of 'Yes!' then I would be inclined to call you a proper brewer already. But how about setting up your own business and selling your beer? Tempted? Read on, because that's exactly what I'm doing at the moment. In fact, by the time you're reading this me and my business partner will have started brewing on a commercial scale and sold our first few cases.

A couple of years ago I was eyeballing new career options. I had been selling whisky in shops for over ten years and, while very much enjoying what I was doing, was trying to make my work life a bit more exciting. The drinks trade, as you would expect, has treated me well and so I was keen to stay in the industry. At home I had been brewing in my kitchen for a few years and had heard the aforementioned exclamation by my friends a few times. I was giving this idea some serious consideration but had to discover that above all I was lacking the money to do it. In a stroke of luck, for me anyway, my friend Moo had been made redundant and seen off with a decent farewell package by his now ex-company. When he heard about my plans for opening a brewery he was very keen to come on board. So between us we had enough capital to start making a business plan and see if it all might work out. It didn't look too bad. You can get plenty of help with your plan and plenty of advice from Business Gateway in Scotland or Business Link in England and Wales. They should be able to provide you with a business adviser. And how much do they charge for that? Not a penny, so definitely worth it.

If you can't quite scrape enough money together to actually buy your own equipment, pay for the rent, etc., you could also consider becoming a so-called 'cuckoo brewer'. These companies rent a brewery for the day and make their own beer to their own specifications (such as Batch Brew – see page 394). Another option is to contract brew, so essentially ask a brewery to brew your beer for you. While you have substantially less outlay with either of these business ideas, you also have increasingly less control over your products and are a lot less flexible.

We wanted to release many different kinds of beer that would require a lot of experimenting (I'm still using my home-brew kit to work on new recipes) and knew flexibility was a necessity, so we decided to splash out on a used, simple but decent six-barrel kit. That should give us about 1,500 pints per batch. There are breweries out there who can run a profitable business on less than that, but I can imagine you'd struggle to sustain anybody else but you alone, not even a business partner. Speaking of which, try and get one. Sharing the workload will often make things easier, and certainly more entertaining. And aren't most of us doing it for the enjoyment and satisfaction that comes with producing your own beer? In our experience brewers are a friendly and helpful lot; every one of our potential competitors we contacted was very happy to show us around their brewery and give us tons of valuable advice based on first-hand experience.

At this stage we also had to work out what would make our beer better and more desirable than most others. If you're not absolutely convinced your beer is going to be great, how can you expect people to pay for it? So you will need a unique selling point. That can be, for example, the perfect location to corner the local market. Some breweries come up with a really good name that will open a niche market for them; others will rely on their muscle and market their beer aggressively. We thought we'd let our beer speak for itself, making unconventional beers different to anybody else's. Sometimes weird, but never gimmicky for the sake of it, and of course always tasty. There are so many beer styles to be found all over the world, why limit yourself to only a handful if you can brew (almost) all of them? As a home-brewer I never brewed the same beer twice; my main motivation behind my hobby was to create beer I couldn't find in any shop. I only started refining and re-brewing my recipes when we made trial brews for our first commercial releases.

So next time you hear your mates say you should go all out and get your own beer on the market, give it some thought. As a proper brewer you have probably made some really good stuff that is a bit different from the norm. We now have over a thousand breweries in Britain, but I feel we still need more great, exciting beer. Too many of these breweries seem to be content to churn out standard Bitters or suchlike which taste good but are remarkably similar to about 537 other British Bitters. If you think you can contribute to the diversity of beer, have an inkling about how to sell it, have a spare bit of cash and are willing to maybe wing it a little, give it a go. What's the worst that can happen?

This is by no means a complete to-do list for opening a brewery. I could have filled a book with that. We made many mistakes along the way and learned a lot. Probably the biggest lesson we had to learn was that commercial leases are really, really complicated and include a lot of pitfalls. Solicitors are expensive, but we were very glad we paid one in the end, otherwise it might have all ended in tears. And take trademarks seriously! I'm pretty confident that it will work out, otherwise we wouldn't have started the whole thing and poured all this money into it. So I'm certain you'll find our beers on the shelf and in pubs very soon, if they're not already there.

Top Out Brewery is located on the outskirts of Edinburgh.

6

DETECTING AND DEALING WITH FAULTS AND OFF FLAVOURS

HOME AND COMMERCIALLY brewed beers can be subject to the same problems – problems that can often be put down to one of three things: bacterial infections, yeast infections and poor brewing practices. Although this section is mostly aimed at the home-brewer, you might encounter some of the same problems with a pint in a pub or bar and you will be within your rights to bring it back. A good landlord might even thank you for it. Although if you are wrong or the beer is supposed to be brewed that way, then you might just come across as a fussy prick. Do be aware that some landlords will flatly disagree with you; just use that as a cause to be smug. Landlords often can't do much about it other than send the barrel back, but home-brewers should certainly be aware of the common faults that can occur in beers, as sometimes they will be able to rectify them.

IS IT REALLY A DUFF PINT?

Sometimes a pint isn't up to scratch and you might have to return it. Sometimes it is meant to taste a bit odd or have bits floating around in it as that is part of the style. Always ask if you are not sure: if the bar is selling something a little unusual then they should be able to tell you. Lambics, for example, have a funny taste and Wheat Beers are often cloudy. A simple 'Should this look/taste like this?' is a non-confrontational enquiry which should get you your answer. A good bar or pub will give you a shot to taste anyway.

BUBBLES RISING FROM THE SIDES OF THE GLASS

This means the glass has not been cleaned properly and the CO_2 is building up in dust particles or small fibres in the glass. It might not necessarily affect the beer itself, but it will affect the head of your beer. You'll be within your rights to bring it back, but in a busy bar you might not be thanked for it.

HAZY BEER

Haziness in beer can be due to the cask being served too quickly. In cask Ales a process known as 'stillaging' should take place. This means the cask should be left for three days before sale and then the beer will 'drop bright' (become clear). It also happens in cask beer if the beer has been tilted too quickly, disturbing the sediment.

A 'chill haze' can also happen if the beer is stored at too low a temperature, causing proteins in the suspension to clump and become visible. Chill haze can easily be rectified by just warming the beer to room temperature. I often find that people from hotter climes will serve me Ales from the fridge and so I'll always get a chill-hazed beer. I'm more bothered that the chill mutes some of the flavour than I am about the aesthetics.

Another haze, protein haze, can be due to poor mashing and we brewers need to take special note of mashing temperature and procedures if it keeps happening. Hazes also occur from sparge temperatures that are too high, wild yeast infection, grain husks staying present and too short a boil. You probably know when you have done any of these and should try to avoid repeating your mistakes in future brews.

However, in the case of certain beers, such as some Wheat Beers, a hazy pint is not a fault. It can be a mark that fruit has been used, or a sign that finings have not been used. It will also tend to occur in 'natural' or vegan beers, but even these should drop bright in a few days; they just might take a little longer than beers with fish guts or seaweed in them.

BEER GUSHES OUT ALL OVER THE PLACE

I've never heard of this happening in a shop-bought beer, but that doesn't mean it couldn't! In bottled beers this is caused by the 'gusher bug' – a rather quaint name for a pain-in-the-arse wild yeast. Somehow the yeast will have got into your beer, often through improper sanitation. The yeast will carry on fermenting in the bottle until there is nothing left. Not only will all your beer disappear, but there will be a build-up of carbon dioxide inside the bottles and they can blow up. As with all active yeasts, refrigeration will slow them down, but if this has happened I'd suggest throwing a quick impromptu party to get rid of the batch just to free yourself from a potential glass-shattering incident.

OFF FLAVOURS

See over if you are interested in why a beer tastes off, but TCP, plastic, celery, solvents, sour, sweat, nail-polish remover, too much butter, overly astringent and cat-pee tastes and smells are all signs of an off beer. Make sure that none of these characteristics has anything to do with the style and, if it hasn't, ask politely for a refund. Suggest that the barman/landlord tries it himself.

TASTES LIKE GREEN APPLES

The green apple taste is due to a chemical known as acetaldehyde, which is also present in coffee, bread and ripe fruit. In beer it's not always considered a fault, as in low quantities it adds a fresh taste. However, it is not always welcome, especially in higher quantities, and can sometimes even result in a solvent-like aroma.

Acetaldehyde can be formed during many stages of brewing, but most commonly during the early to mid part of fermentation. Its presence can be controlled by ensuring that your wort is below 27°C (80°F) when pitching your yeast, not fermenting at too high a temperature, aerating your wort, selecting less flocculent (see page 23) yeast strains and adding nutrients for your yeast.

If acetaldehyde is detected in finished beer don't worry too much, as often it can dissipate in time, so just leave your beer for a little longer.

In a bought pint it is a question of taste, and armed with what you have just read it is up to you if it goes back or not. Remember that if it is just a hint you might fall into the 'fussy prick' category.

BURNS LIKE STRONG ALCOHOL

Even very strong beers don't have to have that hot alcohol burn that belongs to flaming sambucas. It is a problem associated more with brewers in Australia, as one of the causes can be high fermentation temperatures. To rectify it, some Australian home-brewers adapt their equipment so it can be placed in a swimming pool. Most of us don't have swimming pools here, so in a particularly hot summer submerging your equipment in water or moving your fermenting vessel to a north-facing room will help.

In cooler temperatures the problem might be down to yeast health, in which case making a yeast starter to check health will be a good measure to adopt (see page 209). Luckily, this can be another problem that can be rectified with conditioning.

In a bought pint they might have brought the barrel on too soon. Unless it is overbearing, just switch to something else for your next pint.

TASTES ASTRINGENT

If you pull a face like a cat's arse after a sip of beer, the chances are it is slightly too astringent. This can be caused by over-sparging, sparging with water that is too hot, or using water that is too alkaline. Extract brewers can also come a cropper to the cat's-arseness if they steep their grains for too long. Be careful, too, when designing a beer, as using anything with tannins can cause a problem: so too much black malt, spices, fruit peel or high alpha acid hops can all be culprits.

A strong tannin, astringent flavour rather like a teabag can also come from having sparge water that is too hot. Similarly, extract brewers who steep the grains at too high a temperature will have the same problem. If the beer can handle it, leave it to condition for at least a couple more months.

If in a pub, it's not really the landlord's fault, so make a face and switch to another beer for the next one.

A SORT OF FAKE BUTTERY/STRONG BUTTERSCOTCH TASTE

Fake butter or overpowering butterscotch can be due to the presence of diacetyl in your beer. It is not always considered to be a fault; in fact, I've had a few beers where it is rather pleasant, leaving a rounded flavour that complements the malts. However, it can be overpowering and it can ruin a beer, especially if you find it in what should be a crisp, clean-tasting

Lager. Also, commercial brewers need to beware, as it can make drinkers feel full and put them off buying more beer!

Diacetyl is formed during the fermentation process and is normally created then re-absorbed by the yeast. If fermenting at warm enough temperatures (18–21°C/64–70°F) the yeast should sort any diacetyl flavours out. Ensure that you have this temperature range for three days for an Ale and seven for a Lager before racking into a secondary.

Less commonly, a diacetyl taste can be due to an infection of *Pediococcus* or *Lactobacilli* bacteria strains. If the flavour suddenly appears, this is likely to be the case and I'm afraid there is not much you can do about it, other than get used to it and curse yourself for not cleaning and sterilizing your equipment properly.

OXIDATION

This is a problem that manifests itself as a 'stale'. It results from poor handling post-fermentation and means that oxygen has got in. In bottled beers it happens if the crown caps are not affixed properly and in cask beers it can happen if the cask is not drunk in three days. If the beer tastes like cardboard then it has gone 'stale'.

Home-brewers, check your set-up. Remember, don't use hobgoblin-type bottles as they don't take crown caps. In a pub you can take this beer back.

Mind you, sometimes oxidation is a good thing, especially in Old Ales and Barley Wines, as it can add a sherry or honey flavour, so sometimes beers are intentionally oxidized.

SMELLS OF CATS/SKUNKS

Believe it or not, the same chemical that skunks use to repel predators can appear in your beer. It can be caused by a reaction of the blue wavelength of ultra-violet light with the hops. These wavelengths from the sun or fluorescent light will not pass through brown glass but they will through green, so just change the bottles you are using. Unfortunately, once it has happened it cannot be reversed. Serving the beer ice cold might mask it enough to allow you to drink what is essentially skunk piss without noticing it! Mind you, apparently there are plenty of people out there who actually like drinking skunk piss.

WHAT TO DO WITH BEER YOU WON'T DRINK

If you have looked above and you are pretty sure your beer is bad, you might want to pour it down the drain. Before you do, though, consider a few other uses.

Light beers can replace milk in batter for pancakes and fish, and darker beers can be substituted for water in gravy. I find it especially good when making meat pies. However, if the fault is enough to make you gag or is too strong, then it won't be worth ruining your dinner as well as your beer. Cut your losses.

WHAT TO DO WITH BEER YOU CAN'T DRINK

If your beer is undrinkable – so undrinkable that even the men who live in the park turn it down – then it will be no good for cooking and you might now be considering pouring it all down the drain. Whilst this might seem the best thing for it, there are still other options:

1. Kill slugs with it. This is an age-old method for controlling the slug population, as they love beer; in fact, they love it so much that they drown in even the most rancid brew.

Pour some beer into jam jars, or better still Marmite jars, and bury them so that just the top of the jar is level with the soil, or tip them on their sides at an angle so a small puddle of beer can be held in each jar. Fill them with as much beer as they will hold without spilling over and watch the slugs drown (or for those non-serial killers amongst you, return at a later date and pull out the deceased slugs, then put them on your compost heap).

2. Give it to annoying freeloaders. Many of us have a mate who only turns up to drink our beer. Simply stash your undrinkable bottles separately from your other beers and pass him/her one from that area. One of two things will happen: they will stop asking for beer or they will get through yours. Either will be a bonus.

PART THREE

The Gardening Brewer

7

A PINT OF BEER FROM SEED

THE FIRST BREWERS were probably the first farmers too and the first crops would have been similar to our main cereal crops. For a long time it was thought that our ancestors originally grew and harvested these plants to make bread, but new evidence is emerging that suggests beer was first. Indeed, farming cereal crops in order to make beer may precede farming crops for food by around 3,000 years – that's a long time to wait for a fried breakfast.

Back then, around 10,000 years ago, beer was literally considered to come from the gods, and ceremonies and rituals followed each part of the brewing process. In that respect those Mesolithics had a lot in common with us beer-worshippers. But perhaps it went deeper, as to appreciate fully what goes into making a pint of beer down to the last molecule, to grow every ingredient yourself and then to drink it after all that effort is surely an almost spiritual moment. Breaking the earth; getting the soil beneath your fingertips; witnessing your own hops winding up and up as spring turns to summer and then autumn; watching as a gust of wind catches your barley grain until you hear the dry seeds, almost ready for harvest, gently rattling against each other in a symphony of expectation. It's a great and rewarding project to undertake and there is no better way to say 'up yours' to the chancellor than to drink a beer that hasn't had a single penny paid in duty on it.

MAKING YOUR OWN MALT

Many years ago I was on one of the many hikes I used to take with my brother across the Wiltshire countryside. It formed cheap entertainment as both of us were skint. Midway through, we came across a skip on the edge of a farmer's field. It was full of barley grain. Knowing that malt, hops, water and yeast were the four things I needed to make beer, I found myself saying out loud, 'I wonder if I can make beer from this?' I was half joking, but with some intent, as the idea momentarily excited me. We were so broke at the time that we were living off cabbage curries. Even baked beans were a luxury, so you can imagine how out of reach beer felt. Some of the grain had started sprouting in the skip, however, and I decided that this meant it was useless and was probably why it was in the skip.

If I'd known then that germinating seeds from the *Gramineae* family are the basis of all beer, then I may well have enjoyed a skip beer. The *Gramineae* are a family of cereal grains including corn, millet, oats, rice, rye and spelt, all of which have been used either entirely or in part to make beer across the planet for thousands of years.

In the wild, after these plants have gone to seed, their seed will drop and lie dormant for the winter. When the ground warms up it sends a signal to the seed to start growing. The seed then starts to transform, sucking in the surrounding moisture and going through biological changes that start the growing process. In the field this all happens in, or on, the ground. In the modern malting process it is all done in the controlled environment of a silo, which means that all the malt can be germinated at the same rate. Different maltsters will have different techniques, but generally speaking harvested grain is cleaned, steeped in water, allowed to dry, then steeped again a number of times. This process starts the seeds germinating, signs of which can be seen in the tiny rootlets that emanate from the seeds.

The next stage is the germination phase, which will last for four to five days. The grain is kept at a controlled temperature and turned regularly. This prevents the roots from tangling with adjacent grains. At this stage the malt is known as green malt.

The last stage is to kiln the green malt to make grain that can be used by brewers. Hot air is blown through the grains, and by changing the temperature of the air flow different colours and flavour attributes are given to the malts.

It is possible, if a little time-consuming and fiddly, to make your own malted barley for brewing. As home-malting is not as efficient as professional malting, you'll need around one third to half as much again in a recipe as you would if using professionally malted malt. It is worth the extra, though: imagine the satisfaction of sitting there with friends, sharing a beer that you have grown from seed. It will also improve your knowledge of the fermented drink from the gods tenfold, as you'll almost be able to taste the summer that went into growing your grain.

GROWING BARLEY

The amount of barley you grow will ultimately depend on how much space you have. According to the National Association of Allotments & Leisure Gardens, the average size of a plot is 250 square metres. The average garden size in the UK is slightly smaller, at 90 square metres. But as only 15 square metres (bigger than a shed but smaller than a garage) is needed to grow enough barley to make one all-grain batch, then most people who have an allotment or garden will have room to grow at least enough barley for two or even three batches of beer, with plenty of room left over for some sprouts.

Choosing and Buying Seed

Depending on the variety, barley seed can be sown in autumn or in spring. Autumn-sown barley, which for some reason is known as winter barley, is of little use to the brewer, as although it is high yielding the seeds are of poorer quality. Spring-sown barley is harvested in August and, although much lower yielding, the quality of the grain is exactly what is needed to make decent beer.

Buying the seed might prove difficult, as there are not too many people growing barley and so there just isn't the market for it. Home-brew clubs could buy in bulk direct from the farmers' seed merchants, but many will require contracts and big, farmer-sized orders. You could also try asking around on web forums and in real life to find a barley farmer who might sell you some of their leftover seed.

Realistically, the best bet is to buy in bulk from a health-food shop, but you may have to ask them to order some in. They should be able to sell you a 5kg (11lb) bag, which should cover around 148 square metres and will be more than enough for anyone's needs. Unfortunately, due to lack of choice it is likely that this will be the UK two-row barley that we use in brewing, but it will be impossible to know what sort of grade it is.

As some grades won't make great beer, you may want to make just a small batch using your barley seed before you go to the effort of planting and growing it to ensure it makes a decent enough beer; if so, follow the malting instructions on page 116.

Planting, Soil Conditions and Aftercare

Plant in late winter/very early spring when the ground has warmed up a little; a farmer will sow in February. Barley thrives in a soil that isn't overly acidic, but nor should it be alkaline. You will be looking for a pH level of between 5.8 and 6.5, which is generally what most gardens will be anyway. But if your soil is too acidic then you can add lime; if it is too alkaline you can add coffee grounds. The barley will benefit too from a top dressing of well-rotted compost.

As with all plants, weeds will appear from nowhere and want to compete with the barley. The only real option is to rid the ground of as much weed seed and roots as humanly possible the season before you plant and hope that your barley out-competes the opposition. Trying to weed around barley is difficult in the early stages, as you risk damaging the roots of young seedlings.

Barley likes dry soil, so choose your site carefully and ensure it is well drained. Work the soil and rake it to a fine tilth (so the soil crumbles in your hand). Broadcast-sow the seeds at a rate of 250g (9oz) of seed for every 6 square metres; you need about 1 kernel (seed) per 3cm square. Rake the seeds in and then watch all your hard work get eaten by birds. Alternatively, you could hang some CDs from nearby trees to act as bird-scarers, or plant a little more than you need and put some netting over the top. If you do the latter, ensure that there are no gaps and if rodents are a problem you could consider traps. In days of yore farmers would train terriers to get rid of rats.

Apart from watering in dry weather, barley is a fairly strong plant and won't need much attention at all.

Harvesting

Your barley should be ready to harvest around August when it is golden in colour and the straw brittle to the touch. The kernels will be difficult to dent when pressed with a fingernail, the ears will have bent over and the grains will be easily removed. It is best harvested after a dry spell and with a scythe. I realize these are not often found in the average shed, but luckily shears are up to the job too.

Once cut, the ears will need to be collected into bundles that are about 15cm (6in) in diameter and then stood grain end up in stacks of six and left to dry; leave them outside in the sun for two weeks. If, like in many of our summers, there just aren't enough dry days, you could put them in the greenhouse on the days that it rains, but make sure that the temperature in there doesn't exceed 45°C (113°F). You could also just cover them with some waterproof material such as a tarpaulin.

Threshing and Winnowing

At this point the grains are still attached to the dried seed heads and need to be removed. In order to do so you will need to thresh the barley. The easiest way to do this is to use an old 30-litre (53-pint) fermentation vessel, rubbish bin or anything of similar size and smack the seed heads against the side of it until the grain falls off.

If you haven't given up and gone down the pub, the next stage is to winnow your grain. This is pretty simple. On a windy day, or near a fan, pour your grain from one container to another so that the lighter bits of straw fly off.

HOME-MALTING

Anyone with a working kitchen can malt their own grains; it wasn't always the specialized process that it is now whereby just a handful of maltsters serve the planet's beer needs. As with home-brewing, the home-maltster is going through the same process that is done commercially on an industrial scale, but just using what they have to hand. It might take a bit of trial and error, so, especially if you have grown your own grain, I'd strongly suggest doing a little bit at a time. As I've already mentioned, I'd also suggest using a third more, if not doubling up, the amount of grain specified in recipes, as the process can be up to 50% less efficient than when done by a professional maltster.

Soaking

The first step is to weigh your grain so you know how much you are working with. Then wash it, ensuring that all the chaff has been removed; this can be done fairly easily by just putting the grain into a bucket and letting the chaff float to the top.

The next step is soaking it overnight (no longer than 8 hours). You can do this by wrapping up the grains in some muslin cloth and dipping them into an old fermenting vessel. Allow at least 10cm (4in) of water above the top of the grains.

Take out the grain and pour it into another bucket/old fermenting vessel (old to avoid scratching a perfectly good bit of home-brew kit). Soak again and you should see a visible change to the barley grain – small white roots will start to appear. If this doesn't happen, then repeat the process until the grains have expanded and you can see the little white roots sticking out of them, but never allow the grains to soak for longer than 8 hours at a time or you'll kill them. Having soaked in all that moisture they will also be heavier by about 35%. Weigh them again: 1kg (2lb 3oz) should now weigh 1.35kg (3lb).

Germination/Couching

After soaking, you'll need to germinate the grain. For this you'll need a cool (18°C/64°F), moist, well-ventilated area. If your bathroom is big enough the bathtub will be ideal; however, you or anyone else in the house won't be able to wash for the two to five days needed to sprout your grain, which could cause marital or housemate problems. Alternatively, a concrete garage floor, or even a patio covered with a tarp, will do. Watch out for rodents, though.

Whatever cool surface you use, spread the grains out and spray them with a fine mist every now and then to keep them moist but not soaked. Just as the maltsters do at malting, you'll have to turn the grain every 2 hours, otherwise bacteria will turn your hard work into a pointless waste of time. Continue this process of misting and turning every 2 hours until your grains sprout; the sprout should be approximately the size of the grain or a little smaller. Not all the sprouts will be of similar length and not all will sprout, but try to wait until the majority have sprouted sufficiently.

Kilning

Kilning should be less fiddly and a more straightforward part of the process of turning hard work into a beer, and can be done in a normal household oven. What is basically happening is that the moisture levels of the malt are being reduced from around half to around 5%; in other words, you are drying out the grains.

1. Stick your grains in the oven on a baking sheet at the lowest setting (around 40°C/104°F is the ideal temperature) with the oven door ajar for 48 hours. Ensure that the grains don't go above 44°C (111°F), otherwise you will be destroying the enzymes.

2. Weigh the grain after the first 12 hours to see how dry it is. Keep weighing it at regular intervals and when it is the same weight as when you steeped it then it will be dry. The trick to doing this is to set about 100g (3½oz) or so of grains apart from the main 'group', so you only have to weigh that same small quantity each time. They will dry a bit quicker than the main group, but it will give you an indication.

3. The grains can then be dried at 100°C (212°F) for 2–3 hours to make

pale malt, which is the base grain for making your speciality malts. Ideally, the grain should now be left for at least three weeks before being used, and of course it also needs to be crushed.

Other non-caramelized malts can be made by varying step 3, the temperature and drying time. Pilsner (a base malt), for example, can be made by drying at 88°C (190°F) for 2–3 hours; and a roast malt like brown malt can be roasted for 5 hours at 100°C (212°F), then raise the temperature to 175°C (347°F) for 40 minutes. For more of an explanation on the different type of malts, see page 181.

MAKING SPECIALITY GRAINS FROM PALE MALT

In most beer recipes pale malt will be the predominant grain, but if you are making something other than a simple Pale Ale or an IPA then you'll need to create some speciality grain (see the Malt chapter, pages 181–201, for a full description). The host of beer styles, and especially the varying colours of beer, owe more to the choice of other grains that go into the beer than to how they are brewed. There are two types of malts: caramelized and non-caramelized (or roasted). You'll need to follow differing processes to make each.

Chocolate Malt

Soak some Pilsner malt for 30 minutes, then bake it in the oven at 70°C (158°F) for 2 hours. Raise the temperature to 120°C (248°F) for a further 30 minutes to dry the grains. Now to start really cooking the grains, raise the temperature again to 150°C (302°F) for 20 minutes and then to 160°C (320°F) for 10 minutes, before finally increasing it to 240°C (464°F) for 1–1½ hours, depending on how much malt you are roasting.

Munich Malt

A working replica of Munich malt can be made by taking dry pale malt, putting it on a baking tray and baking it at 175°C (347°F) for 20 minutes for a few grams and up to 30 minutes for a couple of kilos.

Crystal Malt

It's actually surprisingly easy to get really good results making crystal malt. Start with any of the base malts. Leave some water to stand for a couple of days, or treat it with a campden tablet to remove any chlorine. Weigh out 1kg (2lb 3oz) of base malt, then soak it in the water for 24 hours. The grains need to have absorbed enough moisture to have almost doubled in weight by almost 50%, to around 1.45kg (3lb 3oz). Don't worry if it's not dead on.

Strain thoroughly, then put into a baking dish, ensuring an even depth of 5cm (2in). Loosely cover with aluminium foil and bake at 70°C (160°F) for 2–3 hours. The easiest way to ensure you have the right heat is to set the oven to around that temperature but then to check with a meat thermometer or food probe, as accuracy within a few degrees is important and oven thermometers are not always that accurate. The real trick is not to let it go over 73°C (163°F). Check and rotate the grains every half-hour.

Take off the foil cover and turn the oven up to 100°C (200°F), again checking your thermometer and allowing for +/– 4°C. Roast at this temperature for 2–3 hours, rotating the grains every half-hour or so, and you'll have pale crystal malt.

If you want darker malts, raise the oven to 150°C (300°F) and rotate the grains every half-hour, ensuring that they all get an even roasting. Keep checking the grains until you have reached your desired malt.

Note: Leave all grains for a few weeks before using. Your beer will thank you for it.

CRUSHING GRAINS

On one of my first ever all-grain batches I accidently bought a bag of whole, uncrushed grains. I wouldn't mind, but it was a 25kg (55lb) bag. Being rather wet behind the ears, I didn't realize they had to be crushed, so I brewed anyway and ended up with a very weak and thin beer. So, although it is possible to make a beer with uncrushed grains, you won't be happy with the results. Expect around 25% efficiency. Some brewers insist that buying whole grains then crushing them means their beer tastes fresher than using pre-crushed grains. If you plan to make only a few batches a year and want to buy in bulk, then whole grain could also be a way forward, but it does mean you have to find a way to crush them.

Most people will recommend getting a grain mill in order to crush, but these are not items to be scrimped on, the cheapest not being fit for purpose, the adequate being rather expensive and the decent coming in at around the price of most people's entire home-brew set-up. But if you are serious about brewing they are a worthwhile investment. However, crushed grains are not really that much different in price from uncrushed, so grain mills are a luxury here in the UK. That said, if you do own one you can experiment with different settings to get different efficiencies with your brews.

Using a blender is another – and far cheaper – option. It doesn't so much crush your grains as cut them up, but having blended 25kg (55lb) I can vouch for it that good beer can still be made.

In a standard-size (1.25-litre/2-pint) blender, place 140g (5oz) of uncrushed grain, so that the blender is half full – there should be enough to stop the grain from flying around but not so much that it clogs the blender. Pressing the pulse button will then start to crush the grains. The grains will fall down towards the blades so there is an even crush. Keep an eye on the centre well as the grains fall; when you no longer see uncrushed grains you are done. If you are fairly new to brewing, it can also be pertinent to have a few crushed grains sitting near to you in order to compare. What you are looking for is an even crush, leaving no whole grains; you don't want it to go too far the other way either, turning your grains into flour.

GROWING YOUR OWN HOPS

Commercial hops are grown up poles, but you can grow them up the side of your house. Hops like sunlight and will require around 8 hours of it every day, so a south-facing garden that gets plenty of light is ideal. They can also grow up to 7 metres (23 feet), or about the size of a typical two-storey Victorian house. They won't tolerate thick clay, preferring a nutrient-rich, well-drained soil. If you do have thick clay, digging in plenty of manure and compost will transform the growing medium into a hop-friendly one. Alternatively, they can be grown in big pots measuring at least 50cm (20in) in diameter and they will need watering more than a ground-planted hop.

PLANTING AND TRAINING

Plant softwood cuttings or rhizome cuttings in spring when the ground is not frozen. Once you have chosen which type of hop suits your needs (see page 156), the search can start. Cuttings can be found on home-brew web forums, from specialist nurseries, by asking members in your local brew circle and on classified websites like eBay or gumtree.com. It is always worth trying to get rhizomes that have been grown as close to your home as possible. This is because plants will naturally adapt to weather and soil conditions, and growing them in the same district just means there are fewer things for them to re-adapt to.

Before planting, ensure rhizomes are nice fat examples and not dried out or disease-ridden. If they are firm to the touch you are on to a winner; you want something that feels like an under-ripe avocado rather than a very over-ripe one. Ensure that the rhizomes are planted horizontally, with the white shoots facing up and the roots facing downwards. If you don't intend to plant them out immediately, then wrap them up in newspaper or damp sawdust to stop them from drying out and check frequently to ensure they don't go mouldy or dry out.

Plant to a depth of 15–20cm (6–8in) and water in well. Adding a mulch of straw or bark will retard weed growth.

Hop bines will need to grow up something. I have used fencing wire, but rope, or even a sturdy old washing line, will do the job. Select the strongest bines and allow them to wrap themselves around the wire; they may need a little bit of coaxing at first but they will get the hang of it after a week or two. To make a trellis, set a 3–4-metre (10–13-foot) pole in the ground and tie the wire to the top, pegging it out at around 1 metre (3 feet) from the base of the pole to form a tepee-like structure for your hops to grow up.

Don't expect too much in the first year – although I did get enough to make a single 19-litre (33½-pint) batch of beer. Prune some of the young leaves in late spring to open up the bines to the sun. Keep varieties separate and feed with an organic liquid fertilizer (or even mulch with spent hops).

PESTS AND DISEASES

Aphids can be a problem. To combat them I picked as many ladybird larvae (young ladybirds) as I could from a nearby lime (*Tilia*) tree and placed them on the bines, where they made short work of the aphids. This is best done as soon as you see any aphids. They are born pregnant and sometimes even with a pregnant aphid inside them, so these little critters multiply quicker than rabbits.

Powdery mildew can also be a problem. This is a fungus that appears in small, circular powdery colonies on the leaves. It grows just like mushrooms do, spreading a web of mycelium (fungus roots). If left untreated, the whole bine can turn white. The fungus can also stop the flowers (or burr) from forming altogether and yields may drop to next to nothing.

Prevention, as always, can be better than cure. As powdery mildew can over-winter on hop debris, ensure all above-ground growth is destroyed each year and consider planting disease-resistant varieties such as Boadicea, Wye Target, Magnum or Newport, or moderately resistant varieties such as Fuggle, Perle and Hallertau. Also, do not over-fertilize with any nitrogen-based fertilizers, as the disease will strike young growth rather than established growth and the nitrogen will aid young, fresh, disease-susceptible shoots. When watering, water just the roots, or consider setting up an irrigation system and water first thing in the morning to stop humidity levels rising – mildew loves high humidity levels.

Inspect plants regularly and, if infected, remove and destroy all infected parts, normally the bottom leaves. This also opens up the hop area and helps to decrease humidity. Some growers have reported good results from spraying with a solution made up of 50% water and 50% cow's milk.

Hops are greedier than city bankers: they will need nutrients and lots of them. It is good to know the warning signs of any deficiency and what to do to rectify it. Leaves turning yellow, leaves falling off or curling, and slow growth are all signs of mineral deficiencies. These can be easily rectified by feeding with a liquid seaweed feed; if that doesn't work, try digging wood ash into the soil around your plants. I'd also suggest using a comfrey feed, which is made simply by adding comfrey to a water butt then watering your plants with the 'tea' – or there is always the less smelly option of mulching with comfrey.

HARVESTING

After your hops have lazily wound themselves up the side of your house, slowly producing small burrs that turn into flowers, they will be ready for harvesting in the late summer to early autumn. You'll know when they are ready as the hop cones (flowers) will feel light, dry and papery, and they will spring back after a squeeze rather than feeling wet to the touch and being about as springy as a ninety-year-old man's skin. They will also appear lighter in colour than they were when they first appeared.

Pick a cone off your bine and take it apart. Look at the base of the petals (bracts): there should be yellow powdery resin (lupulin) which looks rather like the pollen you see on an overladen bee's legs. Give it a sniff: it should be quite strong-smelling, just like the hop smell when you first open a bag from your supplier. This is the part of the hop that flavours our beer, the bit full of those lovely alpha acids. If you have left it too late and the hops are past their prime picking time, then they will turn brown and start to open. It's not a great idea to use over-ripe hops in your beer, as the lupulin will have started to degrade.

To harvest, wait for a dry, fine day. If the hops have been grown on the side of a house, up a tree or wall, then pick from a ladder, placing your hop cones into a clean sack or bag that can be attached to the ladder, or yourself, to aid picking (and holding the ladder). Pick only the ripest cones. You may have seen footage of the hop fields in Kent being harvested, great bines being cut at the base, pulled down and then picked in quantity. This is a great way to harvest if you have multiple bines, as it is very quick; the downside is that you have just one harvest and you'll also be picking some not yet ripe or over-ripe cones.

You'll be surprised just how prolific wild hops can be; I've seen them growing wild from Devon right up to Falkirk. Start looking in the hedgerows around your area and you might get lucky. Harvesting wild hops need not be any different from harvesting home-grown ones. I tend to cut the bine at base level and pull it slowly from the tree before picking off the cones and putting them into a sack. The spent bine can then be placed back in the hedgerow to decay and give back some nutrients for next year's growth.

DRYING

Hops need to be dried in a warm place where there is no sunlight and where air can circulate freely. Traditionally this would be done in an oast house, and if you have ever travelled around Kent you will see these all over the place. They are unmistakable: round buildings with strange, tent-like roofs, with a funny-looking white central, pivoted chimney. These two- or three-storey buildings would have a fire lit at the bottom and the hot air would rise, drying the hops.

Of course most houses are not set up like oast houses, and the home-brewer will have to find another way to dry their hops. The loft (unless it

gets humid), a garage, or a shed can be a perfect place in summer, as they all get hot, have air circulating and are dark. An old (but clean) net curtain tied to a square frame made from four bits of bamboo cane can work as a screen on which to place your harvested hops. They can take a few days to dry. For smaller quantities, 'hop pockets' can be made – these are simply pages from a newspaper folded into pockets and stapled together. The pockets can be filled with hops, sealed and put on your hot-water tank for a few days.

STORING

Hops keep very well in the freezer – I've used hops that were over a year old and haven't noticed any discernible difference in flavour or bitterness. That said, the alpha-acid level will deteriorate over time and it is best practice to buy and use hops as and when you need them.

Before freezing, ensure that your hops are completely dry and store them in resealable freezer bags, ensuring that all the air is squeezed out of the bags before sticking them in the freezer. It is best to keep a note of when your hops were harvested, the alpha-acid levels and the type of hop. I'd also recommend storing your hops in 25g (1oz) bags, as it makes it easier if you don't have to keep opening large bags.

Better than freezing, if at all possible even home-grown hops should be sealed in a foil vacuum pack just as you might buy them from your home-brew stockist. You can buy vacuum sealers and bags on the internet or from larger kitchen shops/catering suppliers.

WHAT TO DO WITH SPENT HOPS

Spent hops can be composted and will break down very well. However, they are far more useful as mulch, which will retard weed growth and add nutrients to the soil. Place them around your plants, but it is advisable to avoid putting them around the stems of young plants as they will scorch.

DRY-HOPPING

Hops added at the start of the boil will increase bitterness, but most of their aroma will evaporate. Hops added towards the end of the boil will add some bitterness and also, as their aromatic compounds stay intact, they will add some aroma and flavour to the finished beer, but unfortunately some of these compounds can be stripped away during fermentation. Therefore when we 'dry-hop' what we mean is adding hops long after the boil, often during secondary fermentation or conditioning. Whole hops, hop plugs or pellets can all be added.

At first this practice does seem to go against all the advice of every brewer, in that it means adding an unsanitized product to your wort/beer. However, hops tend not to carry the types of bacteria considered harmful to beer; nor does what they do carry fare too well in an airless, low pH, alcoholic environment.

The practice isn't new, and brewers during the nineteenth century were dry-hopping; indeed, some of the advice given then still rings true today. In E. R. Southby's book *A Systematic Handbook of Practical Brewing*, published in 1885, he states, '"Dry-hopping" is, therefore, the only means of securing the presence of these highly volatile matters, and without them it is impossible to obtain that delicacy of flavour so much admired . . .' He also rather amusingly advises that 'the proportion of hops is weighed out separately for each cask by workmen who can be depended upon'. Any brewer, home or otherwise, who has a few pints whilst brewing might well take note!

How to Dry-hop

All brewers at every level can dry-hop, even armchair brewers. Simply put a single hop cone into a meticulously clean coffee plunger (one that is used only for beer-related activities will be ideal) and top up with beer. Leave it to infuse for a short while, then pour it into a pint glass and drink. If you've used a beer with which you are very familiar, you'll detect a difference in the flavour and aroma. You may notice a difference in the bitterness, but as dry-hopping doesn't actually affect the bitterness levels this is a matter of perception.

Don't be tempted to try this process by opening and resealing an already fermented bottled beer; it will end up gushing and the flavour will be akin to sucking the floor of a greengrocer's van.

Alternatively, if you are feeling particularly lazy, just pop a couple of (frozen) hop flowers straight into a beer. The amount of time it takes to drink it will mean that as you reach the bottom the hop will have defrosted fully and will be intensely bitter, whereas at the start it will be less so. It's enough to give you an indication of how different levels of IBUs (International Bittering Units – see page 25) will affect your beer.

To dry-hop your brewed beer, wait until the majority of active fermentation has ceased. Then just put the hops directly into the beer sitting in your fermenting vessel – this can be done in either your primary or your secondary fermenting vessel. As I found to my dismay, cones will float to the top and cause a few problems, such as shedding petals and bunging up the airlock or clogging up siphoning tubes. It is easy to rectify this annoyance by encasing the hop cones in a muslin bag, filling the bag with marbles, sewing it up with nylon thread, tying string to the top of the bag and dangling it so that the hops sit perfectly suspended towards the bottom of your beer. Ensure that the hops are not too tightly packed so that they and the beer can get to know each other. This also means that the hops actually get utilized rather than just floating on the surface.

You may want to undertake a few dry runs first, using water and some dried grass, as hops can be quite buoyant and will float quite a few marbles to the top of your beer. I'd also suggest racking your beer directly from your FV rather than trying to fish out the hops first; it is much easier to get them out of an empty FV.

Clogging can also become a problem if you are using hop pellets; however, the pellets will soak up the beer and will sink, and when racking your beer a small muslin square tied to the bottom of a siphon will rectify any clogging. You may need to change the square midway.

The length of time for which you dry-hop and your choice of pellets or cones is just that – your choice. Most brewers will agree that the usual length of time to dry-hop is between three and ten days. However, there is emerging evidence from the Department of Food Science and Technology at Oregon State University suggesting that just one day of dry-hopping with pellets rather than cones will give the best results, as long as the pellets are suspended and are kept circulating.

The amount of cones or pellets to use depends on a few things: the type of hops you are using, the amount of aroma you wish to add to your finished beer, and the temperature. In a 19-litre (33½-pint) batch around 10–15g (¼–½oz) of low-aromatic hops such as East Kent Goldings, Czech Saaz or Styrian Goldings at 15°C (59°F) will of course have much less of an aroma impact than the same amount of a high-aromatic hop such as Chinook, Cascade or Simcoe – which is why you might end up having to use three times the amount to make any kind of dent in your aroma profile. The temperature makes a difference too, as more aroma oils are released at higher temperature. This is why you may notice a real difference to the beers you dry-hop in summer compared with perhaps the same beers that you make in winter.

It's certainly worth experimenting with dry-hopping to obtain the results that you want. Those who brew country wines will be well equipped with 4.5-litre (1-gallon) glass demijohns. These are perfect, as you can dry-hop a 19-litre (33½-pint) batch into four demijohns with varying amounts of hops in them.

As a cautionary note, don't use hops that smell of old socks or like a rabbit hutch, as they will have started to oxidize and that smell will end up in your beer.

CULTURING YEAST

When a sailing barge sank in the English Channel back in 1825 no one could have guessed that a small part of its cargo would be of so much interest to beer lovers when it was recovered over 160 years later. The bounty was made precious by a few wax-sealed bottles of Porter which had survived the wreck. Although stale, undrinkable and with an aroma of 'dead dog', the beers were at least more interesting if not more valuable than any beer available anywhere across the world. These small ale bottles contained a real window into history – or at least their sediment did, as in the sediment there might be some remaining live yeast cells. Often recipes will be passed down the ages, but, as yeast plays such a crucial part in the flavour of a beer, without the authentic yeast strain it is impossible to brew an historically accurate beer.

Over time Dr Keith Thomas and his team at Brewlab in Sunderland carefully cultured the shipwrecked yeast in sterile conditions. Initially, they managed to grow only bacteria, but eventually in one bottle they found sufficient cells to culture into enough yeast to make a starter and then, using malts made without any post-Second World War pesticides, they brewed the most authentic Porter since the First World War. It was known as Flag Porter and, according to Mr E. Poutard, one of the few surviving drinkers of pre-war Porters, 'It tastes like real Porter. It's a good pure drink.'

If yeast can be cultured from 163-year-old bottles from the bottom of the sea, then there is nothing to stop the home-brewer from culturing a yeast from the bottom of a bottle of conditioned beer. There are two ways of doing this and both of them differ from making a yeast starter (see page 209).

It has to be said, though, that it really wasn't easy to culture the yeast recovered from the shipwreck. Yeast will 'eat' all of the residual sugars and minerals left in beer before feeding off dead cell material. Yeast also mutates with time and won't be true to form, so you can't always expect your yeast to work in exactly the same manner as it did when the brewers initially pitched it. It will, however, be close.

First find a bottled conditioned beer with a taste that you really enjoy – there is no use putting all that effort into something you might not like! Keep it in the fridge for a week, then sanitize the top of the bottle and, in a clean environment, remove the cap with a sterilized opener, run a fag-lighter flame across the bottle neck for a few seconds and swab the inside of the bottle with a vodka-infused cotton bud. Gently decant the beer into a glass, leaving just the sediment at the bottom. Swirl the sediment around in the bottom of the bottle, use your fag lighter again and then pour the sediment into a sterile yeast-collection vessel. A small plastic tub will do the job, but it needs to be sterile and scratch-free.

INGREDIENTS
10g (¼oz) dry malt extract (DME)
1–2g (⅓–⅔oz) Japanese agar (available from wholefood shops and Asian supermarkets)
120ml (4 fl. oz) water

EQUIPMENT
2 small saucepans, a funnel and coffee filter, a lab-style beaker, three Petri dishes

with lids, a pressure cooker, sanitizer, aluminium foil, a bottle of your favourite beer (bottle-conditioned), an inoculation loop and slant tube (can be purchased from eBay or laboratory suppliers), a fag lighter, a steady hand and lots of patience

1. Rehydrate the agar for 30 minutes.

2. Meanwhile, whisk the DME in the water and bring to the boil, keeping a careful eye that it doesn't boil over. Pour this through a coffee filter into another clean pan, add the agar and bring back to the boil, stirring occasionally until the agar is fully dissolved. Pour into a beaker through the coffee filter.

3. Put the three Petri dishes (also known as agar plates) and the beaker with the agar/wort in it into the pressure cooker with 3–5cm (1½–2in) of water. Allow the pressure cooker to do its stuff and start making a noise, then turn the heat down to very low and leave for 15 minutes. Turn off the heat and leave to cool.

4. Place the Petri dishes and beaker on to sterilized foil. Pour the wort into the dishes, keeping the amount of time the lids are off to a minimum. Wait 2 hours until the wort has solidified.

5. Condensation will have formed on the lids, so hold them near a heat source, such as a gas hob, in order to dry. Run your inoculation loop through a flame, but don't allow it to get hot, then let it cool for a few seconds. Dip your loop into your sediment as this contains the beer yeast you want, then using your loop draw a continuous zigzag line backwards and forwards along the agar plates. Replace the lids and turn the dishes over. Leave at room temperature in a dark location for three or four days.

6. On return to your yeast, it should have visibly cultured and you will see marks on the agar plate. Boil some water and let it cool. Then, using the inoculation loop, pull out any good-looking colonies of yeast and place them in a beaker with 10ml (⅓ fl. oz) of the boiled and cooled water.

7. Make up a wort solution identical to the previous one and place this

into a slant tube, which is basically similar to a test tube with a lid. You could use a meticulously cleaned and sterilized white lab yeast vial. Using the loop again, put your healthy colonies into the tube and leave it in a cool, dark place for another three or four days. This can then be taped up and left in the fridge for months.

8. When you want to use the yeast, pull out your trusty loop and build up a yeast starter, starting at 10ml (⅓ fl. oz); see page 209 for how to do this.

8

GRUIT ALES

Β RITISH BEER IS always being influenced by new ingredients. Before the fifteenth–sixteenth-century invasion of the hop we used to brew with herbal mixes. These are generically called 'gruit mixes' and they were used to flavour and preserve Ale. Various botanicals are used to make a gruit beer, but a 'true' Gruit Ale is always made with yarrow, (wild) rosemary and bog myrtle. Interestingly, hops were sometimes used, as well as other botanicals, which could also include juniper, mugwort, wormwood, heather, liquorice, henbane and sage.

When making a Gruit Ale I find that the sweetness of a Scottish Ale works very well in balancing out the bitter herbs. It is also worth experimenting, changing the herbs to others that can be used in brewing (see Other Ingredients, page 140). Especially considering that when Gruit Ales were all the rage the Church would closely guard their mixes and recipes would change hands for vast sums of money, who knows – you could come up with something that hasn't been brewed since Robin Hood was running around.

Although you can essentially use any herbs as a mix, the basic three – yarrow, bog myrtle and rosemary – work as a good basis for other herbs. Just as you would if brewing with hops, the more bitter herbs can be used at the start of the boil, while the more fragrant will offer aromas when used towards the end. You can also enhance the flavour by 'dry-herbing' – which, just like dry-hopping, means adding herbs during the last few days of secondary fermentation.

The most interesting part of Gruit Ales, I find, is people's mental reaction to them. Each of the herbs has mild narcotic effects and the drunkenness from Gruit Ales is very different from those using hops. But that said, hops do have a soporific effect, too. Any medicated guests at a party probably need to be told what they are drinking, as some herbs can interact with prescription drugs.

GRUIT ALE RECIPES

Don't expect this to taste like a normal beer – it really isn't. It is something quite different and quite unusual. This recipe is meant as a guideline to making the basis of a Gruit Ale, to which you can add your own take by including other herbs and spices.

Extract Gruit

INGREDIENTS
80g (3oz) chocolate malt
160g (5½oz) crystal malt
4kg (9lb) pale malt extract

Steep the grains, then boil 17 litres (30 pints) of water, adding the water from the steeped grains and the pale malt extract. Boil for 60 minutes, adding the herbs at the following times:

40g (½oz) dried yarrow leaves @ 45 minutes (which means after 15 minutes' boiling, with 45 minutes left)

20g (¾oz) dried rosemary @ 15 minutes (i.e. after 45 minutes, with 15 minutes left)

0.5g (0.02oz) dried bog myrtle leaves @ 15 minutes

20g (¾oz) yarrow flowers for the last three days of fermentation

10g (¼oz) rosemary for the last three days of fermentation

Ferment for two days at 19°C (66°F) and then two weeks at 18°C (64°F) using 2 vials of WLP028 Edinburgh Ale yeast or 1 packet of Danstar Nottingham dried yeast.

All-grain Gruit

INGREDIENTS

5kg (11lb) Golden Promise (4 EBC) 93.3%

240g (8oz) crystal malt (120 EBC) 4.5%

120g (4oz) chocolate malt (885 EBC) 2.2%

Target OG 1.064

Target PG 1.014

Mash for 75 minutes at 66°C (151°F). Add herbs at the following times:

40g (1½oz) dried yarrow leaves at 45 minutes

20g (¾oz) dried rosemary at 15 minutes

0.5g (0.02oz) dried bog myrtle leaves at 15 minutes

FOR DRY-HERBING

20g (¾oz) yarrow flowers and 10g (¼oz) rosemary

Ferment using 2 vials of WLP028 Edinburgh Ale yeast. Ferment at 19°C (66°F), raising the temperature to 21°C (70°F) after 48 hours. Secondary ferment after two weeks as long as the majority of fermentation has ceased. Dry-herb with 10g (¼oz) rosemary and 20g (¾oz) dried yarrow flowers after three weeks. Allow to condition for at least two months before drinking.

GRUIT ALE HERBS

BOG MYRTLE (*MYRICA GALE*)

Also known as sweet gale, bog myrtle likes to grow near running water, generally on marshlands, and therefore it is a plant that is foraged rather than grown. It can be found in quantity in Scotland, Wales and north-west England, and occasionally in the east of England, Surrey and Devon. As well as its leaves being one of the predominant herbs in a 'gruit' mix ale it is said that bog myrtle can also be used as an excellent insect repellent.

Having tried a beer brewed with two lots of 25g (1oz) of bog myrtle put in at the start of the boil and at the end, I'd suggest that, if using it experimentally, it's best to go easy at first. It has a very strong and over-powering, astringent medicinal flavour and can drown out any other aroma if used in quantity – let alone repel any insects. It should be used during the first part of the boil to bitter, or to dry-herb.

Bog myrtle is also said to have relaxing, stupefying and narcotic properties, which might account for its popularity with ancient brewers.

ROSEMARY (*ROSMARINUS OFFICINALIS*)

Ordinary garden rosemary is very easy to grow. It can be raised from seed, but since germination rates are erratic at best and it takes ages to grow, it is much easier to pick up a plant from a garden centre and plant that. Or you could grow from cuttings. Cut a 7cm (3in) piece and take off the bottom leaves. Dust with hormone rooting powder and plant in a compost/coir/grit mix. Don't overwater but don't allow to dry out either. Plant out when established in well-drained, neutral to alkaline soil in full sun. Prune to encourage new growth and protect in the harshest of winters. But if you forget, prune off the black, frost-scorched leaves in spring.

However, there is no need to grow a plant in order to have a great supply of rosemary. If you have a walk around your neighbourhood you will no doubt find some growing semi-wild in parks and gardens. If you end up picking from someone's front garden, be sure to ask first (far be it from me to suggest you do it at night when no one is watching).

Rosemary is at its most aromatic when it is in flower during the winter months, as it is higher in essential oils then, so use half as much in a recipe as you might the rest of the year.

You could also use shop-bought dried rosemary if you have money to burn, but in my opinion the results are not as good. Simply put it in a muslin bag to use.

Use in: Gruit Ales or in place of hops in Pale Ale.

Yarrow (*Achillea Millefolium*)

Having planted yarrow in my herb garden I can safely say that once it takes you'll have it for ever. It spreads by root and seed and can often be found growing in all but the most highly sprayed and carefully managed lawns. Sow seeds in the autumn in pots in a greenhouse or indoors before planting out in the spring. It is drought-tolerant, survives in most soils and even comes back after continual cutting when it spreads into the lawn.

As it is such an invasive plant it grows well in the wild too, so can be easily foraged.

The dried leaves of yarrow can be used as a bittering agent and the dried flowers as an aroma if dry-herbed.

GROWING AND USING OTHER INGREDIENTS

Before hops were commonplace all manner of herbs, spices and wild plants were used in beers. Just as some brewers will closely guard their recipes now, so brewers of old used to be secretive about their gruit mixes.

The modern brewer might most commonly obtain a whole array of flavours from carefully choosing and blending hops and malts, but a Porter can be set apart by having an extra bit of spice, or a Wheat Beer can be more refreshing by the addition of some coriander. These herbs and spices can be added at various stages, just as hops are. Adding during the last part of the boil, dry-herbing during the last few days of secondary fermentation, or adding infusions are all great methods for introducing new flavours.

MAKING AN INFUSION

The easiest way to make a flavour infusion is to make a herbal tea by infusing 15g (½oz) dry herbs or 30g (1oz) fresh with 250ml (8 fl. oz) of boiling water. Allow it to cool, then add it to your beer during the last 10 minutes of the boil.

You can also add some herbal teabags (1 bag per 4.5 litres/ 1 gallon) – but avoid doing this if you are using a pungent herb.

If you are simply experimenting, make a quarter of a cup of very strong herbal tea and add this to a beer. The tea will water down the beer, but at least you'll see if your beer style and chosen herb match.

BAY (*LAURUS NOBILIS*)

Useful for adding a touch of spice to darker beers. Bay leaves are available all year round and can be easily mistaken for other types of laurel leaves which should not be used. To aid identification, go to a garden centre, find a bay tree, sneak a leaf off and crush it in your hand to smell it. You may also find bay trees growing like lollipops in front of hotel doorways; if you are going to sneak a leaf, ensure the doorman is not about.

If planting, don't forget bay can grow up to 20 metres (66 feet) tall. It doesn't need much attention, but heavy pruning will keep it in check. It is easier to buy one rather than starting from seed.

Use in: Porters, Stouts and ESBs.

CHAMOMILE (*MATRICARIA CHAMOMILLA*)

German chamomile is the variety most widely grown for its flowers. This is a herb that grows very easily from seed. Plant after the first frost and water when dry. With any luck it will self-seed in the same spot year after year.

You can use the fresh flower heads in beer – these will start to bloom from early summer. Alternatively, pluck the heads off and dry them on newspaper in a well-ventilated room away from direct sunlight and store in an airtight container. Use about 2 teaspoons of fresh chamomile or 1 teaspoon of the dried herb towards the end of the boil.

However, perhaps the easiest way to get chamomile is to buy some teabags! You can make an infusion with a few chamomile teabags and throw it in towards the end of the boil; teabags themselves can also be used to dry-herb, or towards the end of the boil.

The flavour of chamomile can be rather subtle, but it does help to accentuate some of the characteristics of the Noble Hops (see page 178).

Use in: Wheat Beers, Pale Ales.

CORIANDER (*CORIANDRUM SATIVUM*)

As long as you keep slugs at bay in the early stages of growth, coriander is very easy to cultivate. Ensure you buy a seed-producing variety.

A handful of seeds, crushed and placed in a muslin bag during the last 10–15 minutes of the boil, will impart plenty of flavour to your beer. Don't worry if you are not a gardener, as shop-bought coriander seeds are fine to use and can be found cheaply in supermarkets.

Use in: Old Ales and Wheat Beers.

GROUND IVY (*GLECHOMA HEDERACEA*)

This plant grows in partial shade and so can be found along forest floors, by hedgerows and on verges.

Ground ivy is also known as ale-hoof due to its use in Ale 'on the hoof', or after the wort has boiled. Once you have boiled your wort throw in some ground ivy, leaving it in the boiler when you transfer the wort to the fermenting vessel. Anecdotal evidence suggests it makes a good clarifying agent. It also imparts a peppery taste and can be used in place of or as well as aroma hops.

Use in: Anything for which you have used rye malt – a Mild, for example.

WOOD AVENS (*GEUM URBANUM*)

Also known as herb bennet, which comes from Benedictine and means 'holy herb', it was thought to ward off evil spirits and help protect against the plague. Perhaps the meaning is more likely to derive from its use by Benedictine monks in brewing. It can be found growing under trees and shrubs as a pernicious weed, so there is no real need to grow any. I've found it in every garden and allotment I've ever cultivated.

Dig up the root and cut off the leafy green part. Wash the root, soak it in vodka, put it in a muslin bag and add to your beer during the last few days of fermentation or during the last bit of the boil. It will impart a clove-like flavour. As it's a wild plant there is no real uniformity of flavour, so it's best to rely on your nose. If your avens smell strong, don't use more than 1 teaspoon in a 19-litre (33½-pint) batch and double that for weaker-smelling avens. Less is more in this case – unless you want your beer to taste solely of cloves.

When used centuries ago the herb's antiseptic properties were reported to help stop beers from souring, so it is worth experimenting with it in unhopped beers.

Use in: Porters and Milds.

PART FOUR

The Ingredients

9

HOPS

UNLESS YOU ARE tuned into the botanical goings-on in the hedgerows, you'll fail to see wild hops growing until they are in flower. They seem to creep secretly around trees and shrubs, winding themselves slowly up and up. It's this somewhat devious, secretive nature that earned them the title of 'wolf of the hedgerow', which is reflected in their Latin name *Humulus lupulus* (*lupus* being the Latin for wolf).

There are some vague, and some sources suggest unfounded, references suggesting that hops were used in beer 3,000 years ago, but the first real, solid, written evidence is not until January AD 822. The reference comes from the French monastery of St Peter and St Stephen at Corbie, which had been a well-known beer-drinking monastery ever since its inception in the seventh century. It is stated that the practice of using hops in beer is well established by this point, so its origins could indeed be slightly older, though impossible to find out without a time machine.

The use of hops spread like hop bines through an unsuspecting hedgerow, and by the fourteenth century they had made their way to Britain via Belgium. Brewers used to making herbal beers, which would spoil within a few weeks, found that they kept for longer if hopped. This is certainly the case, as I've found even high ABV herbal beers made to all the modern sanitizing standards can turn in a matter of weeks if hops are not used.

WHAT ARE ALPHA ACIDS?

When your hands get a yellow sticky substance on them after handling hop cones (flowers), it is because of a resin contained in the hop called lupulin. Alpha acids are found in this resin, so they make up a certain percentage of what's in the hop, hence the AA percentage on the side of hops bought from reputable sources.

Bitter alpha acids are made up of other chemicals, each of which imparts a different type of bitterness to the beer. The two most important are humulone, which in high levels is thought to give beer a 'clean' bitterness, and cohumulone, which in high levels is thought to give your beer a harsher bitterness. However, I've not met anyone who can tell me what this harsh bitterness really means (see Alpha Acids, page 16).

CALCULATING ALPHA ACID LEVELS FROM HOME-GROWN OR WILD HOPS

Brewers can calculate how many IBUs (International Bittering Units) their beer will have by looking at the alpha acid level of the hops they plan to use and calculating the proportion of those alpha acids that will be utilized (see page 25 for calculating IBUs).

Most home-brewers don't have access to a laboratory in which they can test the alpha acid levels of their hops. This means that when using wild, home-grown or poorly labelled hops it can be impossible to work out their bitterness levels. So your Mild might become a black IPA and your prize pale IPA a pale Mild. If you are just making beer for yourself and your friends and you are not too fussy about the level of bitterness, then fine. If you want to enter competitions or to impress that mate who just knows everything about beer, then it is another useful variable to tweak in order to make exceptional, well-balanced beer rather than OK, drinkable beer.

To calculate the AA level, you could make a simple Pale Ale (see Simcoe, page 170) and just test the bitterness by drinking it and comparing it to shop-bought beers, or home-brewed beers for which you know the bitterness level.

Although drinking beer is an enjoyable method, it's perhaps not the most accurate. Instead you may want to do as brewers of yore did. Make two teas using 250ml (8 fl. oz) of water per cup and 30g (1¼oz) of two different hops – one for which you already know the AA level and the one you want to find. Tip out 60ml (2fl. oz) of the most bitter of the teas and dilute it with 60ml (2fl. oz) of water. Keep diluting until it tastes around the same as the other tea in terms of bitterness. For each 60ml (2fl. oz) calculate 1% AA. So if it was diluted three times, drop 3 alpha acid percentage points from the level of the hop for which you know the AA content.

So, for example, your bought Centennial hops state 10% AA on the packet so you use this as a benchmark for your home-grown Fuggles hops, which will be much less bitter tasting. After diluting the Centennial tea five times you find them to be comparable. This means your Fuggles will have around 5% AA.

BITTERING, AROMA AND DUAL-PURPOSE HOPS AND HOW TO USE THEM

'Bittering', 'aroma' and 'dual-purpose' are generally used as something of a shortcut to describe the characteristics of hops and how they are used in beer. As you can probably work out, bittering hops are used to impart bitterness and aroma hops are used to impart aroma; dual-purpose can do both. In actual fact, all hops can be used in all parts of brewing – it's just that over time brewers have favoured certain hops for different jobs.

Alpha acids need to be isomerized (see page 26) in order to impart their bitterness into the beer. The longer they are boiled, the more alpha acids are isomerized to become bitter iso-alpha acids. For this reason bittering hops are generally boiled from between 45 and 90 minutes. Isomerization is the process of transforming the existing molecules into new molecules, so the process of boiling turns alpha acids into iso-alpha acids which are four times more bitter than alpha acids. This might all sound a little complicated, but in plain English all you really have to know is that hops need to be boiled in order to be bitter. Think of them like a teabag. Plonk a teabag in cold water and nothing much happens. Pour over hot water and bingo – you have tea.

Hops that are high in alpha acids are often used as bittering hops, as you can use fewer hops to get higher levels of bitterness. For example, Fuggles often have around 5% AA and Target 10%, so you'd need half the amount of Target to get the same level of bitterness. Indeed, if a commercial brewer gives you a recipe they will often say something like 'enough hops to hit 30 IBUs', regardless of the variety.

Hops that are lower in alpha acids are often higher in the essential oils needed to create aroma. These are best used at any point during the last 15 minutes of the boil, or even after the boil through dry-hopping (see page 128).

Aroma hops can give your beer a variety of flavours and aromas, including marmalade, tropical fruits or even blackcurrant. High-flavour IPAs are often loaded with aroma hops.

Many hops are known as dual purpose and can be used for bittering, aroma and flavours. The truth really is that all hops can be used for both purposes, it's just that some will have properties that lend themselves to be used as one or the other in particular.

BUYING HOPS

The first time you go shopping for hops can be a daunting experience as the choice is massive. What's more, it's a choice that is forever growing as new strains are introduced on to the market. The list below is fairly exhaustive now, but I am certain that if you are reading this ten years after I have written these words the list will be a drop in the ocean, as even as you read new strains are being grown and tested across the world.

Some home-brew shops will try to pass off hops that are past their best. Ideally they should be stored in a freezer in an airtight vacuum pack; however, this does not always happen, especially if there is a high turnover. Some home-brew shops will let you smell samples – sounds daft, but make sure that you do smell something, and perhaps cross-check it with the list below. Also, reject any hops that are turning brown, as the amount of alpha acid present will be significantly reduced.

LEARNING BY DRINKING

Most brewers will agree that it is one thing visiting a well-stocked home-brew shop or a hop merchant to get to know your hops, another to make a hop tea – but really you need to drink the hops in a beer. Luckily, many brewers do make single-hopped beers. Brewers that are doing this on a regular basis include:

Marston's, Wolverhampton, West Midlands

Royston Fine Ales, Royston, Hertfordshire

Seren Brewing Co., Rosebush, Pembrokeshire

Arbor Ales, Bristol

Oakham Ales, Peterborough, Cambridgeshire

Pictish Brewing Company, Rochdale, Lancashire

Ascot Ales, Camberley, Surrey

George Wright Brewery, St Helens, Lancashire

The Kernel, London

Along with the above, I've also suggested a beer or two to go with each hop description. In some cases hop flavours and aromas might only be apparent in the background as a bittering hop; in other cases the hop aromas will be obvious as soon as you take a whiff. After a while you should be able to start pinpointing the characteristics of each hop. It could take years of practice, but it's hardly an arduous task!

BREWING A SMASH BEER

The practice of single-hopping is obviously not reserved just for the commercial brewer, and a method adopted by many home-brewers has coined the term SMaSH brewing – that is, brewing with a Single Malt and a Single Hop. It is certainly a great way to get to know your hop properly: once you have made a few SMaSH beers you should be able to pinpoint hops from beers across the pub.

You might want to alter the hop additions relative to their alpha acid levels to make beers with similar bitterness. So 3 × 38g (1½oz) of Fuggles (4.5% AA) will give you a beer that has 26 IBUs and using 3 × 12g (¼oz) of Admiral (14% AA) will give a beer with a similar 26.6 IBUs (see page 25 for how to calculate IBUs). This is my 19-litre (33½-pint) version.

4.5kg (10lb) pale malt (6 EBC) 100%

Mash for 1 hour at 66.7°C (152°F). Boil for 1 hour. Then add hops as follows:

12g–50g (½–2oz) hop @ 60 minutes

12g–50g (½–2oz) hop @ 10 minutes

12g–50g (½–2oz) hop @ 5 minutes

Yeast: Safale American US-05

OG 1.048, FG 1.010, ABV 4.8%

British Hops

The buzz in the brewing world at the moment is about New World (American and New Zealand) hops. Drinkers, and therefore brewers, are demanding more and more exotic flavour in their beers. The British hop, once grown across thousands of acres, is now grown across hundreds and seems to be falling out of fashion. I asked Ali Capper, a hop farmer who is helping to promote British hops, a few questions about how British hops are faring in the world market.

Do British hops have a chance, considering the excitement around New World hops?

British hop varieties have predominantly been developed to impart the wonderful English Best Bitter, Pale Ale and Mild flavours and aromas and over the last hundred years hop-breeding programmes have been focused on developing hop varieties that replicate Fuggles and Goldings. The flavours are delicate, complex and, most importantly, produce commercially successful, drinkable beers. With so much experimentation in brewing these days, and the wonderful aromas that British hops offer, every hop variety should be reconsidered for its aroma potential.

Aromas in British hops include: orange, floral, grapefruit, blackcurrant, sage, citrus, apricot, minty, chocolate, marmalade, pepper, pears and lemon.

So, for example, Target is traditionally seen as a bittering hop; it's being used more and more as a late or dry-hop addition, as it gives wonderful sage and citrus flavour notes. Lots of brewers are revisiting British hops for single-hopping. It has been done successfully with most of the UK varieties in recent years and every brewer gets a different result.

In addition, we have some varieties like Admiral, Bramling Cross, Pilgrim and Endeavour that create really powerful flavour if brewed in the right way. Overseas, US, European and Asian craft brewers are getting very excited about the potential that British hops can offer and there is a good export market opening up. British provenance is a very important asset to the UK hop industry. We also have some very exciting new varieties with great flavour potential coming through.

What about organic hops? I'm finding that brewers are getting hops imported from as far afield as New Zealand in order to get certified organic hops. Are there really that many problems with growing organic hops here?

New Zealand is very lucky. Because their plant-health border controls are so tight they have no verticilium wilt and very little other hop pest or disease to contend with, so being organic is easier. In truth, though, their production is not entirely 'organic' in the true sense of the word; but they do use fewer crop-

protection products than in the European or the US hop-growing regions.

True organic hops are produced by a few farms in the UK, and various varieties are available, including First Gold, Sovereign and a small quantity of Fuggles and Target. These are available through hop merchants.

Are there many brewers that use just UK hops?

Ninety per cent of breweries would use some British hops. And a majority of the volume of hops used in a recipe will use British hops, as the large regional breweries would have British hops at the heart of most of their recipes. Quite a lot of craft breweries are using British hops as a majority or exclusively. And quite a few are very proud of their hops' British provenance.

As you can imagine, though, as brewers get more and more keen to experiment, introducing new beers, seasonals and trial beers, the publicity often goes behind the new hop that's come in from New Zealand or the US. So the effort to promote British hops is just about redressing the 'excitement/publicity' balance.

Hops grown in different climates take on different characteristics. Are there characteristics unique to the UK?

The British maritime climate is unique amongst all the hop-growing regions of the world. Most other hop-growing regions have a Mediterranean climate with hotter summers and colder winters, and almost all other regions rely on irrigation to grow hops. These Mediterranean climates do produce different flavours, but they rely heavily on a natural resource to produce hops, which with the climate change forecast may become harder and harder to justify and to achieve in practice.

So the British climate suits hop-growing and our maritime climate tends to produce gentler aromas that produce delicate, complex and deliciously drinkable beers. Beers that you can drink another glass of, that quench your thirst. No wonder we are renowned throughout the world!

It seems that there are always exciting new varieties coming from the States and New Zealand, but what of the UK – do we have any new varieties originating here?

Yes, lots. The most recent success from the Wye Hops programme is Endeavour, which is a Cascade cross and has wonderful grapefruit citrus aroma but is gentler than US Cascade. On that theme, British Cascade is now available and it too is gentler than its American cousin.

There are quite a few brand-new varieties that we are assessing very carefully and that, hopefully, will make it through farm trials. And we are revisiting the National Hop Collection to find old varieties that may be of interest to brewers. The new and old varieties programme is continual, predominantly funded by British hop-growers and run by the British Hop Association through its subsidiary company Wye Hops.

Tell me about the new 'Made with British Hops' logo. Will it soon be a familiar sight on beer-bottle labels and pump clips?

The 'Made with British Hops' logo came about because brewers who had heard talks or seen articles about British hops got in contact to ask if there was anything they could use to promote the British hops in their beer. So we created something. And it was immediately picked up by Hook Norton, Hart Family Brewery, Wye Valley Brewery and many, many more brewers. It would be amazing to think that we might see the logo on bottle labels, pump clips and on marketing materials in breweries, pubs and shops around the UK.

THE HOPS

Each hop has a different character, with different flavours that it will impart to our pints. Just like grapes and wines, some of these flavours are subject to the tastebuds of the drinker, while some are subject to the conditions in which the hops were grown and harvested. However, it does help when tasting or brewing a beer to have some sort of idea of a starting point. Some brewers are beginning to let us drinkers know what hops they are using – a practice that I applaud – so next time you have a pint try to find out which hops have been added and cross-reference the following list. That way you might soon learn if you are a fan of Bramling Cross, or Citra, First Gold or Simcoe hops, just as some wine drinkers know that they love a Merlot or a Pinot Noir grape.

BRITISH HOPS

Admiral, AA 14–16%, Bittering

Bred in the UK at Wye College and released in 1998, Admiral is mostly used as a bittering hop due to its relatively high (for a UK hop) alpha acid content. Citrus aroma, clean orangey bitterness and some earthiness.
Beer profiles suited: Pale Ales and IPAs.
Can be found in: Seafarers 3.9%, Fullers; and, although not showcased, the Wild Rider IPA, 5.5%, Kelham Island, is an example of how it can be used in combination.

Beate, AA 4–6%, Aroma

This relatively new hop is reported to have honey, apricot and even artificial sweet aroma. Use late in the boil or loose.
One to watch out for.
Beer profiles suited: Pale Ales.

Boadicea, AA 6–9%, Aroma

Another relatively new and delicate aroma hop, recommended for dry-hopping and for use late in the boil. In an attempt to be environmentally friendly, Adnams have used Boadicea in their East Green Carbon Neutral Golden Ale.

Beer profiles suited: Golden Ales.

Can be found in: Old Ale, 4.1%, Adnams; soon to be favoured in a selection of beers from Stroud Brewery. Also used in Best Bitter, 4.2%, Ashley Down Brewery.

Bramling Cross, AA 5–8%, Dual

Part Monitoban (a wild hop variety) and part Bramling, this is another hop from the Wye stable, first produced in 1927. It imparts a lovely black-currant edge when used for aroma but can also be used for bittering.

Beer profiles suited: Christmas Ales, Imperial Stouts and Golden Ales.

Can be found in: Bramling Cross, 4.3%, Broughton Ales; also the berry-fruit qualities are excellently showcased in Trawlerboys, 4.6%, Green Jacks.

Cascade (UK), AA 5.3–6.8%, Dual

Not to be confused with the US Cascade. These were first introduced from the States in 2002. Essentially a less intense version of US Cascade (see American Hops, page 164).

Beer profiles suited: IPAs.

Can be found in: Incubus, 4%, Hopdaemon; and in Hophead, 3.8%, Dark Sar, the floral aromas are highlighted.

Challenger, AA 5–9%, Dual

Want spice, get Challenger. Green tea aroma, and if you are wondering where you might have had it before, think Bass, as they embraced it during the 1970s.

Beer profiles suited: Brown Ales, Stouts, Barley Wines, Pale Ales.

Can be found in: Incubus, 4%, Hopdaemon; Loxley Ale, 4.2%, Milestone. Mendip Spring, 3.8%.

East Kent Goldings (EKG), AA 5–9%, Aroma

When used for aroma, EKG offers floral, spice, earthy and herbal notes to a beer. If used for bittering, it tends towards the sweeter, more honey-like. Developed in Canterbury in 1970.

Beer profiles suited: all English-style Ales and Bitters.

Can be found in: Gadds No. 3 Premium Pale Ale, 5%, Gadds the Ramsgate Brewery; Double Maxim, 4.7%, Maxim; and in Holt Two Hoots, 4.2%, Holt Brewery.

Endeavour, AA 8–10.5%, Dual

Very new and not on release as yet for the home-brewer. Blackcurrant aroma and subtle bitterness. Look out for commercial single-hopped examples.

Beer profiles suited: uses unknown as yet, but certainly Pale Ales.

First Gold, AA 6.5–10%, Dual

The summer of 1995 was a long, hot one with little rainfall and therefore was fairly magical. It was also a magical time for hops, as it was when First

Gold first appeared. Despite the proliferation of US hopped beers on the UK market, First Gold is one of the few hops that is gathering steam across the pond, partly due to its all-round versatility: clean and crisp when used for bittering and plenty of citrusy, spicy and floral notes when used for aroma. All in all, makes it a great hop for dry-hopping too. Unlike many UK hops, First Gold is also available organically.

Beer profiles suited: use in any beer style.

Can be found in: Lakeland Gold, 4.4%, Hawkshead; Ruby, 4.5%, Yeovil. Broadside 4.7%, Adnams, uses only First Gold.

Fuggles, AA 3.5–5.8%, Dual

Mr Fuggle might sound like the made-up name of a character from a children's book, but Mr Richard Fuggle actually existed and in 1861 he selected the seedling that we now know as the Fuggle hop. Or is this just another unsubstantiated 'pub fact'? Questions have arisen around the authenticity of this story and as yet it remains just that – a story. There is no hard evidence either to substantiate or disprove it.

Fuggles was originally used for bittering but is now mainly used for aroma, mainly because bittering with a hop with such a low AA is rather expensive. Expect a very typically British, earthy, herbal and spicy aroma.

Beer profiles suited: use in most traditional English Ales.

Can be found in: Owd Oak, 3.5%, Hydes. Adnams Southwold Bitter is dry-hopped using Fuggles. Black Panther, 4.8%, Moorhouse, uses only Fuggles.

Northdown, AA 6–9%, Dual

Northdown is the offspring of Northern Brewer and despite this is considered very versatile and a contender for dry-hopping. Cedarwood earthiness on the aroma profile along with, sometimes, a hint of mint and pine.

Beer profiles suited: most traditional Ales but especially Dark Milds, Old Ales and Barley Wines to give a berry-fruit flavour.

Can be found in: Flack Catcher, 4.4%, Flack Manor; Falling Stone, 4.2%, World Top.

Phoenix, AA 9–12%, Dual

A seedling of Yeoman and another hop from the prestigious Wye College. Released in the year of the Spice (Girls) 1996, Phoenix hops offer more aroma for your buck (or pound, rather) than most, with very interesting spice, floral, chocolate and even molasses characteristics to boot.

Beer profiles suited: Bitters, Pale Ales, Stouts.

Can be found in: Original Port Stout, 4.8%, O'Hanlon's.

Pilgrim, AA 9–13%, Dual (But Mostly Used for Bittering)

Released in 2001. Think fruit – imparts a lemon/grapefruit aroma, but also don't be surprised to find pears, berries and grassy spice too.

Beer profiles suited: IPAs, Stouts, Bitters and Porters.

Can be found in: Innkeepers, 4.5%, Coach House; and Otter Ale, 4.5%, Otter.

Pilot, AA 7–10%, Dual

Formerly known as S24 and named in 2002 by Charles Faram & Co. Ltd, this hedgerow variety has aromas of lemon and spice and clean bittering. A hop that is 'different' from most UK hops and can be used in American-style beers.

Beer profiles suited: APAs, IPAs and most Pale Ales.
Can be found in: Merry Mount, 3.8%, Morton Brewery; Summerskills Blondie, 4.6%, Summerskills.

Pioneer, AA 9–12%, Dual

Distinctive lemon citrus aroma; herbal and cedar present too when used as an aroma hop, but still asserted as a very British hop. When used for bittering it is considered rather clean.
Beer profiles suited: IPAs and Pale Ales.
Can be found in: London Fields PA, 4.0%, Brodie's, excellently highlights the use of Pioneer.

Progress, AA 5–8%, Dual

Bred as an alternative to Fuggles and released in 1951. As such, is pretty similar to Fuggles with grassy, floral, pine and earthy aromas. However, unlike Fuggles it is often used for bittering too.
Beer profiles suited: Porters, Stouts, Pale Ales, Bitters, Scottish Ales.
Can be found in: Try This, 3.7%, WharfeBank; Falling Stone Bitter, 4.2%, World Top; and Hopping Mad, 4.7%, Wood's, uses only Progress.

Sovereign, AA 4–7%, Dual

Grassy, earthy and floral, but with some surprising flavours too, such as peach. The granddaughter of Pioneer yet often compared to Progress and Fuggles. A bit of a Marmite hop – although most don't love it at all.
Beer profiles suited: Bitters, Pas Ales and the bin.
Can be found in: Sovereign, 4.3%, Andwell Brewing.

Sussex, AA 4.3–5.8%, Aroma

Grown by the Cyster family, who have been farming hops for over a hundred years and regularly win prizes at hop exhibitions. Peter Cyster found Sussex growing in a hedgerow and, as he thought it looked 'promising', he subsequently cultivated it. Perhaps a future hop for the home-grown market as it is very vigorous and very easy to grow.

Considered to be a wild variety after studies suggest it is unlike any other hop, although with a similar aroma profile to Fuggles.

Beer profiles suited: Pale Ales.

Can be found in: Iron Horse, 4.8%, Sussex.

Target, AA 9–13%, Dual (But Generally Used for Bittering)

The most widely grown hop in England during the early 1970s after it was released, partly due to its heavy cropping. Also considered to be part of the vanguard for high alpha acid hops and therefore quite interesting to experiment with for dry-hopping (see page 128), but could be considered earthy and spicy. Earthiness less evident when using for bitterness.

Beer profiles suited: IPAs, Brown Ales, Barley Wines, ESBs, Bitters.

Can be found in: one of the hops in London Pride, 4.7%, Fullers; also used in Farriers Best Bitter, 3.8%, Coach House; Oxford Gold Organic Beer, 4.6%, Brakspear.

WGV, AA 5–7.5%, Aroma

WGV stands for Whitbread Golding Variety – a sign that 'owning' or having a trademark on hops is nothing new, as these were of course owned by Whitbread. Woody and floral notes when used for aroma.

Beer profiles suited: Pale Ales, Scottish Ales, Bitters.
Can be found in: 80/–, 4.1%, Caledonian. Old Cocky, 4.3%, Weltons, excellently blends WGV with Northdown.

AMERICAN HOPS

There are a few reasons for the rise and rise of American hops, one of the most interesting being Jim Solberg, an ex-Nike executive with very deep pockets. He bought up land that used to grow acres of hops for Budweiser and his company Indie Hops is funding research into new strains – hops that taste of coconut, blueberry and, perhaps most strangely, garlic. These are exciting times for the future of hops.

Ahtanum, AA 5.2–6.5%, Aroma

A great choice for the brewer who wishes to give an aroma/flavour of grape-fruit, citrus and pine. Similar to Cascade and Amarillo but without all that bitterness. An excellent choice for dry-hopping.
Beer profiles suited: Lagers, IPAs and Pale Ales.
Can be found (in abundance) in: Jaipur Indian Pale Ale, 5.9%, Thornbridge.

Amarillo, AA 8–11%, Dual

Huge amounts of money can go into developing new strains of hops, so you can understand why their growers sometimes want to protect their investment. Which is why there are proprietary hops – hops that are trademarked and can be grown only under licence. It's not really a new idea, as I've mentioned with WGV, which were grown only by Whitbread. What it does is create in-built scarcity and therefore these proprietary hops can often demand higher prices on the open market. Amarillo is such a hop (as are Ahtanum, Simcoe, Warrior, CTZ and Citra). But in the case of Amarillo it was found growing wild, suggesting that there is gold in them there hedgerows.

There are various oils in hops that give the beer flavour. One of them, Myrcene, is particularly high in Amarillo at around 70%. It is the same oil that is found in lemongrass and thyme. When used in beer it gives some citrus, melon and other stone-fruit flavours.

Beer profiles suited (if you can find it): Wheat Beers and 'Hop Bombs'.
Can be found in: Knight of the Garter, 3.8%, Windsor and Eton.

Apollo, AA 15–19%, Bittering

Originating as a crossbreed between Zeus and the catchily named 98001 x USDA, Apollo is a grower's dream. It is high-yielding, resistant to powdery mildew, retains a large percentage of its alpha acids whilst stored and has compact cones which are easy to pick mechanically.

Fruit, particularly citrus, passionfruit and mango flavours, is prominent, as is spicy resinous flavour. Something this 'big' in alpha can go very well in strong IPAs, although here in the UK Stuart Ross (Magic Rock) seems to have set a trend, being one of the first brewers to use Apollo. Whilst he was head brewer at the Castle Brewery in Sheffield he used it to make a low-alcohol, single-hop beer and that tendency still continues.

Beer profiles suited: IPAs and Golden Ales.
Can be found in: Cabarrus Gold, 3.6%, Olde Slewfoot.

Bravo, AA 14–17%, Bittering

If you find yourself reincarnated as a hop you'd better be strong, as only those showing favourable characteristics will be selected for survival. Take

#01046, for example: despite being high in alpha acids and resistant to downy mildew, it took eight years for #01046 to be named Bravo and to go into commercial production.

The citrus notes that many associate with American hops are non-existent; instead this will add floral, piney notes to any beer.

Beer profiles suited: IPAs and Pale Ales.

Can be found in: Nerotype #3 Bravo Black IPA, 6%, Summer Wine Brewery; Bravo, 4.7%, Pictish Brewing Company.

Chinook 12–14%, Dual

There were some momentous happenings for the senses in 1985. It's the year that *Back to the Future* was first shown, 'Meat Is Murder' by The Smiths was first heard, and Chinook hops were first tasted. These Cold War hops helped to kickstart a flagging US brewing industry after being embraced by craft brewers and subsequently becoming known as the hallmark of American hops.

Very good bittering hops and bred for that reason, they are now used in the middle of the boil too in order to offer some great spice and pine flavours.

Beer profiles suited: IPAs, Porters, Stouts, Barley Wines.

Can be found in: Posh Pooch, 4.2%, Ascot Ales.

Citra, AA 11–14%, Dual

To call this hop dual purpose is almost to do it a disservice, as it does both wonderfully and is great as a dry hop too. Named after the Citra area in Florida, home to the pineapple orange – which goes some way to suggesting the flavours this hop gives. Expect lemon, lime, passionfruit and other tropical flavours. Unfortunately, this is one of those hops that sells out on occasions and can command rather high prices too.

Beer profiles suited: Saison, Pale Ales, IPA.
Can be found in: Pale Ale Citra, 5.1%, The Kernel.

Columbus/Tomahawk/Zeus (CTZ), AA 14–18%, Dual

One of the problems that can arise when hops become an investment rather than a plant is the rise of disputes. You can patent a hop, but once it grows somewhere else it can subtly change. The question is: does it change enough to become a new hop altogether? In 1979 Chuck Zimmerman, one of the pioneers in the new wave of hop breeds, left his job with the USDA Hop Program to join the Hop Union. At the time there was no one else left to run the programme and so, as Chuck thought one particular new hop so valuable, he 'borrowed' it and it continued to flourish. Chuck then left Hop Union and joined Yakima Chief. Hop Union pushed to get a patent on the hop that they were now calling Columbus, much to Chuck's dismay, and at this point he and Yakima Chief were calling the exact same hop Tomahawk. To muddy the waters even further, a third company came along with a hop that was very similar to the other 'two' hops. SS Steiner called their hop Zeus. Some tests have shown it to be genetically different from Columbus, but in reality it is so similar that they are often bunched together.

Although due to the high alpha acid content CTZ is excellent as a bittering hop, there is a strong grassy, citrusy aroma. As you'd expect, it is bitter, but the bitterness is shortlived, clean and crisp. Flavour-wise, some people suggest an earthiness with a hint of tobacco and cloves, along with typical Washington State clean citrus flavours. CTZ is a good choice for dry-hopping as it has a high oil content.

Beer profiles suited: IPAs, Pale Ales, Stouts.
Can be found in: Tomahawk, 5%, Titanic Brewery; Columbus, 3.8%,

Mallinsons Brewing Company; The Kernel Pale Ale Columbus, 5.3%, The Kernel.

Delta, AA 5.5–7%, Aroma

An interesting new hop, as it signifies a move away from producing mostly high alpha acid hops. Born as a cross between Fuggle and Cascade hops. Expect flavours of malts to be complemented and a Fuggle floralness amplified. It's almost the hop equivalent of food-matching, offering a great balance with darker malts.

Beer profiles suited: Pale Ales.

Can be found in: Blackwater Delta, 4%, Farmer's Ales.

Horizon, AA 10–16%, Dual

The half-sister of Nugget, it has a low amount of cohumulone. When used for aroma it will help to give beers some spice and floral characteristics.

Beer profiles suited: Light Ales, Lagers, Porters and Christmas Beers.

Can be found in: Deck Aid, 4%, Newby Wyke Brewery.

Liberty, AA 3–5%, Aroma

Considered to be an American Noble closely resembling its family members from the Hallertauer family of hops. Considered by many brewers to be a great hop for late-boil (aroma) additions due to its floral, herbal aromas and vanilla flavours.

Beer profiles suited: Wheat Beers, Kölsch and German-type Lagers.

Can be found in: Liberty, 4.5%, Batemans.

Millennium, AA 14.5–16.5%, Dual (But Mostly Bittering)

Released in the year 2000. A result of a crossbreed between Nugget and Columbus and similar in aroma profile to Nugget.
Beer profiles suited: IPAs, Pale Ales.
Can be found in: Stone the Crows, 5.4%, Lymestone.

Mount Hood, AA 4–7%, Aroma

Just as David Hasselhoff was influencing the fall of the Berlin Wall in 1989, so were other collaborations between Germany and the USA – in this case, the release of this hop bred with the German Hallertauer variety. Expect coriander and spice.
Beer profiles suited: Lagers, Wheat Beers and German beers.
Can be found in: Newby Wyke White Squall, 4.8%, Newby Wyke Brewery.

Newport, AA 13.5–17%, Bittering

An odd hop this, as due to the high cohumulone (see page 148) content of up to 38% it can add some off flavours – even balsamic vinegar! However, this hop is something of a hero as it helped keep the world in hops back at the turn of this century when more than 20% of the planet's hops were succumbing to powdery mildew.

These hops are great if you want to give a beer bitterness and nothing else; it's very smooth in that respect. Due to the high AA content you'll need less hop to reach higher IBUs and therefore it makes Newport a cost-efficient choice.
Beer profiles suited: IPAs, Pale Ales.

Can be found in: Single Hop Newport, 4.6%, Ascot Ales; West Coast IPA, 6.2%, Black Iris Brewery.

Simcoe, AA 12–14%, Dual (But Excellent for Flavour and Aroma)

Another licensed hop, meaning that you have to pay licensing fees in order to grow them. At the time of writing only three farms in Washington State, covering a total of 237 acres, are able to grow Simcoe. This means that the company controlling the production controls the price too and there are also frequent shortages.

But you do get a flavour unlike any other hop when using Simcoe – a fruity, lychee-like flavour that does such a number on your tongue that you can forget the bitterness.

Beer profiles suited: IPAs and American Pale Ales.

Can be found in: Simcoe, 4.7%, Liverpool Organic Brewery.

Summit, AA 16–19%, Bittering

Dwarf variety brought into production in 2003, Summit is part of the new wave of New World hops often typified by high alpha acids. Often used to add tangerine/citrus flavour to strong IPAs and APAs (American Pale Ales). It has been called a 'grapefruit bomb' by many drinkers.

Some report an onion/garlic aroma, which can happen if the hop has been harvested a little later than it should be, but this can dissipate as your beer ages. I've heard reports that it's not altogether as unpleasant as it sounds.

Beer profiles suited: IPAs and American flavoured Stouts.

Can be found in: Summit, 4.5%, AllGates; Dark Horse, 4.3%, Loose Cannon.

Super Galena, AA 13–16%, Bittering

A pretty, natural hop, used mainly for bitterness. It is another cost-effective hop for the brewer, as the high AA levels mean you don't have to use quite so much. More citrus than its less-super gran Galena. Championed by growers for producing more alpha acids per acre than many other hops.
Beer profiles suited: IPAs.
Can be found in: Captain Smith's, 5.2%, Titanic.

Warrior, AA 15–18%, Dual

A clean bittering hop with not much flavour or aroma. Most brewers will favour it as a bittering hop, as due to its very high alpha acid content and low cohumulone (see page 148) it will give you high IBUs, bitter without having to use many. Just 14.5g (½oz) addition at 60 minutes will give you around 30 IBUs, which is as bitter as a pint of Best Bitter!
Beer profiles suited: Pale Ales, Porters, Barley Wines.
Can be found in: American Pale Ale, 5%, Slater's.

Willamette, AA 4–6%, Aroma

Known to some as the American Fuggles, to which it is similar, it went from being the country's favoured hop to being less popular. Not so similarly to Fuggles, this was because of one brewery and one beer: Budweiser, the beer of choice for over half of all American drinkers and exported all round the world. Anheuser-Busch InBev, the company that owns Budweiser, decided to cut back their use of Willamette in 2008. But all was not lost and Willamette was accepted into craft brewing circles with open arms. It still accounts for around 20% of the hops used in the States.

Just like Fuggles, it is excellent to use as an aroma hop (late in the boil). As with many English hops, think earthy, spicy, herbal and floral.

Beer profiles suited: all Ales, Bitters, Stouts – almost anything, really.

Can be found in: Premier Bitter, 3.7%, Moorhouse.

NEW ZEALAND HOPS

Hops were introduced to New Zealand around a hundred years ago by English and German settlers who quite rightly didn't want to do without beer. The remote nature of New Zealand means that the hops are isolated from disease such as powdery mildew and pests like aphid; therefore they can be grown organically on a massive scale and most of the world's organic hops come from New Zealand.

Green Bullet, AA 11–14%, Dual

Despite being high in alpha acids, Green Bullet is also well known for its aroma qualities and has often been touted as the poster child for NZ hop qualities. It has a unique citrus aroma, edging towards the fresher lemon side of the citrus scale rather than orange or marmalade, but with a punch.

Beer profiles suited: Lagers, Bitters, Stouts.

Can be found in: Cheshire Gold, 4.1%, Coach House.

Moteuka, AA 7–8%, Aroma

Another hop that asserts its difference from its cousins with strong hibiscus flower, tropical fruits, lemon citrus and a touch of spice flavours and aromas. A hop that really does define 'aroma hop'. Certainly worthy of late-addition copper experimentation.

Beer profiles suited: Lagers, Barley Wines and Ales.
Can be found in: Slater's Haka, 5.2%, Eccleshall Brewery.

Nelson Sauvin, AA 12–13%, Dual

Dubbed 'the wine of hops' as it helps to impart a grape flavour, as well as gooseberry, tropical fruit (mango) and to a lesser extent late-blossoming elderflower when used for bitterness. But don't expect any of these characteristics to be subtle; it really just adds something to most other hop combinations. Rather like cooking with butter, sugar or nuts, you can't really fail (unless you don't want any hop character).
Beer profiles suited: Ales.
Can be found in: Wild Mule, 3.9%, Roosters; Decadence, 4.4%, Brewsters.

Pacific Gem, AA 13–15%, Bittering

New Zealand Hops Ltd suggest that this hop 'makes its presence throughout'. That is certainly true, and the novice brewer can easily mess up using this, as its bitterness can be harsh and will cut a delicate beer like a light Lager to pieces. That said, put it in at the start of the boil, in a beer with a high malt profile, or a beer that you wish to age, and it will do wonders. Oaky, blackberry aromas coming through.
Beer profiles suited: Ales, Bitters, Blondes.
Can be found in: many beers, including Festival Special Bitter, 3.9%, Mighty Hop Brewery; Winter Warmer, 5%, North Curry Brewery (winter only); and Long Wall Mouse Organic Blonde, 5%, brewed for Suma by Little Valley Brewery.

Pacifica, AA 5–6%, Dual (But Lends Itself More Towards Aroma/Finishing)

For orange-marmalade citrus, Pacifica is the hop of choice – although expect floral aromas too. Blends very well with caramel malts.
Beer profiles suited: German clean Lagers, Pale Ales and Saisons.
Can be found in: All Black, 3.6%, AllGates.

Riwaka, AA 6–7%, Aroma

In getting to know the differences between the citrus characteristics that hops can give, Riwaka would be the choice to learn grapefruit citrus. A hop much sought-after by brewers everywhere.
Beer profiles suited: Pilsner and Lagers to make something very different. Also good in Pale Ales.
Can be found in: Riwaka IPA, 5%, Acorn.

Southern Cross, AA 11–14%, Dual

The result of a cross with the lesser-known American 'Cali' hop and UK Fuggles. Soft bitterness and a subtle resinous quality. The aroma lemon peel and fresh pine needles, with the characteristics of the Fuggles perhaps offering a spiciness. Overall a delicate balance of citrus and spice.
Beer profiles suited: Lagers.
Can be found in: Southern Cross, 4.1%, AllGates.

Super Alpha, AA 10–12%, Dual

Released when I was two years old (1976) and soon became a favourite for Asian Pacific brewers. A nice clean bitterness, and when used for aroma/flavour expect lemongrass and pine.

Beer profiles suited: IPAs, Lagers, Bitters, Winter/Christmas Ales.
Can be found in: India Pale Ale Super Alpha Pacific Jade, 7.3%, The Kernel.

REST OF THE WORLD

The 35th–55th Parallel North and below the 36th Parallel South offer the perfect growing conditions for hops. Not every country on those parallels has taken such full advantage of these conditions as the UK, USA and New Zealand have. However, throughout the world there is a great diversity of hop-growing countries, which at present are: Armenia, Australia, Azerbaijan, Belarus, China, Czech Republic, France, Georgia, Germany, Japan, Kazakhstan, Kyrgyzstan, Moldova, North and South Korea, Russia, Slovenia, South Africa, Tajikistan, Turkmenistan, Ukraine and Uzbekistan.

Production varies from country to country. North Korea and China grow mostly for their own consumption and some of the other countries listed grow on such a small scale that it is unlikely you will find any of their hops in a beer near you. Others, like Germany, used to grow on a fairly massive scale but have seen similar declines in demand as British hop-growers have experienced. But perhaps as our thirst for new tastes continues apace, and as climate change favours new growing conditions elsewhere, we might start seeing Greenland IPAs or even Icelandic hopped Best Bitters.

Aurora, AA 7–9.5%, Aroma, Slovenia

Also known as Super Styrian. Many report similarities to Cascade.
Beer profiles suited: most Blondes, Pale Ales, Golden Ales.
Can be found in: Stadium Bitter, 3.8%, Mallinsons, uses a combination of Perle, Aurora and Amarillo hops.

Bor, AA 7–10%, Bittering, Czech Republic

Used to give additional clean bittering, although with an aroma reportedly similar to Saaz.
Beer profiles suited: Bitters and ESBs.
Can be found in: solely in Old Scrooge 5%, Arundel.

Hallertau (traditional), AA 4–7%, Aroma, Germany

Although a German hop, there are various other Hallertau variations, many of which are grown in the USA. Their family includes a Hallertau Blanc which imparts a grape quality. This is perhaps the opposite of many USA or NZ hops, as the aromas/flavours are extremely subtle. Expect floral and spicy.
Beer profiles suited: Golden Ales, Lagers, Pilsners.
Can be found in: Lomond Gold, 5%, Traditional Scottish Ales; Jersey Liberation Ale, 4%, Jersey Brewery.

Lublin, AA 3–5%, Aroma, Poland

An early-maturing hop, named after the city of Lublin and also known as Lubelski. The relatively high amount of farnesene oil gives this hop hints of lavender and magnolia. Rather interestingly, the same chemical is emitted by aphids as a sign of threat and for this reason Lublin hops are less troubled by aphids as the smell repels them from the plant.
Beer profiles suited: Lagers and Golden Ales.
Can be found in: look out for many seasonal summer beers single-hopped with Lublin.

Perle, AA 4–9%, Dual, Germany (Also Grown in USA)

When cinema-goers were getting scared out of their wits by films like *Dawn of the Dead* and *Halloween* back in 1978, so the Hüll Hop Research Institute in Bavaria released Perle. When used in bittering it is non-aggressive and its aroma can be considered 'minty', although it also has some characteristics similar to traditional English hops, with a hint of the 'Noble' about it.

Beer profiles suited: all types of Lagers.
Can be found in: Gentleman's Wit, 4.3%, Camden; Red Kite, 4.3%, Vale Brewery.

Strisselspalt, AA 3–5%, Aroma, France

Resembles Hersbrucker, to which it is thought to be related. Also goes by the names Alsace, Elsasser and Précoce de Bourgogne.
Beer profiles suited: Lagers and Wheat Beers.
Can be found in: Strisselspalt IPA, 5%, Acorn.

Qindaodahuo, AA 6–8%, Dual, China

As with many things in China, an approach to hops was adopted, time and resources were thrown at the problem, results were calculated and a plan of action formulated. After twelve years of research from 1954 to 1966, it was decided that Qindaodahuo was to be the hop of choice and that it would be grown in north-west China to feed the nation's ever-growing demand for beer. By 2004 they were producing an annual yield of 10,379 tons, mainly for their own consumption, and thus China had become the third largest hop-producer in the world. Since it is for their own consumption, it is unlikely that you'll find Qindaodahuo hops outside China and therefore it is difficult to find any taste notes or beers that use them.

Find in Chinese beers, use in Chinese beers.

NOBLE HOPS

Want to wind up a beer snob? Start talking about Noble Hops. This is another hotly debated subject. The term has only really been in use since the 1980s and there is no set definition, nor can everyone agree which varieties actually are Noble Hops – although, with some reluctant general consensus, it is suggested that five hops can be called Noble: Tettnanger, Saaz, Spalter, Mittelfrüh and Hersbrucker. They all impart a clean bitterness and offer a heady mix of floral, spice and spruce aromas with a complexity unlike many other hops.

Recent DNA evidence suggests that Tettnanger, Saaz and Spalter could all have evolved from the same plant, but due to the lack of any historical evidence it is impossible to find out if this truly is the case. But they are noteworthy hops and can really transform a beer.

Hersbrucker, AA 2–5%, Aroma, Germany

Named after the small town of Hersbruck in central Franconia, Bavaria, the hop is also known as Hersbrucker Spät. Although it was one of Germany's most important aroma varieties in the nineteenth century and is very disease resistant, it is grown only in small quantities. Floral and fruity notes.

Beer profiles suited: Lagers, Pilsners, Golden Ales.
Can be found in: Golden Sun, 4.3%, Caledonian.

Mittelfrüh, AA 3.5–5%, Aroma, Germany

Also known as Hallertau Mittelfrüh and mostly replaced by the disease-resistant Hersbrucker. Mainly used in Pilsners. Floral, citrus, apricots and spicy aromas, but compared with most of the stronger aromas of modern hops this once-prized variety is considered by some to be too mild. It is a shame, as the aromas, just like those of the other Noble Hops, are simply and delicately special.

Beer profiles suited: Pilsners, Lagers and Wheat Beers as a finishing hop.
Can be found in: some UK brewers have single-hopped using Mittelfrüh, but at the time of writing none was available.

Saaz, AA 3–6%, Aroma, Czech Republic

Accounting for 83% of the Czech hop harvest in 2011, this is an individual, mild, earthy, grassy and spicy hop. Its smooth taste lends itself towards Lagers and Pilsners. It is the Genghis Khan of the hop world, and many other hops can trace their lineage back to Saaz.

Beer profiles suited: Lagers, Pilsners.
Can be found in: Blonde, 4.0%, Saltaire. Sunchaser, 4%, Everards, uses a combination of Hallertau, Saaz and Tettnanger.

Spalt(er), AA 4.5–5%, Aroma, Germany

Not as widely distributed as the other Noble Hops. Mild spice flavours. Compared with many other hops it has taken something of a back seat, but styles and tastes always ebb and flow and, just like flared trousers and platform shoes, it will no doubt rise again.

Beer profiles suited: Lagers, Pilsners and Helles, or in most Ales.
Can be found in: Original Bitter, 4.1%, Hereford (used in bittering).

Tettnanger, AA 2.5–5.5%, Aroma, Germany

A hop originating from the small town of Tettnang in Germany. Genetically similar to Saaz, it is used for its floral/spicy flavours and aromas, but with some unexpected flavours of bergamot, cognac and chocolate too. Not to be confused with the US Tettnanger, which is woodier and much more reminiscent of the Fuggle.

Beer profiles suited: Lagers, Pilsners, Schwarzbier.

Can be found in: Devil's Advocate, 4.2%, Caledonian, uses a mix of Hallertau, Hersbrucker and Tettnanger.

10

MALT

WHEN WE BREWERS talk of 'malt', we are generally talking about malted barley and sometimes wheat, which are the most commonly malted grains. However, any grain that has been modified through steeping, germinating and kilning in order to develop the enzymes needed to change its starches into sugars can be considered to be malt.

When growing naturally, a grain's seeds will lie dormant for the winter and will be triggered by the warmth of the spring sunshine to absorb the surrounding moisture they need to start growing. The seeds will then put out roots and shoots ready to become plants. The maltster will mimic these conditions and halt them just in time, so that instead of using its potential to make a new plant, the grain can be used to make a beer. See Part Three, The Gardening Brewer, for a full description of the malting process and how to malt your own grain.

There is a similarity between malts and grapes, or hops for that matter, in that they are all plants and therefore can display different characteristics depending on the time they are sown, the weather and the soil conditions. The summer of 2012, for example, was cool and moist, meaning more starch and less protein for our barley. For this reason the brewer may find inconsistencies, even when using the same grain, if it has been harvested during a different year or has been grown in a different area. This is why when buying grains from a good supplier they will let you know the colour (EBC – see page 43), moisture content, nitrogen content and the soluble nitrogen ratio. These are all things that will help the professional brewer or good home-brewer to be consistent with their flavours.

WHAT DOES THE 'GRAIN BILL' MEAN?

You may have heard brewers or read beer bloggers talking about the 'grain bill' and been afraid to ask what they mean. Put very simply, it is the sugars that go into making your beer – or, in other words, the ingredients that will ferment. The grain bill can be made up entirely of malt extracts, or malt extract and some grains, or just grains, depending on your level of brewing. The grains used will be base malts, roasted or speciality malts, and adjuncts.

BASE MALTS

Base malts normally make up between 60% and 100% of the total grain bill. They are grains that contain enough amylase enzymes to convert their own starches into fermentable sugars. That might be gibberish to all but the more advanced or well-read brewer. So to try to explain further, amylase enzyme conversion is something that most people will experience every day, as the amylase enzyme is present in human saliva and it helps us to digest food. Foods that contain lots of starch but not much sugar can be converted in your mouth whilst you chew; this is why foods such as rice or potatoes, for example, can become sweeter as you chew. The same process is happening during the mashing stage of beer-making (see page 28). During this process complex sugar chains (starches) are broken down into less complex sugars/shorter chains which yeast cells can happily ingest and turn into alcohol.

Interestingly, the amylase enzyme in our saliva was once used in brewing, as the brewer would chew on some of the grain before spitting it back into the wort – a practice that the modern drinker might struggle with.

PALE ALE MALT

Pale Ale malts are the basis of much of the UK brewing industry and can be malted from more than one two-row barley varieties. In a Pale Ale or an IPA it can make up to 100% of the grain bill, although often other malts or adjuncts are added to increase head-retention or improve the beer in some way. There are various Pale Ale malts – USA pale malt, Belgian pale malt, Golden Promise – differing slightly from the UK pale malt in colour (around 2 EBC). Each grain will differ slightly year to year and this is why maltsters might blend more than one variety in order to get consistent characteristics each year. As I've said before, this is no different from different grapes being blended to make wine taste consistent.

Pale Ale malts are traditionally light-coloured, but not as light as Pilsner/Lager malts, with a range of 6–12 EBC and generally towards the lower end of that scale. The strain or type of barley used can make a difference in the overall taste of the beer, especially when the malt character is something the brewer wishes to profile. There are some common strains of barley used for Pale Ale malts and often the final malted barley will reference the name; these include Maris Otter, Golden Promise, Halcyon and Optic.

Maris Otter

The year was 1966, and whilst Scotland cursed and England celebrated a 4–2 victory over West Germany, Dr G. Bell and his team at the British Plant Breeding Institute (BPI) on Maris Lane in Trumpington, Cambridgeshire, quietly introduced a type of barley they called Maris Otter. Often described as a thoroughbred malt, Maris Otter is highly prized and is now used by many home and commercial brewers in the UK. Indeed, as Bath Ales brewer Gerry Condell told me, 'A good beer needs quality ingredients, which is why we use Maris Otter.'

Maris Otter is a traditional two-row, low-protein, winter barley. Its dominance in the UK market is down to a few reasons. Firstly, it doesn't grow well away from the British maritime climate; and secondly, it is an excellent grain to work with for both malting and mashing. That aside, due to its low yields and low disease resistance, it's not a grain praised by farmers and as such production nearly ceased during the early 1990s. The rights to grow the grain were then bought up by a group of canny farmers and maltsters who started producing the grain exclusively as a brand.

Maris Otter can give beers a rich, nutty or biscuit flavour and it can be used on its own. The colour is rather light at around 4–6 EBC, and due to its low levels of nitrogen it is less likely to contribute to haze formation. Most brewers agree that using Maris Otter will ensure a beer that is full-bodied and clean-tasting.

Stout, 4.5%, Quantock, and Artisan Choice, 4.4%, Collingham Ales, are two of the numerous beers that use Maris Otter.

Golden Promise

When Shakin Stevens (1980s pop singer and Welsh icon) was called 'the Elvis of Wales', he'd have been allowed to be a little disappointed, as it put him firmly in the shadow of such a massive star. Similarly, if Golden Promise could talk it might bemoan being called 'the Maris Otter of Scotland' – especially as Golden Promise was around before Maris Otter and was the first variety to be protected under the 1964 Plant Varieties and Seeds Act, an Act that gives proprietary rights to anyone who discovers or breeds new plant varieties, allowing them to restrict growing to licence holders.

The Maris Otter comparison is also unfair as brewers using Golden Promise instead of Maris Otter claim that it is superior, giving beers a greater depth of flavours, which are sweeter, slightly more caramelly and cleaner than beers made with Maris Otter. Whilst this may be true, it is like saying a sports car is better than a four-wheel-drive car: each will favour different conditions and neither is really better than the other. Each grain fits the style of drink you wish to brew: Golden Promise works well in Scottish beer styles, giving the right characteristics from the malt, and is also much favoured in the whisky industry. To be honest, some people will argue that there is no real noticeable difference between Maris Otter and Golden Promise in the final beer, but that, I'm sure, is fighting talk.

Golden Promise is an early-maturing barley and is towards the lighter end of the scale for Pale Ale malts, at around 4–5.5 EBC.

Use in Scottish beers such as 60/– and 70/–, Bitters, Best and Extra Special Bitters, Milds and Stouts. The experimental brewer might also want to have a go at using it in a Lager. Timothy Taylor's Landlord is made using Golden Promise malt, or for something a little different try Golden Promise IPA, 5.5%, Wapping.

Halcyon

Another classic two-row winter barley from the BPI in Cambridgeshire, and a child of Maris Otter. Favoured by farmers and brewers alike due to its disease resistance and low protein levels. Beers brewed using Halcyon are less sweet – some even suggest sharp – whilst also having a more biscuity flavour. EBC is approximately 5.

Use in all British Ales. Dinting Arches, 4.5%, Howard Town, uses Halcyon along with Maris Otter.

Optic

If you see barley growing in a British field there is a strong chance it will be Optic, as it has become the most widely planted in the British Isles. It is considered to be a very aromatic malt that flavours well in the brew house. Its slightly plumper kernels offer fuller and richer flavours (some say biscuit) than its contemporaries.

Can be used as the main ingredient in Pale Ales, Milds, Bitters and Stouts. It is also favoured stateside for IPAs and APAs.

EBC is 5–6. One of the most accessible examples of a beer that uses Optic is Old Empire, 5.7%, Marston's.

OTHER BASE MALTS

Although Pale Ale malts are versatile and can lend themselves to many styles of beer, there are lots more base malts available to us brewers.

Lager/Pilsner Malt

As Lager malt is the accepted British version of Pilsner malt and they share many of the same characteristics, I have lumped them together. That said, Lager malt does differ slightly from Pilsner insofar as it is kilned at a slightly higher temperature. Lager malt in the UK is mainly derived from two-row barley and Pilsner malt is always made from two-row.

The term 'Lager malt' does arise from its predominant use in making pale Lagers, but it can be used in any style. Some report a slightly grainier flavour when using in an Ale in place of pale malt and good results are found when using it in low-alcohol beers and Blondes. The colour may be much lighter too due to the EBC being around 2–4. Beer made using Lager/Pilsner malt will offer very delicate flavours. It also gives the beer good head-retention and mouthfeel.

A pleasant example of Pilsner malt can be found in Pilsner, 4.4%, Meantime Brewing Company.

Mild Malt

Due to their unique kilning process, mild malts will produce relatively high levels of dextrin in the wort. This makes them ideal for use in Milds, which may require a sweeter-than-average malt flavour. It also has a slightly higher-than-average nitrogen content, meaning that up to 25% of adjuncts can be used. Mild malt is rather mild in colour too, with an EBC of 6–7.

Midshipman Mild, 4%, Nelson Brewery, will give you a taste of Mild malt.

Munich Malt

Originating in Germany (funnily enough), Munich malt is used mainly to produce sweeter beers associated with Bavaria, and also some Belgian beers. Some British brewers are starting to use it, however, as it can enhance some of the other malt flavours used; indeed this is one of its finer qualities and it is therefore used in many Oktoberfest beers. That said, it can be used without any other grains in a brew, but in general a brewer will use it for only 10–25% of the total grain bill, even though up to 80% is possible; but as it doesn't add anything to the body of the beer, it is rarely used to such a high percentage. Munich malt adds a golden-orange colour and a richer, grainy sweetness – some say toffee flavour – to the overall profile of a beer.

When we refer to Munich malt we think of a pale, 12–17 EBC, malt, but two slightly darker Munich malts are also sometimes available to the brewer: Munich II, also known as Munich 10L, and Munich III, also known as Munich 20L or Dark Munich. They are 20–25 EBC and 50 EBC respectively. At the time of writing they are harder to find in the UK, but I suspect this will change as brewers demand an increasingly varied pallet of ingredients. They will do much the same as Munich, but add a darker profile to your beer colour.

Use in Pale Ale, Amber, Brown Ale, Stouts and dark beers, Bocks. At around 30–50% of the total grain bill, experimental brewers are using it in lower ABV beers, such as Milds, and reporting great results.

Baltic Red, 4.2, Downton, is a lovely example of the use of Munich.

Vienna Malt

Slightly lighter than Munich malt at 6–8 EBC, this has been called the Euro equivalent of pale malt, but it has a higher protein content which can account for the protein haze in some Euro-beers.

Can be used in Oktoberfest and Märzen beers, but also great in Lagers using up to 100% Vienna malt, as it adds something unique. Think rich, bready and clean malt flavours. Lower amounts, around 10–30%, will go in an IPA or Pale Ale pretty well too. More frequently, though, Vienna is used in conjunction with equal amounts of Munich and Pilsner/Lager malt to make very good Lagers. I'd suggesting finishing off with Noble Hops (see page 178) for a good clean Lager.

Try a Pale Ale made with Vienna, such as High Spy, 4%, Jennings.

Wheat Malt

Wheat malt accounts for between 50% and 60% of the base malt in a German Wheat Beer (Hefeweizen or Weizenbier), but in our Wheat Beers we tend to use much less. It is apparently possible to use 100% wheat in a beer, but this is a feat for the true brewing élite as it requires some serious expertise to get right. Wheat contains more proteins than barley does, so it can contribute to a protein haze – something that can be a feature of Wheat Beers. It also works well to add a little bit of wheat – perhaps around 5% – to the overall grain bill to help aid head-retention. EBC is normally in the range of 3–5 for malted wheat.

Use in any beers to aid head-retention and, perhaps very obviously, use in Wheat Beers. Experimental brewers might want to try making a wheat wine, a high-ABV Barley Wine equivalent.

Dark Wheat, 3.6%, Tiger Tops, is a dark Mild made using wheat malt.

GREEN MALTS

Green malt is grain that has been softened by being steeped in water and allowed to germinate, then dried, but has not yet been kilned. To say it is not widely used by brewers, either home or commercial, would be an understatement, but that is not to say that it is never used. Some commercial brewers over in the States and in Germany have been experimenting using green malts in order to make light-bodied, high-alcohol beers.

For more information on using green malts I found this paper online:http://onlinelibrary.wiley.com/doi/10.1002/j.2050-0416.1963.tb01925.x/pdf

ROASTED MALTS

Rich Tea biscuits, fresh coffee, bitter chocolate and caramel are all flavours that come from using different roasted, also known as speciality, malts. They contain no enzymes so they cannot be used on their own in the mash but have to be used with base malts. Roasted malts are created by drying at a low temperature (60°C/140°F) and then kilning at a high temperature (160–220°C/320–428°F). It is these high temperatures that make the enzymes inactive.

Darker colour in beer also comes from roasted malts. Without them we wouldn't have Stouts, Porters, Dark Milds or Brown Ales. Dark roasted malt can be finely ground and added to beers in small quantities to give them some colour without adding too much flavour, although if used in excess they can offer a dry and burnt, bitter flavour. High amounts can also mess with the lautering process (see page 26), as the grains are dry and brittle and fall apart easily.

To make your own roasted malts, turn to page 118.

BROWN MALT

Porters were once frequently made using brown malts and many older recipes will call for an addition of brown malt. It can also be used in Scottish Ales, Milds, Bitters, Brown Ales and Stouts. It's a grain that will add a real 'British' flavour to your beer. Think dry, biscuity flavours and that's about right. EBC is approximately 160, but can vary from maltster to maltster within a range of 100–200. At one time brown malts were always made by rapidly curing over open fires, which would give them a smoked quality; alas this is not the case now, but if you are after a touch of smoke use brown malt in conjunction with the German grain Rauchmalz, which is readily available.

Porters made with brown malt will have a taste of Marmite. If you've never tasted it, it sounds pretty awful; but imagine it without the salt and just with that savoury bite, the touch of umami, that you get with Marmite – not as an upfront flavour. I think it adds an extra dimension to a beer, though it can be rather overpowering if 10% or more is used in a batch.

For many traditional recipes and more information on using brown malts, see *Old British Beers and How to Make Them* by Dr John Harrison and the Members of the Durden Park Beer Circle. Also try Double Stout, 4.8%, Hook Norton.

BLACK (PATENT) MALT

Black malt, also known as black patent malt, is the darkest malt available and is used in very small quantities to give beers some colour, without imparting any colour to the head of the beer. In larger quantities, up to 10%, it can have an astringent quality and so is rarely used at such high levels. Instead, a range of 3–5% is typical, at which it will give some roasted qualities to your beer.

It is made by roasting at 230°C (446°F) without burning the grains. The term 'patent' comes from one man, Daniel Wheeler, who in 1817 converted a coffee-roaster to roast malts at higher temperatures without charring them, so creating black malts. This was patented, hence the name black 'patent' malt.

The colour is generally around 1300 EBC. Use in Porters, Stouts, dark Milds, darker Scottish Ales and black Lagers. Many beers use black malt, but why not try Ace of Harts, 3.9%, by Harthill Village Brewery?

CHOCOLATE MALT

Fairly essential for making modern Porters, chocolate malt gives a nutty, toasted quality to the aroma and flavours for Stouts, Brown Ales and dark Milds too. It has similar characteristics to black malt, but is roasted for a slightly shorter period of time. This means it is less bitter and the harsher flavours sometimes associated with black malt are not as pronounced.

To approach the chocolate flavour in beers, use 6% along with sweeter malts such as crystal malt. Indeed, chocolate malt can be used to counteract the real cloying sweetness associated with high levels of crystal malts, even when used as a smaller 1.5% addition. On its own you are more likely to get coffee flavours. As with all roasted malts, use with base malts.

Minotaur, 3.3%, a Mild by Milton Brewery, uses a 'lavish' amount of chocolate malt.

BISCUIT MALT

Belgian in origin, biscuit malt adds a toasted, some say biscuit, flavour to your beer. It is also sometimes used in Nut Brown Ales to give that extra quality of nuttiness, although this is more common in American Brown Ales. In Pale Ales it can give a nice bready quality, and it adds an extra dimension to IPAs. In general, don't use more than 10% in any recipe, as it can be overpowering.

It is made by roasting at the lower end of the scale at around 160°C (320°F) and so is much lighter than the other roasted malts, at around 50–60 EBC.

Biscuit malt has been used in Northumbrian Gold, 4.5%, Hadrian Border Brewery.

CARAMELIZED MALTS

Caramel malts are created between germination and kilning. The green malt is mashed at a temperature range of 64–72°C (147–162°F) and this process creates a sugary liquid that is trapped beneath the husk, caramelizing the grain. The grain is then dried at between 90°C and 200°C (194°F and 392°F), depending on how dark the maltster wants the resulting malt to be. This doesn't just affect the colour, but the flavour too.

Caramel malts are generally used in the ratio 5–15% of the total grain bill; any higher and the result is a ludicrously sweet beer.

CARAMUNICH MALT

It doesn't take a brewing genius to guess that CaraMunich malt is caramelized malt from Munich. It is obtained by roasting green Lager malt at 110–130°C (230–266°F) and is often used to add an extra dimension to dark Lagers. Expect light roast flavours and toffee to come from using CaraMunich.

Use 5–10% for dark beer and 1–5 % for lighter beers. Used in Pale Ale, 4%, from Camden.

CRYSTAL MALT

For many years here in Britain the only crystal malt available to home-brewers was one known simply as 'crystal malt'. This means there was only one set of characteristics that brewers could expect to impart when using crystal malt: a light toffee/caramel flavour and some extra body and improved head-retention. Meanwhile, American brewers were starting to enjoy a full range of crystal malts, which were numbered using the Lovibond colour-rating scale (see page 43). American crystal malts range from 10L (20 EBC) to 150L (300 EBC). In the UK we have now started to have more of a range and ours seem to take on different names depending on where they are bought from. This is a rough translation, but the darker the crystal malt you use, the more 'burnt toffee' rather than 'sweet malty' flavours you'll get.

Crystal malts aid head-retention and increase body. Generally, use 5–10%; any higher and the beer can be overly sweet and pretty vile.

Use the different crystal malts in the following ways:

Crystal malt, also known as medium crystal malt, 120–140 EBC (US 60L), is what to use if a recipe simply says 'crystal malt'. More rounded caramel flavours.

Pale crystal malt, also known as light crystal malt, 50–70 EBC (similar to the US 30L), will add a sweet caramel flavour.

Low-colour crystal malt, 100 EBC (US 50L), will give medium caramel colours and flavours.

High-colour crystal malt, also known as dark crystal malt, 200–400 EBC (US 120L or 150L), gives burnt toffee flavours and adds a darker caramel, even ruby, colour to beer.

Crystal malts are used in many UK beers, but to pluck one out of the air with particular caramel flavours, try Polly Folly, 4.3%, by Buffy's of Norwich.

SPECIAL B

I have head brewers literally rave on about Special B. It does differ from many of the other crystal malts available in that it can give your beer some of the flavours more associated with darker beers. Think dried fruits and cloves. If it's a touch of malt complexity you are after, then this is your man, or rather your malt.

Originating from Belgium, Special B gets its unique characteristics from undergoing a second roasting. With an EBC of around 300 (sometimes more), it can also add some darkness to a beer. Use experimentally in Brown Ales, Milds, Red Ales and Porters, or in classic Belgian styles.

The wonderfully named Dr Paracelsus' Bombastic Indigo Elixir, 8%, from the Summer Wine Brewery, contains Special B (along with liquorice root, Turkish pepper and black cardamoms).

ADJUNCTS

Adjuncts are extra, non-standard ingredients in beers. They can be used to lighten or darken a beer; to enhance or add to the flavour; to improve head-retention; or, in the case of some sugars, to save some money on the final grain bill. Adjuncts are the 'extras'; if a beer could be made without using an ingredient, then it is an adjunct. So, for example, malted barley could become an adjunct in a sorghum beer.

The term is more often used to describe sugars and syrups, such as sucrose (or candi sugar), honey, inverted sugar, maltodextrin, corn syrup, or dextrose, and solid or cereal adjuncts like barley, wheat, corn, rice, oats, buckwheat or sorghum. The cereal grains can be whole, torrified (heat-treated), malted, flaked or even in the form of flours. The term 'adjunct' can also be used to describe water treatments, spices and clarifying agents.

CANDI SUGAR

Used primarily in Belgian beers, such as Dubbels and Tripels, to raise the alcohol level without stressing the yeast or producing any undesirable characteristics. When yeast breaks down normal sugar it needs to work a little bit harder, producing an enzyme called invertase before it can get on with fermenting. When using candi sugar it doesn't have to make this enzyme and so can make lots of lovely alcohol instead. It's kind of like having a fuel injection in your beer.

CANE SUGAR (GRANULATED SUGAR)

Once the adjunct of choice for all home-brewers in the UK: one tin of hopped malt extract + 1 bag of sugar and some dried yeast = beer. It was the only equation needed. Sadly, the beer wasn't great, because although sugar does increase the ABV, if used as half of the fermentables it can make the beer thinner, unless in the hands of a consummate professional. Used correctly, it can reduce sweetness and help accentuate hop bitterness.

For a commercial example that uses cane sugar, try Theakston's Hogshead Bitter.

FLAKED BARLEY

This is raw, unmalted barley and it is used to add a smooth, grainy flavour to beer, as well as improving head-retention and foam stability. Up to 20% can be used, but increased levels can cause hazy beers. Use in Porters and Stouts. It really needs to be mashed, but if using in extract brewing it needs to be steeped for 45 minutes. The flaked aspect means that the barley will yield enhanced extracts compared with whole barley; in other words, it's easier to get the stuff out of it you need to.

FLAKED MAIZE

Added to reduce malt flavours in Lagers, up to 40% can be used in the mash. With a low nitrogen content, it also helps clarify beer and can increase alcohol but not flavour.

FLAKED OATS

High protein means more body and smoothness when used in Stouts. Use up to 10%.

Toasting porridge oats in the oven until they are golden-brown is a cheaper alternative to buying flaked oats.

FLAKED RYE

Used in rye beers to give a crisp character.

CLARIFYING AGENTS

These are agents that are used to reduce haze in beer.

IRISH MOSS

The forager in me knows this red seaweed found in rock pools around the shores of Britain and Ireland as 'Irish carraigín', an edible seaweed that can help stop a bout of the shits! It has also been used in the brew kettle for over 200 years to help clarify beer. It works because it has an electrostatic charge that gathers oppositely charged materials, such as proteins, into clumps, which helps them settle at the bottom of beer or wort. In all, quite a remarkable plant.

ISINGLASS

How on earth the swim bladders of fish have ended up becoming something that is used to clarify beer is anyone's guess. Apparently a fisherman – probably a forefather of someone like the chief bottler at BrewDog – may have kept his beer in the swim bladder of a fish and subsequently found it clearer. But this stuff really does work, which is why most of the brewing fraternity in the UK subscribe to its use. It works by causing the yeast to flocculate (clump) into a jelly-like mass, which settles at the bottom of a cask.

Many of us have vegan friends (or you might be one), in which case the idea of drinking a beer that uses swim bladders could be rather abhorrent, but not all brewers use isinglass. For a list of beers that don't, try www.barnivore.com/beer.

THE DIFFERENCE BETWEEN TWO-ROW AND SIX-ROW MALTS

Put simply, two-row malt comes from barley which has two rows of seed along the flowering head – and guess how many are on six-row! Two-row barley tends to have larger kernels, lower protein levels and lower starch to protein ratios. Six-row tends to be favoured over in the States and two-row almost everywhere else. Six-row barley is also often used for caramel and roasted malts, whereas two-row is more suited for use as base malts.

Interestingly, barley is made up of around 30,000 genes, but only one (or two, depending on who you talk to) of those genes determines whether the plant will become a two- or six-row crop. This makes it very easy to develop new strains using any type of barley.

HOW TO TRANSLATE A MALT ANALYSIS SHEET

There have been many advances in home-brewing over the last five or ten years, giving home-brewers as much information as the professional brewer. Some of the better home-brew shops and the maltsters themselves will show you a malt analysis sheet when you are trying to choose your grain. This is a sheet with various numbers and percentages on it – very useful information that can make a difference to the taste and even the final ABV of your beer, and therefore to the cost of production. If one is not available when you buy, a search on the malting company's website should supply one, even if you have to ask.

The most important bits of information for the brewer are: moisture content, protein/nitrogen content, extract yield and colour.

MOISTURE CONTENT

The amount of moisture in a grain is important to the brewer for several reasons. Firstly, storage. If the grains have a high moisture content then they won't store well, so grains with a moisture content of 1–2% will store for longer than grains with up to around 6–7%. This is because moisture can attract mould spores, which will of course render your grain useless. Drier grains also retain flavours and aromas, and moisture-rich grains are likely to give more off flavours.

If you are buying grains you also don't want to be paying for water and sub-standard grain. In practice, this means refusing base grains that have a moisture content that doesn't fall into the accepted range of around 1.5–5% – slightly higher for speciality grains, but still not above about 6%, with 7% being the absolute limit.

PROTEIN AND NITROGEN CONTENT

As proteins are comprised of nitrogen-rich amino acids, the two values can be interchanged and 1% of total nitrogen (TN) is equal to 6.25% of protein. Despite brewers of that specific time period known as 'yore' reportedly adding all sorts of bits of dead animals or even falling into fermenting vessels and allegedly improving the beer beyond all recognition, protein doesn't have too much brewing value other than for enzymes and head-retention; in fact, too much can give a beer haze problems. This is why you may see more use of clarifiers in American recipes, as their six-row malt has around 2% more protein than ours.

Soluble Nitrogen / Soluble Protein

Normally expressed as SP (soluble protein) or SN (soluble nitrogen), this figure refers to the percentage of protein or nitrogen that is soluble in water and is used to calculate the soluble total. It is an indicator of how much germination took place during that phase of malting. Figures above 45% S/T (soluble total) can result in thin-bodied beer. Around 35% is really what the brewer should be looking for.

EXTRACT YIELD

The term 'extract' when applied to brewing generally means sugars, and maltsters will take a sample of their malt to work out its maximum extract yield, or maximum sugar yield. They work out the maximum possible extract rate as a percentage by mashing the grains. This is done by finely grinding the grains and mashing under laboratory conditions, and will be shown as 'FGDB' or 'fine grind dry basis'. You may also find data for 'fine grind as is'. This can be considered very useful, as it gives you the extraction rate with moisture intact – in other words, just as you'd buy it rather than with a moisture level of nothing.

Some maltsters will give you even more useful information and you'll see 'coarse grind dry basis' and 'coarse grind as is'. This reflects more closely the grind (how much the grains have been crushed) that the brewer is likely to be using, although this will still be the maximum possible yield and we brewers can expect to knock off around 5–15 percentage points from whatever the total is. Again, the 'as is' figure will also more accurately reflect the brewhouse reality.

The range will be given as a percentage, from 60% to 85%, and reflects the extraction rate of starch from the grains. The higher the percentage, the more starch and therefore the more potential sugars you'll have in your grains compared with husk and protein. So if you are offered bags of base malt and one is cheaper but only has an FGDB of 76%, while the more expensive is 85%, then you may find that actually the more expensive is the more cost-effective.

COLOUR

This may be expressed as EBC or Lovibond (L). I've gone into more detail about colour on page 43, but very roughly EBC is normally around twice the Lovibond scale. The range of colours extends from 2.5 EBC for the very palest Lager and Pilsner malts and up to 1500 EBC for some black malts. The darker your malt, the darker your beer.

The colour reflects how long the grains have been roasted or kilned, and can vary from maltster to maltster. Sometimes the maltster will purposely create slightly different malt colours from their competitors in order to keep returning business from brewers who don't wish to change their popular beer recipes too much. However, it does also mean that the brewer has a wider choice when it comes to malt diversity.

11

YEAST

IN BAVARIA, IN southern Germany, there is a famous beer law that was passed by the Bavarian Duke Wilhelm IV in 1516. It is known as *Reinheitsgebot*, which roughly translated into English means 'purity law'. It decreed that brewers could use only hops, water and barley to make beer. The omission of yeast is rather telling. Not only did brewers not know of its existence, but they didn't really know how brewing happened, the accepted wisdom being that some sort of spontaneous fermentation took place.

It might seem very odd to us now, but before 1836 all brewers believed that something divine was happening when their worts and musts started to ferment. Which is where the antiquated term for yeast, 'Goddesgoode' or 'God is good', comes from, and perhaps it also helps to explain why the Church managed to keep such a monopoly on brewing in Europe for so many years.

But all that changed in 1836 when a clever French inventor named Cagniard de la Tour showed that yeast cells were living things necessary in making alcohol, so dispelling earlier beliefs of spontaneous generation. Louis Pasteur later built on de la Tour's research and in 1876 he published *Études sur la Bière*, meaning 'Studies on Beer' and translated as *Studies on Fermentation*. Despite the Frenchman's dislike of beer, it was this book that changed the face of brewing for ever. In it he described how beer can be contaminated by bacteria and wild yeasts and gave 'means of preventing them'.

We now know that spontaneous brewing is actually down to yeast: strains of wild yeast looking for a place to infect and sweet wort as a prime breeding ground. However, not all wild yeasts are good and not every batch of spontaneously fermenting beer will ferment, which is possibly why beer and the fermentation process was considered sacred. It is likely that the wild yeasts utilized by ancient brewers were *Brettanomyces lambicus* ('Brett' for short), a type of wild yeast favoured by some brewers in the Flanders region, just a skip away in Belgium.

Although most likely the original Old Ales/Stock Ales were made using Brett, few modern brewers rely on wild yeasts and, besides, the sour and sometimes sharp beers brewed using it are an acquired taste and not one that has been acquired (at least *en masse*) by drinkers in the UK. Even if you have never tried a beer from Flanders, you will have an idea of the taste if you have had a pint that has soured; chances are it has been infected by *Brettanomyces* at some point (if not a bacterium such as *Lactobacillus* or *Pediococcus*). The majority of beer in Britain is therefore brewed used either *Saccharomyces cerevisiae* or *Saccharomyces pastorianus*.

Saccharomyces cerevisiae is widely used to make Ales and can also be referred to as a 'top-fermenting' yeast. The term comes from the behaviour of the yeast as it clumps together, forming and rising to the top of the fermenting vessel. This makes it possible to 'top crop' the yeast by scooping some off and inoculating a separate batch with it. Top-fermenting yeasts will ferment at fairly high temperatures (16–25°C/61–77°F, but sometimes up to 30°C/86°F) and in this country it often means the home-brewer only really has to find a room with a steady temperature in order to brew decent beer. But, as there always seems to be an exception with every aspect of beer and brewing, Kölsch yeasts are top-fermenting yeasts that prefer colder temperatures.

Saccharomyces pastorianus, on the other hand, is known as a bottom-fermenting yeast, or Lager yeast. Many brewers, both commercial and home, will have to set up a controlled environment in order to make a decent Lager, as Lager yeasts prefer a range of 5–10°C (41–50°F). At these temperatures the yeast works very slowly and will settle out on the bottom of the fermenting vessel.

SOME YEAST TERMINOLOGY

Attenuation

Yeast is a sugar fungus and it consumes sugar. Generally it will consume between 65% and 80% of the sugar depending on the strain (type) of yeast and the gravity (strength) of the wort (unfermented beer). Different beers need a different balance of sugars against the other ingredients in order to taste true to style. A Mild, for example, needs some residual sweetness and so is considered properly attenuated when 65% of the sugars have been consumed, whereas a Lager is closer to style when more sugars have been consumed and so the beer is drier; therefore a Lager yeast strain might consume up to 90% of the sugars before it has attenuation considered true to style.

Flocculation

The clumping together of yeast cells which then by force of gravity fall to the bottom of a fermenting vessel. Yeast cells that do not flocculate well will remain in suspension – that is, they will hang in the wort, taking ages to clear.

Lag Phase

The period of time between pitching your yeast and the start of fermentation. It can last between 3 and 15 hours, during which time the yeast cells become acclimatized to their new environment, absorbing much-needed oxygen and other compounds which will help them to reproduce rapidly. During this time the wort is unprotected and open to infection, therefore it is important to do everything possible to reduce the lag phase.

Log Phase

This comes after the lag phase. All tanked up and ready to reproduce, the cells will rapidly multiply.

Pitching (Yeast)

The act of adding yeast to wort (unfermented beer).

CHOOSING THE RIGHT STRAIN OF YEAST

It would seem obvious to use a Lager yeast on a Lager and an Ale yeast on an Ale, and whilst that is correct, some brewers are finding that when making an IPA, for example, they can produce a clean bitterness which accentuates the powerful, high alpha acid (see page 15) hops that they are using. But really this is complicating matters, and Ale and Lager yeasts should be used on their prospective beers. Generally speaking, using an Ale yeast on a Lager will make it too fruity and a Lager yeast on an Ale will mute many of the characteristic fruity and malt flavours that you are after. Interestingly, I have also used a dry champagne yeast to make an Ale with good results; the resulting Ale was drier than usual, but not quite a Lager.

Different strains will also give different characteristics to your beer. British Ale yeast strains tend to make the beer fruitier, whilst American Ale strains will offer a 'cleaner' taste.

DRY YEAST

The first choice is between a wet or a dry yeast. Liquid yeasts are often given undue reverence amongst brewers, despite the fact that some of the best beer in the world is made using dry yeast and I've even heard stories of professional brewers leaning over fermentation tanks and sprinkling dry yeast on to the unfermented wort below. Although this might not sound too outrageous to many kit brewers or beginners, the more experienced brewers reading this will be twitching and shaking their heads with dismay.

You see, there is an idea that dry yeasts are not as good as liquid yeasts, but this is simply unfounded: they are both yeasts that get to work on turning the sugars present into alcohol and both do it well. The real reason that many people will turn to liquid over dry is quantity rather than quality, as there is a much wider range of yeast available in liquid form. That said, I know many brewers who prefer using dry yeasts and they make world-class beer.

Dry yeast has many advantages over liquid. Firstly, it often works out cheaper than liquid; and secondly, you often don't have to make a starter (although you can), as the number of yeast cells per packet is a perfect match for the average-sized wort. If another reason were needed, dry yeast has a longer shelf-life too, lasting years rather than months, and on top of that, because it is created with large amounts of air, there is no need to aerate before pitching dry yeast. I certainly suggest having a pack or two stashed away, if only for emergency use.

LIQUID YEAST

In 1986 David and Jeanette Logson started a yeast bank in order to supply home-brewers with quality yeast and so Wyeast Laboratories in Oregon, in the USA, was born. Arguably this was one of the factors that helped change the face of home-brewing, as home-brewers could now have access to yeast strains hitherto the conserve of the master brewer. Nine years later another American liquid yeast company started – White Labs, who at any one time are culturing hundreds of yeast strains and opening the pool of yeast available even wider. These two companies currently dominate the liquid-yeast market, but their products differ slightly, Wyeast offering a 'smack pack' and White Labs a vial.

The smack pack or Activator™ was designed to create an active yeast culture directly to wort, thus helping to cut down on lag time. It contains some yeast nutrient and yeast slurry, which are kept separate inside a pouch. When the pouch is smacked, the nutrient feeds into the slurry and activates it. The beauty of these pouches is that they start producing CO_2 within a couple of hours so you know if your yeast culture is viable.

White Lab vials are pre-forms of 2-litre (3½-pint) plastic bottles (pop bottles that have not been moulded) used to house some yeast slurry.

Often neither of these liquid yeasts contains enough cells to inoculate a batch of beer and therefore a yeast starter has to be made. It is considered best practice when making a batch of beer to make a yeast starter and many pro-brewers swear by this practice.

PITCHING YOUR YEAST

There are a few very important factors to consider when pitching your yeast. Remember you want to create the ideal conditions for the cells to thrive. Yeast is a lot like a human: overwork or stress it and you'll get poor results.

For healthy yeast cells, ensure that you pitch at the correct rate for your wort: for beers 750 million cells per 1 litre (1¾ pints) of Ale wort; and 1500 million cells for every 1 litre (1¾ pints) of Lager wort. This is the rate for re-pitching yeast harvested from previous batches, and you'll need to halve that if using fresh yeast; this is because more cells will be viable. Just as a note, I'd also suggest using a bit more if using a yeast vial that is more than a month old, as the yeast culture will rapidly die off. Also, more yeast is needed when you increase the gravity of the beer as the cells will be working that little bit harder.

As it is important to get the right number of cells into your beer, there is an equation you can use in order to work out the right ratio. Even if you have never used degrees Plato before, it is fairly straightforward, being $1 \times 1 \times 1$. That is, 1 million cells $\times$ 1 degree Plato $\times$ 1 ml wort. 1 degree Plato is roughly equal to 4 brewer's points ($4 \times .001$), degrees Plato being just another measurement (like brewer's points) for measuring sugar density in wort. So let's take a batch of wort that has been measured at 1.048 and divide it by 4 to get the right degrees Plato measurement: $48 \div 4 = 12$. So using this calculation for a 19-litre (33½-pint) batch of beer with an OG of 1.048 would mean 1,000,000 (cells) $\times$ 12 (degrees Plato) $\times$ 19,000 (ml of wort) = 228,000,000,000, and that is how many viable yeast cells you'd need.

If you are finding yourself re-reading that last paragraph, try not to worry too much as there are about 20 billion cells per gram for dry yeast and most packs are 11.5g (¼oz), meaning you'll have to pitch one pack for the figure above. In the case of liquid yeasts there are often 100 billion cells per pack and so two packs will be needed. You'd also look at doubling that to make Lager or beers with high OG (ABV). Luckily, there are resources out there that can help so you don't have to keep referring back to this page and I would highly recommend using a resource like the Mr Malty's Pitching Rate Calculator™ – mrmalty.com/calc/calc.html – which will accurately calculate the number of yeast cells needed. In time you'll get to know your yeast and this will become second nature.

But why are pitching rates important? Low pitching rates increase the lag time, which will leave your beer open to infection; it will cause slow and sluggish fermentation and off flavours. It's like sending in a single bricklayer to build a block of flats – the job will probably get done and the bricklayer will probably get done in. High pitching rates mean the yeast will run out of sugar before it completes the fermentation cycle, and this will result in off flavours and poor head-retention. If pushed, I'd suggest that over-pitching is better than under-pitching as long as you don't go mad.

The range of temperature to pitch Ale yeast at is around 18–27°C (64–91°F) but, that said, you will get problems at either end of that scale. Ideally you are looking to pitch as close to 21°C (70°F) as possible (16°C/61°F for a Lager). Pitching at a higher temperature will stress the yeast and lead to off flavours.

YEAST STARTER INSTRUCTIONS

This size of yeast starter will make roughly 200 billion yeast cells from either a smack pack or vial. Although it is still (just) lower than the pitching rate needed for the average beer, it will reduce lag time and result in more cells completing their cycle, resulting in much better beer. However, do remember that if you are using yeast that isn't fresh the viability will be reduced – over three months and you might need an extra vial or pack to make a healthy starter.

200g (7oz) dried malt extract (DME), or 70g (2¾oz) if planning to culture up yeast from a bottled beer
1g (0.04oz) yeast nutrient
2 litres (3½ pints) water
ice
liquid yeast

1. Mix the DME with 2 litres (3½ pints) of cold water in a saucepan and stir well. Add the nutrient and boil for 15 minutes.
2. Put the pan into a sink of iced water and cool down to 21°C (70°F).
3. Using a sanitized funnel, pour the wort into a sanitized half-size demijohn (2-litre/3½-pint Westons Scrumpy Cider bottles are great substitutes), beaker or even a 2-litre (3½-pint) pop bottle as long as it has been sanitized. Add yeast and place some sanitized aluminium foil over the mouth of the demijohn/beaker/bottle (or screw the cap on). If you have access to an aquarium pump, then adding oxygen to the starter (remember to keep everything sterile) during fermentation will be highly beneficial. If not, then giving it a shake now and then will help. Ensure that your starter doesn't foam over. Keep it at 18–24°C (64–75°F).
4. Wait 24–48 hours then refrigerate until the yeast settles to the bottom of your container. When it does, carefully pour out the spent wort. The yeast can then be poured into the wort, although to pitch it the wort should be within 3–6°C of the starter temperature, so you will need to take it out of the fridge before you start your brew day.

AERATING THE WORT

Oxygen can ruin a beer, so why would you add it? Well, yes, in most stages of brewing you try to limit the amount of oxygen that comes into contact with your wort – except for the time just before you pitch your yeast. Yeast needs oxygen and since when you boil wort you take the oxygen out of it, you need to put it back in again.

Once you have transferred your wort into the fermenting vessel, this can easily be done either by using a sterilized electric whisk and whisking until you have a nice layer of foam on the top; or, if you don't have a whisk and are fairly fit and strong without any history of back trouble, you could have a go at picking up your fermenting vessel, ensuring the lid is firmly attached and shaking it up. Remember to bend your knees!

RE-USING YEAST

By far the easiest way to re-use yeast is to pitch on to the 'yeast cake' after siphoning off your fermented beer. The trouble is, this can lead to over-pitching and that can cause some undesirable flavours. Another suggestion would be to use a standard-size (250ml/8 fl. oz) sterilized cup, scoop up the slurry from the bottom of the fermenting vessel and pour that into a 1-litre (1¾-pint) plastic bottle, pushing all the air out and sealing it, then putting it into the fridge until you need it. It's best to use the yeast within a week, as the viability of the cells will start dropping off.

Ale yeasts can be top-cropped – that is, the yeast is collected from the top of the fermentation vessel. During the second or third day of fermentation is a good time to harvest. Simply get a large sterile spoon and skim off the surface foam. Skim off the first two or three layers and discard, then put the rest into a sterile container. Remember that, since dust particles can fall into your wort, you don't want to be messing about doing this for too long, so ensure you have your container at the ready and turn up just half of the lid. If using a narrow-necked glass fermenting vessel (carboy) rather than a brewing bucket, you can use a sanitized turkey-baster to get enough yeast out. Again, use within a week. If intending to keep for longer, refrigerate.

12

WATER

DIFFERENT AREAS OF a country can become synonymous with beer styles. Think Porter and you might think of a London Porter; think Bitter and you might think of Yorkshire Bitter; and think of Wee Heavies and of course you think of Scotland. The development of these styles in their respective areas doesn't have as much to do with the differing tastes of the inhabitants – although that does help – as it has to do with the water available to the brewers. When these styles of beer were first developed there were no real water treatments available and so the brewer was at the mercy of the water to which he had access.

To simplify matters, a region can have hard or soft water, two terms that describe the amount of (or lack of) minerals in your water. Your likelihood of having one or the other is based on the geology of the area. Soft water has travelled through hard rock and so picks up very little mineral content, while hard water can be much older, having taken years (sometimes) to get to your tap, travelling through soft rock so more of the mineral content has mixed with the water. This is why areas with a bedrock of limestone (calcium carbonate) will have hard water and places rich in granite will have soft water.

A simple test for working out if you have hard or soft water is to look at your taps or the bottom of your kettle: hard water will leave white scale deposits on them. If you are still not sure, look in your bath: if you constantly get a soap ring going around the tub, then you have hard water, my friend.

But why is hard or soft water so important in brewing? The type of water affects brewers in a number of different ways. Firstly, it can affect the perceived bitterness and hop utilization; it can also affect the flavour of the wort, along with how much sugar you can extract from your grains; and lastly the flavour of your water can affect the flavour of your beer. Simple water treatments available to brewers can ensure that your water is as near perfect as possible for whatever style of beer you choose to make.

IMPROVING YOUR WATER – REMOVING CHLORINE AND CHLORAMINE

All brewers, from kit to commercial, will benefit from removing chlorine and chloramine from their water, as often these chemicals can react with the beer, making it taste more like root beer with that strong medicinal flavour. You will need to obtain a free water report from your water company in order to ascertain what is in your water (see page 402 for water company details).

Removing chlorine is easy: water can be boiled for 15 minutes before you make your beer, or to save on your energy bill it can be left in an open container overnight.

Chloramine is a bit more of a bugger to remove and as such will need more of a shoehorn to get it out of your beer. Commercial brewers use a carbon filter; these are also available for the home-brewer (see page 381 for suppliers). Alternatively, you could boil your water for 15 minutes, or leave it to stand for four days.

A home water-filter jug, such as Brita, will remove up to 90% of chloramine and chlorine and could be a consideration for reducing the amount rather than removing totally.

Sulphites in the form of a campden tablet (potassium metabisulphite) at 1 tablet per 91 litres (20 gallons) of water are also an effective and cheap treatment and will work in less than 5 minutes. I am always reluctant to offer chemical treatments above any other method as I believe beer should be as pure as possible; however, in this instance the concentrations are low and the benefits are high, but the choice is yours.

Lastly, you can add 25g (1oz) sodium metabisulphite to a Pyrex jug and top it up with 225ml (7½ fl. oz) of water that has been pre-boiled then cooled to hand hot. Mix well and place in a suitable sanitized bottle. You can use ½ teaspoon to treat 25 litres (44 pints) of water and this will help remove both chloramine and chlorine.

WATER TREATMENT FOR KIT AND EXTRACT BREWERS

For extract brewers, tap water – provided it tastes OK – will be OK in your beer. You may wish to remove the chlorine, especially if it has a strong chlorine smell – see above. You could also put your water through a Brita filter to ensure other contaminates are neutralized if you can be arsed, but this does take time.

WATER TREATMENT FOR ALL-GRAIN BREWERS

The first step in treating your water is to get a water report so you know what you are dealing with. I've included the address and website details of all the main UK water companies at the back of the book (page 402) to help you find access to yours. However, as some areas will switch water from one source to another, especially in times of drought (interestingly, people notice only when the companies switch back to the original source), it could be useful to do your own test. You can buy water-testing kits from aquarium suppliers. The important ions to consider are calcium, magnesium and bicarbonate.

Calcium is good stuff for the brewer – it is the most important ion, since it will lower the pH during mashing, enhance the beer stability, clarity and flavour, and also work as a yeast nutrient. It is desirable to have in the region of 50–250ppm (parts per million), although the famous Burton upon Trent water has 295ppm. To increase calcium levels, add gypsum to your mash: normally 1–2 teaspoons will be enough in soft-water areas. To reduce levels, water-softening systems can be attached at source. These may seem like a costly option, but as they can prolong the life of washing machines, boilers, kettles and dishwashers, they can pay for themselves. Water-softening devices are pretty nifty too; I like the waterimp.co.uk which the manufacturers insist can reduce heating bills. Perhaps the cheapest way to remove calcium and magnesium, though, is to let your water sit over night and siphon off all but the bottom 10cm (4in).

Magnesium also contributes to water hardness, but more importantly it is a critical yeast nutrient if within a range of 10–30ppm. High levels of about 125ppm will give you the shits and even levels of above 50ppm will sour your beer. To treat for too high levels, see above.

The range of bicarbonates needed changes for different beers, from none to 50ppm for pale beers made without any speciality grains and light Lagers; 50–150ppm for slightly darker beers made using caramelized malts; and up to 250ppm for dark beers made with roasted malts. The easiest way to produce bicarbonates in your beer is to dilute it with distilled water at a rate of 1:1. Essentially, this means people with hard water who want to make Lagers or Pale Ales should be diluting their beer. If you don't have access to distilled water you can boil tap water then siphon off the top three quarters, discarding the rest.

I have really only touched on water and water treatment, but, as John Palmer said in *How to Brew*, a whole book could be written about it – which is probably why he and Colin Kaminski wrote *Water: A Comprehensive Guide for Brewers*, a must for home-brewers wishing to find out more.

PART FIVE

The Beers

13

BITTERS

T HE DISTINCTIVE RED triangle on a pint of Bass was the first ever registered British trademark and Bass also happened to be my first ever pint. I was thirteen and I'd just finished my first day's work helping out on a market stall in Northampton. The owner of the stall was pleased with my work and so treated me to a pint in his working man's club. I felt like I'd become a man. Unfortunately I got a little pissed on that one pint and my rather embarrassed boss never bought me one again.

My first experiences of Bitter help to sum up one of the reasons why it (along with Mild) is a beer that sometimes has an 'old man' or 'fusty' image. The market trader I drank mine with was well into his sixties and we drank in a sparsely decorated, nicotine-stained bar populated only by older men sitting individually at their tables. It is an unjust image, as Bitter is one of our greatest exports, the bread and butter of the beer world; indeed Fuller's ESB (Extra Special Bitter) is one of the beers that helped spark the American craft-brewing scene. Craft brewers over there still rate it as a pint to emulate, a standard to reach.

It is surprising, therefore, that such a British institution has only been around since the early nineteenth century and that we started to recognize the term 'Bitter' only around the time of the Cuban Missile Crisis. The terminology had more to do with the lack of pump clips than anything else, as, when ordering, punters needed to differentiate these beers from the

Milds, Pale Ales and Stouts on offer. They started to ask for pints of 'bitter beer'.

The term eventually stuck and beers such as Pedigree and London Pride started to be called 'Bitters' rather than 'Pale Ales' by the brewers, and thus a style was born. Although, of course the great style controversy continues and some Bitters are still called Pale Ales (Landlord, for example). The confusion starts from the fact that all Bitters are Pale Ales but not all Pale Ales are Bitters!

Bitters range from around 3% to 6% ABV and there are three subcategories denoted by their alcohol strength. Ordinary Bitter will be on the weaker side at around 3–4% and is produced to be drunk in quantity as a 'session beer'; Best Bitter is brewed to be slightly stronger, often to about 4.5%; and Extra Special Bitter or ESB will be brewed at a strength of 5–6% ABV and is more of a weekend beer. Some may still call it a session beer, but they will either weigh over 20 stone or have the sort of sessions that end in supermarket trolleys, ripped clothing, the inability to see and a pneumonia-inducing park-bench snooze.

Bitters generally have some aroma coming from the malt – this can often be biscuit or caramel, but fruity aromas are not uncommon. They are almost always bright beers (clear) unless there is something wrong with the barrel. There should also be a fine balance between the malt and the hops which will, contrarily, not be overly bitter.

SOME OF THE FINEST BITTERS AND BEST BITTERS

These are the beers for which Britain is known the world over. Almost every brewer will have a Bitter of some sort in his or her portfolio. Some are very much the same, some really do stand out.

Landlord, 4.3%, Timothy Taylor, Yorkshire

This is a beer that is difficult to classify, typifying the fine line that often exists between beer styles. I could be so bold as to suggest that it was one of the Pale Ales that some of the punters in the 1950s and 1960s were referring to as 'Bitter' instead of Pale Ale. Even the late Michael Jackson (the beer guy, not the monkey-loving singer), who was instrumental in beer classification, refers to Landlord as a Pale Ale/Bitter.

At the start of my quest for the perfect pint, a Landlord was my number one. In some ways this pint, which was first brewed in 1952, is still difficult to beat, despite numerous examples of new and fantastic flavours – but beer isn't always about a new flavour every time. It should also be about unpretentious, easy drinking, a beer that doesn't split the room, a beer that can be enjoyed by everyone.

There is a very small pub in a village just outside Cirencester that sells one beer, Timothy Taylor's Landlord, and nothing else. It's had two owners since Victorian times, the present one starting when he was just sixteen. The pub consists of one table and has no bar. Rich landowners rub shoulders with labourers and the occasional city worker and they all drink Landlord. It's a great leveller and everyone just chats across the table. The lack of choice is a bonus, as it means there is no beer snobbery; it saves time when ordering, 'Pint or half?' being the only question needed; and it's simply a good pint. I do love the choice in the new breed of ale houses and at festivals, but sometimes it's nice just to have a good pint, and for me that's a pint of Landlord.

Dry-hopped with Styrian Goldings, giving it that unique earthy, rose/floral flavour that sets it slightly apart from many other Bitters/Pale Ales, this is entwined with sweetish caramel and biscuit malts. Unfortunately, and rather ironically, Landlord often gets mistreated by landlords and as a result can be an appalling beer when not served correctly; for this reason I'd recommend trying it again if you didn't like it the first time, especially if you bought it in a pub that doesn't know how to serve a decent pint.

Available from most good off-licences and many British pubs across the country. To find a Timothy Taylor pub, visit timothy-taylor.co.uk/OurPubs.aspx.

Magus, 3.8%, Durham Brewery, Bowburn, Co. Durham

Durham Brewery have a religious theme to many of their beers as a nod to the monastic brewing traditions of yore. Their beers include Redemption, Evensong and Temptation, or in this case Magus – a 'magus' being one of the wise men who first introduced capitalism into Christmas by giving lavish gifts, including gold.

Magus in the sense of this beer is indeed a golden-coloured, light Bitter, but what this lacks in ABV it certainly makes up for in hop flavour. Lemon curd, limeade and bitter Seville marmalade flavours gently assault your senses in this my perfect Bitter.

Available from specialist bottle shops, online at the durham-brewery.co.uk and on cask at the Black Horse and Bodega, Newcastle upon Tyne.

Yorkshire Square Ale, 5%, Black Sheep, Masham, North Yorkshire

Another story that every British beer enthusiast should have in their repertoire is the one behind the Black Sheep Brewery. Back in 1986 a small town in Yorkshire with a population of between only 1,000 and 2,000 people had just one brewery, Theakston. Theakston was a family-run business until 1987 when what are being called 'family disagreements', involving high courts and merchant bankers, forced a series of decisions leading to the eventual buyout by brewing giant Scottish & Newcastle. Paul Theakston was offered a job elsewhere in the company but didn't feel comfortable working for such a mega-corporation.

Alienated from his family members, Paul licked his wounds for some time before deciding that he wanted to carry on not just brewing, but brewing under the shadow of Theakston just a stone's throw away in the same town. Using money from a business expansion scheme, he set up his own brewery in 1991 and at his wife's suggestion he called it Black Sheep. And so a good story and a brewing legend were born.

Yorkshire Square Ale has to be my favourite of the Black Sheep Ales. Initially slightly harsh bitterness rests to reveal strong, soft caramel sweetness and a popcorn buttery feel. I seem to be alone in suggesting that all Black Sheep Ales have a mineral quality that really does remind me of slate. Maybe at one time, before the square slate fermenting vessels gave way to modern stainless steel, I might have been on to something, but essentially, like many authors, I might just have an overactive imagination.

Occasionally available at Black Sheep pubs nationwide, it is also widely distributed across the country at good off-licences (and some terrible ones), or direct from Black Sheep at blacksheepbrewery.com.

Funky Monkey, 4%, Milk Street, Frome, Somerset

The Milk Street Brewery is situated at the back of the Griffin pub in Frome – a simple, one-room pub with oak beams adorned with hop bines, friendly bar staff and an excellent view across the nearby countryside. As with much of Frome, it's a friendly place and I've never left the Griffin without having sparked up a conversation with a local farmer or architect!

Funky Monkey is the flagship beer of the Milk Street Brewery. Head brewer and founder Rik Lyall cut his teeth at the Cotleigh, Stonehenge and Hop Back breweries before setting up on his own. He's been brewing since he was fourteen and for him good beer is all about balance. Funky Monkey is one of Rik's favourites. He was looking for a session beer and at that time had a great Blonde called 'Beer' and a great-selling Bitter called Nick's, which was 4.4% but still a bit strong for a session, so he was looking for something a bit weaker. He had spent quite a few years at the Hop Back Brewery and was a devoted fan of GFB, which inspired him to create a 4% copper-coloured Best Bitter brewed with Styrian Goldings as a single-hopped beer. Initially the name for this brew was Hedge Monkey, which is what Somerset locals call hippies. Rik says, 'It wasn't long on the bar when the locals christened it Funky Monkey, which is a much better name and soon stuck.'

With Funky Monkey what Rik has certainly achieved is a beer that is full of depth, texture and complexity. If you want to teach yourself about balance, Funky Monkey is the beer for the job. Take a sip and think about what is happening in your mouth. As the roof of your mouth gets coated in toffee fudge flavours, this will start to subside, leaving an Opal Fruit (Starburst)/tangerine bitterness behind and a long, lingering, dry finish.

Available at the Griffin and Market Yard in Frome, The Brewhouse in Poole and the Bristol Red Lion Pub Company, or as a polypin direct from the Griffin.

Wot's Occurring, 3.9%, Great Oakley, Tiffield, Northamptonshire

From the first sip I had of Wot's Occurring I could see why it got its name. It's one of those beers that you end up holding in your hand and looking at as if somehow you'll instantly know how it was made. Certainly an unusual

Bitter, with some herbs but also a lovely mixture of fruits – zesty grapefruit, apricot and peach – balanced with a toffee caramel. It's a shame that this wasn't being made in Northamptonshire when I lived there.

Available at the Malt Shovel, Northampton, and in bottles from www.greatoakleybrewery.co.uk.

SOME OF THE FINEST PREMIUM AND EXTRA SPECIAL BITTERS

Extra Special Bitters are one of our greatest exports, as brewers in Australia and the USA will often have an ESB as their flagship beer.

ESB (Extra Special Bitter), 5.9%, Fuller's, London

Just like your first teenage fumble, you should always remember your first pint of ESB. Mine was in the Victoria near Paddington, London, with my good friend Harry. A quick pint sneaked in before the last train to Bristol on a cold winter's night.

I knew that ESB was a beer that I wanted to tick off my (mental) list. I ordered this rich mahogany Ale of true equipoise, delighting in each sip. I found out then that ESB is a beer that walks a remarkable balancing act, allowing the 5.9% ABV to slip down a treat. Breaded malts sit with such bitter breakfast marmalade hops that you can almost smell the crease being ironed into a newspaper, all nicely finished with a long floral aftertaste.

Glad that I'd ticked one off my mental list, I ordered five more and slept all the way back to Bristol.

ESB is readily available in over 500 Fuller's pubs (see fullers.co.uk) and widely available in most places that sell beer.

Radgie Gadgie, 4.8%, Mordue, North Shields, Tyne and Wear

Radgie Gadgie is classed a Premium or Best Bitter. Although fairly similar to Funky Monkey, my mate Paul from the Waen Brewery stated, 'That's dry, that – that's really dry.' Certainly has a feel of morning breakfast too, with toasted malt notes carefully balancing the dry, bitter marmalade hops, with a touch of floral about it too. The hops used are part American Willamette and part English Challenger.

Available at the Crown Posada, the Head of Steam, The Quayside and the Union Rooms in Newcastle upon Tyne. Also in bottles from specialist bottle shops.

Identity XSB (Xtra Strong Bitter), 6%, Revolutions Brewing Co., Castleford, West Yorkshire

What I was expecting when I picked up this highly stylized bottle featuring the retro cool image of a C60 cassette was a take on Fuller's famous ESB. I wasn't disappointed. At first the two drinks were interchangeable, then I started to taste the last forty years of advancement in brewing practices. Full of caramel at first, leading to a peppery spice which carries on and on, more like a C90 on the finish. Closer to something that I might drink in Belgium – a hint of a peppery Saison, a soupçon of Tripel and a huge great dollop of British Bitter. An unexpected delight of an Ale that continues to evolve.

Occasionally available from Shakespeare, Sheffield, the Station Hotel, Castleford, and in bottles from beerritz.co.uk.

BREWING BITTERS

Getting your head around brewing a simple Bitter can be a great starting point for any brewer. The reasons for brewing them at home are pretty similar to the reasons why regular brewers have Bitter on their books: it's a beer that most Ale drinkers will enjoy. What's more, with possibilities of dry-hopping and super-charging your Bitter to become an ESB, it is a style that is good to play about with.

MALT

Pale Ale, amber and crystal malts are used in Bitters and a small addition of black malt can be used for colour adjustment without having to use darker crystal malts that might offer too much of the wrong flavours.

HOPS

The characteristic English hop is used in a Bitter, East Kent Goldings and Fuggles being two very typical examples. But similar hops can be an excellent choice – think Progress, Styrian Goldings, Tettnanger and Willamette. A Bitter shouldn't have an overly strong hop profile, but to break with tradition and go with something 'off style' try using high alpha acid hops such as the American 'C' varieties like Chinook and Cascade; this is what many commercial breweries are doing now with some fantastic results. Dry-hopping is an especially good idea for Best Bitters and ESBs, as it gives beers that extra edge.

YEAST

As Bitter is such a ubiquitous style, there are plenty of strains of yeast to choose from when making it. From Wyeast try for something a little fruitier with 1968 London ESB Ale or 1099 Whitbread Ale; for something a little cleaner use 1275 Thames Valley; and for nutty, fruity, dry beers experiment with 1469 West Yorkshire Ale yeast. From White Labs WLP026 gives something extra special to ESBs – expect more fruit, but it can be very dry too, often giving a much lower FG than other strains. If you can train the beast, Windsor can be something to experiment with, but for a safer bet use Fermentis Safeale s-04 if you wish to use a dry yeast.

It is always worth making a yeast starter the day before brewing if using vials or smack packs (see page 209), unless feeling rich and lazy, in which case 2 vials are generally enough for the average 19–25-litre (33½–44-pint) batch. Pitch yeast at 19°C (66°F) and ferment between 16°C and 21°C (61°F and 70°F). Condition for at least four weeks.

WATER TREATMENT

Treat with gypsum or Burton salts for about 100ppm Ca.

BITTERS FROM KITS

My first ever kit was a Bitter, but that was back in the bad old days of brewing and I made what can only be called passable beer. If I had only known that there are many things that make a huge difference when brewing, maybe I would have had better beer, more friends and perhaps a better sex life – who knows? Improving beer is easy: swapping unnamed yeast for a good strain such as Danstar Nottingham; keeping the fermentation temperature at a steady 22°C (72°F) for the first day, then reducing to 20°C (68°F); allowing for slightly longer in the fermentation vessel too – up to two weeks; and leaving to condition for up to six weeks are just some of the things you can do.

Landlords Finest Bitter, Festival

Festival make very good kits and this is no exception. The finished product has more than a passing resemblance to its namesake, Timothy Taylor's Landlord. It's much better if left for a while. Although it's not a bad pint when drunk young – think Butcombe Original –after two months in the bottle or barrel it is transformed into a pint of Landlord.

Best Bitter, John Bull

If you just want to dip your toe into kit brewing, then the John Bull kits are quite a cheap way of creating a pretty drinkable beer. As with all kits, a little extra investment will make all the difference. Using Muntons Beer Kit Enhancer instead of granulated sugar will give you a pint with a little more body. Veteran kit brewer Dave Glass suggests that if 1kg (2lb 3oz) of sugar is asked for, use 500g (1¼lb) of beer kit enhancer/spray malt and 700g (1½lb) of brewing sugar, a specialized sugar that is available from home-brew stockists. This is very sound advice from Dave.

BITTER RECIPES

There are full instructions on steeping grains on page 89, but it is very easy and will help turn a dull beer into a great one. Basically, just keep your grains in a muslin bag in a pot of water on the hob at a constant temperature of between 65°C and 75°C (149°F and 167°F) for 20–30 minutes, then add to your final wort. You can experiment by adding steeped grains to kit beers too.

Best Bitter

This is a pretty standard Best Bitter; the chocolate malt addition is purely to add a little colour. If you don't have any in stock, it can be omitted and instead a darker malt extract can be used. For an ordinary Bitter, reduce the extract to 2.25kg (5lb) and the Northdown hop addition to just 20g (¾oz) at the start of the boil. For an Extra Special Bitter, increase the extract to 4kg (9lb) and use 50g (2oz) Northdown or the bittering hop of your choice.

INGREDIENTS
3kg (6lb 9oz) pale malt extract (16 EBC) 92.7%
200g (7oz) crystal malt (120 EBC) 6.1%
40g (1½oz) chocolate malt (1240 EBC) 1.2%
40g (1½oz) Northdown (8.5% AA, 30 IBU) @ 45 minutes
15g (½oz) East Kent Goldings (5% AA, 4.3 IBU) @ 15 minutes
2 vials WLP002 or 2 Wyeast 1968 smack packs; if using dried I'd recommend
1 packet Safale s-04

1. Steep the grains for 30 minutes at 68°C (154°F).
2. Bring 21 litres (37 pints) of water to the boil and add the water from the steeped grains, pale malt extract and the Northdown hops. After 30 minutes add the East Kent Goldings and boil for a further 15 minutes.
3. Cool the wort to 19°C (66°F) before pitching (adding) the yeast. Ferment at 19–23°C (66–73°F) for fourteen days and ensure correct final gravity has been reached before bottling with 100g (3½oz) sugar. If you can, leave well alone for at the very least two weeks before drinking.

Estimated ABV 4.6%, OG 1.048, FG 1.013; for Bitter ABV 3.5%, OG 1.036, FG 1.010; for ESB ABV 6.2%, OG 1.064, FG 1.016.

All-grain Best Bitter

This is an all-grain recipe, but make it your own. Change the hops – you may want to bitter using Fuggles and use East Kent Goldings for aroma. The black malt is used just to darken the beer up a little and so it's not imperative that you use it; I just like to have my Bitters slightly darker. Most English Ale yeasts will do the job so, again, experiment.

INGREDIENTS

3.8kg (8lb 6oz) crisp Pale Ale malt (5.7 EBC) 92%

300g (11oz) crystal malt (118.2 EBC) 7.3%

30g (1¼oz) black malt (1300 EBC) 0.7%

45g (1¾oz) East Kent Goldings (5% AA) @ 90 minutes

14g (½oz) Fuggles (4.5% AA) @ 10 minutes

1 smack pack Wyeast 1275 Thames Valley or 1 vial White Labs WLP 023 if using a starter, or use 2 packs/vials if not; or 1 packet Danstar Nottingham dry yeast

Mash at 66°C (151°F) for 75 minutes.
Boil for 90 minutes.

OG 1.045–1.046, FG 1.010, est. ABV 4.6%.

Cool wort to 19°C (66°F) before pitching the yeast. Ferment at 19–23°C (66–74°F) for fourteen days and ensure correct final gravity has been reached before bottling with 100g (3½oz) sugar.

Irish Red Ale

Irish Red Ales are a bit of a rare beast in Britain, but Smithwick's (now part of Guinness) over in Ireland do brew a particularly good one; Fuller's Red Fox is also well worth seeking out. The Irish Red is another style that owes its existence to Michael Jackson (the beer hunter and writer, not the one who befriended children), who went over to Ireland in the 1960s and reported back on a style of beer that he saw as common. Coors picked it up and ran with it, creating Killian's Irish Red, with many American breweries following suit and making their own.

These are basically red-coloured session beers with a light malt that leans on crystal malts to give it more flavour. Irish Red is not without its critics, dubbed a bland beer brewed without much hop or malt profile in order to save money. That said, the experimental brewer can play about with the style to create a sessionable, tasty beer.

This recipe was sent to me by award-winning home-brewer Tom Evans from Donegal in Ireland. He's a man after my own heart who grows not only six varieties of hops but his own grain too! Much of his brewing is chronicled on his blog, homebrewindonegal.blogspot.ie.

INGREDIENTS
3.1kg (7lb) pale malt 81%
500g (1¼lb) light crystal malt (40 EBC) 13%
75g (3oz) CaraRed malt 2%
120g (4oz) roasted barley 4%
35g (1¼oz) Fuggles (5.1% AA) @ 60 minutes (bitter)
20g (¾oz) Fuggles @15 minutes (aroma)
Irish moss

1. Mash with 9.95 litres (17½ pints) at 72–73°C (162–163°F) to achieve 65–66°C (149–151°F); OG 1.038, FG 1.011; IBU 22.

2. Mash for 1 hour, with water that isn't too hard, checking the temperature doesn't dip below 65°C (149°F).

3. Sparge with water at 75–80°C (167–176°F) until the wort runs out at 1004, or until sufficient wort has been collected. Bring to the boil and boil for 1 hour, adding the hops and a dose of Irish moss (see packet instructions).

4. Cool and strain into a fermenting vessel. Depending on how much sugar you have extracted during your mash and sparge phases, you may not be hitting the desired OG of 1.038; if this is the case you need to top up with water. Use the equation below to achieve desired OG in the fermenting vessel, rather than volume. You may need to under- or over-fill:
(current volume ÷ desired gravity) × current gravity = final volume required

5. Pitch the yeast as directed, either 2 vials White Labs WLP004 Irish Ale Yeast (liquid), or 1 packet Danstar Nottingham Ale (dry).

6. After fermentation stops, which should be c.1011, rack into bottles, secondary fermenting vessel or keg. It will be ready after two weeks, but will benefit from three weeks. Carbonate with 100g (3½oz) of granulated sugar.

Extract version

INGREDIENTS
1.9kg (4lb 3oz) light dry malt extract
40g (1½oz) CaraRed malt
260g (9½oz) light crystal malt
35g (1¼oz) Fuggles @ 60 minutes
20g (¾oz) Fuggles @ 15 minutes
1 packet Nottingham dried yeast

1. Put the CaraRed and the light crystal malts in a sealed muslin bag, place in a small pan of water and steep the grains for 20–30 minutes at 68°C (154°F).

2. Meanwhile, bring 25 litres (44 pints) of water to the boil. When boiling, add the water from the steeped grains and 35g (1¼oz) of Fuggles. After 45 minutes add the second lot and boil for a further 15 minutes.

3. Cool to 19°C (66°F) before pitching a packet of Nottingham dried yeast. After fermentation stops – which should be around 1011 – rack into bottles, secondary fermenting vessel or keg. It will be ready after two weeks, but will benefit from three. Carbonate with 100g (3½oz) of granulated sugar.

14

BROWN ALES

I F YOU WERE living in seventeenth-century Britain you would be forgiven for saying that all beer is Brown Ale, as it wasn't until the eighteenth century that pale malts started to be used in beer. Before then Brown Ales – or, rather, brown beers, as they were hopped beers – were made using 100% brown malt. By all accounts these were not great beers and when Porters, Pales and Stouts started to be made they soon took over as the drinks of choice. Brown Ales just couldn't compete and they all but disappeared, not emerging again until the start of the twentieth century, albeit as very different beers with only the style name intact.

It is easy to see a recurring theme with regards to British beers and their decline, and Brown Ale is no expectation, as after the First World War beer was forced to lower its ABV and the style suffered as a result. However, unlike Milds and Porters, Brown Ales have not really made much of a comeback here in the UK. However, if brewers here continue to be influenced by activities across the pond, then we might well see a return to Brown as American brewers have really embraced the style.

The war didn't completely kill off Brown Ales, though, and as blending was still in fashion between the wars and since Brown Ales often came in bottles rather than casks like most Ales, they were a good stable mixer for the draft beers which landlords struggled to keep from spoiling. This gave Brown Ales a brief hiatus back in the limelight. As the century progressed, though, they fell out of fashion, even in bottles, suffering a similar fate to Milds in being considered the refuge of the cloth-capped industrial workers who themselves, or rather their jobs, dwindled into relative obscurity.

A taste of the times is still produced by Mann with a Brown Ale similar to what has been produced since the 1920s. There is of course one other specific and notable exception that has become synonymous with this beer style, or at least with the name Brown Ale. Maybe due to the fact that heavy industry still showed some strength in the region during the latter part of the last century, so did the Brown Ales favoured by the manual worker. Newcastle Brown Ale, despite production being bought up and moved, has clung on in the changing face of the North East. The beer still remains very popular, not just up north but as a recognized world brand.

Newcastle Brown Ale might be known the world over as the 'One and only [Brown Ale]', but does it really define the style? Brown Ales fall into the same murky liquor of beer definition as many of our styles do. The late and notable patron saint of writers on beer styles, Michael Jackson, states that there are two types of Brown Ale in the UK, one in the north and one in the south. The latter is the weaker at 3–3.5%, sweet and dark brown, whereas its northern counterpart is stronger at 4–4.5%, drier and reddish brown. But that is not the end of the story, as there is some confusion over what is really being described. Is it just the colour? In which case an abundance of beers could fit into the 'Brown Ale' category. It has been said that using the term 'Brown Ale' to describe a style of beer is as useful as saying 'red wine'. Indeed, considering that not only are the northern and southern styles very different but that American Brown Ale can be different again, and even German Altbier can fit into the 'Brown Ale' category, it is a valid point.

Brown Ale is therefore another beer that it is difficult to define. In this respect they are similar to Porters or Summer/Golden Ales in that there is a wide scope of interpretation to the style. Yes, northern and southern Brown Ales are very different – but then Robust, Imperial and Brown Porters are all very different, yet we still call them all Porters. Argument around beer styles is an already bloody ring into which to throw your hat, and in the case of Brown Ales I'll add just this massive cop-out: if the brewer insists that it is a Brown Ale and that is what's on the pump clip, then let's respect his/her definition, sit back and enjoy a pint (of whatever it is).

SOME OF THE FINEST BROWN ALES

Stone Brood, 4.4%, Lymestone Brewery, Stone, Staffordshire

When setting up a brewery a beehive is not generally at the top of someone's list, yet when 'Brad the Brewer' found that a swarm had decided otherwise, he invited local beekeeper 'Lee the Bee' to create a hive for them and now there are three. Using honey from said bees, Brad has created a beer that balances honey with chocolate malts to create an unusual Brown Ale. I wasn't sure during the first few sips, but I must have served it (the bottle) slightly cooler than I intended because as it warmed I got a remarkable beer. Nutty and a little smoky and deeply earthy with hints of lychee, and the honey evenly balances everything else that is going on in the Ale. Almost as an aside, if you have ever made your own honeycomb and burnt it a little bit, then this beer will bring a flood of memories of the pan you made it in. It's difficult to get honey in beer right, especially if any strong flavours are evident, and I can only assume that Lee the Bee's bees feast on just the right diet of wild flowers and blossom.

Available seasonally and all year round in bottles from select bottle shops such as www.bestofbritishbeer.co.uk.

Nut Brown Ale, 5%, Samuel Smith, Tadcaster, North Yorkshire

Nut Brown Ale is brewed using the traditional Yorkshire square fermenting system which arguably adds to this beer's unique character. You may have heard of beers being called 'hop-forward', 'malt-forward' and perhaps even 'yeast-forward'; in this case Sam Smith have created a 'nut-forward', full-bodied beer (despite there being no nuts in it). Hazelnut, beech and pecan are all evident and sit with caramel, toasted malt and some fruit flavours – cherry and dried figs. A slight floralness is evident from the hops but is certainly not bold – a fleeting appearance, you might say, with the nuts dominating.

Available from Sam Smith pubs nationwide and in bottles from many major bottle shops and off-licences.

Brown Ale, 2.8%, Manns (Brewed by Marston's, Wolverhampton, West Midlands)

A Brown Ale with a chequered history. First brewed in 1902 and known as the 'sweetest beer in London', it quickly became Londoners' drink of choice, although back then it was brewed to a stronger 4%. The two subsequent world wars and the malt shortages they brought helped bring this (and many other) beers down to its present-day 2.8%.

The Mann Brewery itself no longer exists, but trying to chart the history of every brewery that ever brewed Manns Brown Ale is a complicated business and a real eye-opener in terms of the mergers and acquisitions that can go on in the brewing world. The Mann Brewery merged in 1958 with Watney Combe Reid & Co., who took over many other breweries, including Ushers, who were charged with brewing Manns Brown Ale. This company then merged with Grand Metropolitan in 1972. Ushers was then subject to a management buyout in 1990 and lasted until 2000, when the business was deemed to be 'not cost effective'. The brewery itself was sold for £1.5 million to North Korea and it now functions as the Taedonggang Brewery, which sits just outside Pyongyang, and its beer is apparently drunk in quantity by Kim Jong-un.

But this wasn't the end. Refresh UK was set up after the closure of Ushers and brewed its beers under licence until it too was then taken over by Marston's Beer Company in March 2008, and now Marston's brew Manns Brown Ale. All of which goes to prove that sometimes finding the answer to what seems a very simple question, like who brews a certain beer, is not always that straightforward.

Considering that this Brown Ale must have made a lot of people a lot of money over the years, it begs the question, is it any good? Well, yes, as a matter of fact. Although rather delicate on the nose, there is still some toffee and roast coming from this very dark Brown Ale. I wasn't sure what to expect at all as I drank; it felt as if accepting that I even liked this beer would be an acknowledgement of my age, the start of a decline into wearing slippers all weekend, betting on greyhounds and of course supping this beer rather than something stronger and far cooler. Instead I was very pleasantly surprised to find a relatively good Ale of which I could drink a couple and not even have the slightest chance of a hangover. Its lightness also lent itself to easy drinking: raisins up front, which then gave way to a sweet caramel followed by a lightly spiced malty biscuit and some molasses, with a dry, short-lived finish.

Only comes in bottles, but is very widely available from many off-licences, although many good bottle shops may be slightly too snobbish to stock it as it is rather unfashionable at the time of writing.

BREWING BROWN ALES

MALT

Often Brown Ales will have a base grain of around 80% pale malt, such as Maris Otter. Brown malt is not always present, but somewhere between 2% and 6% makes for a great addition, as do small amounts of other roasted malts: 2–5% chocolate, for example, will also add an extra bit of depth, but if using remember to leave the beer to condition for a few months.

A touch of sweetness from around 5–15% crystal malt is usual too, with lower amounts in a northern Brown Ale. Older home-brew recipes sometimes include caramel, which is added into the boil; this will bring some colour to extract recipes. Mash at 67°C (153°F).

HOPS

Relatively low IBUs – around 15–25 – from traditionally English hops are the way forward for a Brown Ale. Use Fuggles or Goldings as aroma and perhaps Progress as an early addition. Look towards the lower end of the scale for a northern Brown Ale and the higher for a southern.

YEAST AND FERMENTATION

A British Ale strain such as White Labs WLP005 could be an interesting choice. It will require some patience, though, as it can take its time to really get going. I'd suggest making a yeast starter. Also, leave your beer for two weeks in the primary fermenting vessel before moving to a secondary.

Another yeast to try is Danstar Windsor dry yeast, which comes with a warning as well as a recommendation: it works very well for beers made at a low ABV but can be sluggish and you will need to be patient.

BROWN ALE RECIPES

Northern Brown Ale from Extract

INGREDIENTS
3.25kg (7lb 3oz) pale liquid extract

210g (7½oz) crystal malt (120 EBC)

80g (3oz) chocolate malt

50g (2oz) East Kent Goldings (AA 5%) @ 60 minutes

13g (½oz) Fuggles (AA 4.5%) @ 15 minutes

1 packet Windsor Ale dry yeast, but as this can be temperamental try 2 vials White Labs WLP005

Brown Ceas All-grain

This recipe for an American-style Brown Ale comes from Adrian Chapman, a garage brewer from the Keighley area of West Yorkshire who also works at the Saltaire Brewery in Shipley.

INGREDIENTS
3.38kg (7lb 7oz) lager malt 72%

230g (8oz) wheat malt 5%

230g (8oz) crystal malt (120 EBC) 5%

330g (11½oz) caramalt 7%

380g (13½oz) CaraPils malt 8%

90g (3¼oz) chocolate malt 2%

50g (2oz) pale chocolate malt 1%

Mash at 69°C (156°F) for 60–90 minutes.

Boil for 60 minutes, adding hops as follows:

INGREDIENTS

26g (1oz) Aramis (first wort hops; 8.9%) @ 65 minutes

40g (1½oz) Saaz (3.95%) @ 35 minutes

30g (1¼oz) Columbus (Tomahawk, 16.5 %) @ 0 minutes (end of the boil)

30g (1¼oz) Cascade (7.9 %) @ 0 minutes

60g (2¼oz) Chinook (12.5 %) @ 0 minutes

Yeast: Safale US-05

Dry-hop with 20g (¾oz) each of Cascade and Amarillo for three days.

Northern Brown Ale All-grain

This is loosely based on a recipe for an 1812 Brown Ale from the excellent book *Old British Beers and How to Make Them* by Durden Park Beer Circle, but theirs is much hoppier and paler than the original would have been. Using the brown malt will give some harsh roasted flavours and therefore it is certainly advisable to allow this beer to condition for at least four months.

INGREDIENTS

4.23g (0.15oz) pale malt 92%

270g (9½oz) brown malt 5.9%

100g (3½oz) chocolate malt 2.2%

Mash for 75 minutes at 66°C (151°F).

Boil for 60 minutes, then add hops as follows:

INGREDIENTS

40g (1½oz) East Kent Goldings (5%) @ 60 minutes

10g (¼oz) Fuggles (4.5%) @ 15 minutes

Yeast: Wyeast 1028 London Ale smack pack

OG 1.046–1.052, FG 1.011, ABV 4.7%–5.3%

15

GOLDEN (SUMMER) AND BLONDE ALES

THE 1980s WERE dark times for 'Real Ale' drinkers. CAMRA was still in its infancy and mass-marketed Lagers were becoming the toast of the town. Breweries needed to tempt drinkers back to Ale and the trick up their sleeve was a new style brewed with just pale malt – a Golden or Summer Ale, lighter than many beers and as golden-amber in colour as the Lagers they were competing against.

Summer Ales soon took off, led by Exmoor Gold (4.5% cask and bottle), a one-off celebratory Ale from the Golden Hill Brewery in Somerset (now Exmoor Brewery), back in 1986. It was closely followed in the same year by another Golden Ale: single-hopped with East Kent Goldings and called Summer Lightning, it was (and still is) brewed just across the Levels in Salisbury by the Hop Back Brewery (5% cask and bottle). Soon other breweries followed and a style was born.

However, the story of Golden (or Summer) Ales goes back much further. There are references to Golden Ales back in 1842, when the William Saunders Brewery in Burton upon Trent was advertising a 'Golden Ale'; and even earlier, in 1838, '24 dozens of Golden Ale, and 17½ dozen other beers' were in the inventory of the passenger ship *Emerald Isle*. Whether or not these Golden Ales were anything like our present-day beers is anyone's guess, but I prefer the fact that a style dates from when I was first sneaking the odd pint, so let's not let these early references get in the way of good yarn over a pint of Golden!

Blond(e) beers, on the other hand, often get bunched in with Golden or Summer Ales, as there often isn't much more than a brewer's (or marketing department's) prerogative to tell them apart. Indeed, sometimes brewers will call what is essentially a Golden Ale a Blonde Ale – Butcombe Blond, for example. Often they are around 4–5% ABV and have low to moderate hop bitterness of around 15–25 IBU. A tendency has developed, especially amongst new breweries, to achieve this using high alpha acid New World hops too. Actually, though, a true Blonde is a style famed across the Continent and should be made with Lager or Pilsner malt, perhaps with a touch of Munich or Vienna malt, and using ale yeast. What complicates matters further is that Lagers can also be called Blondes – George Wright brews Pure Blonde, for example. One thing is for certain, when you buy a Blonde in the UK it will be pale, but beyond that really it's anyone's guess.

SOME OF THE FINEST GOLDEN (SUMMER) ALES

Summer Meltdown, 4.8%, Dark Star, Horsham, West Sussex

At the risk of offending a continent, if there is any one race of people who love their bad Lagers it's the Aussies (sorry, Aussies). I worked on a radio station with an Aussie called Tom Spence and after our show we'd nip to an Arbor Ales pub and sink a few jars. He'd insist on having a generic Lager despite my pleas for him to try anything else. One magical afternoon, as Tim Henman took a medal in the Olympics, I passed him a pint of Summer Meltdown instead of his usual. He reluctantly took it and stated that it 'wasn't as bad as I thought it might be'. Which is possibly the biggest compliment an Ale might get from an Aussie.

Meltdown is brewed with stem ginger, but this doesn't mean it tastes like a ginger beer, as the ginger is muted by nutmeg, heather and bitter, zesty grapefruit. The ginger does, however, hang around right to the finish. It has that dangerous quality in a beer of not tasting as strong as it is, meaning it is very easy to sink a few before realizing quite how pissed you are.

To find your nearest pint during the summer months, try the Dark Star beerfinder at darkstarbrewing.co.uk/beerfinder. Mostly available in the South East and Home Counties. Not currently available in bottles.

Scarlet Macaw, 4.4%, Oakham, Peterborough, Cambridgeshire

Sitting with two builders at the Hop Bine in Cambridge on one of the few hot summer's days of 2012, I was first introduced to Scarlet Macaw and the joy that is Oakham Ales — one of the best things to come out of Peterborough since Erasure and David Seaman. Scarlet Macaw pours to a perfectly clear golden colour and sharp grapefruit is delicately balanced by a Rich Tea biscuit malt. But there is more going on besides: wood shavings, pine, lychee and peach are all evident too, leading you to a neat, grassy finish.

Simply a great beer, perfect for supping in the summer.

Available all year round as a guest Ale around the East Anglia region (I highly recommend trying the Hop Bine in Cambridge). Also available in bottles from good bottle shops, including the Bacchanalia in Cambridge.

Carnival, 4.3%, Magic Rock, Huddersfield, West Yorkshire

Stuart, the man who brews Carnival (and many other amazing beers for Magic Rock), is rather modest about his talents. However, it's no coincidence that every brewery he's worked for – namely Crown (Sheffield), Acorn (Barnsley) and Kelham Island (Sheffield) – have all won international acclaim for their beers. 'I seem to have a natural talent for knowing what ingredients go together – it seems to come very easily to me,' he told me over a couple of pints. 'I had a lot of time to experiment too at Kelham Island Brewery and that obviously helped.'

Stuart is a man of few words, but a man who sees brewing as something of an art form. Like most artists, he can be prone to some rather odd behaviour: he once 'courted' fellow beer writer Zak Avery's friendship by following him around with a big bag of Scotch eggs. He was also found one Halloween on a pub crawl around Leeds wearing just a one-piece swimming costume and a top hat. Of course Stuart didn't become one of the best brewers in the world by being like everyone else!

For those who are fed up with the high ABV of many IPAs but who still enjoy the flavour, then Carnival is your drink. Think of it as a reduced IPA – less of a punch of citrus hops and kinder to your morning-after head too. That is not to say the hops don't let themselves be known; this is certainly one of the beers that you can smell long before you taste it – aromas of pine and tropical fruits emanate from this Golden Ale. Lightly carbonated yet still with plenty of body; grapefruit, tangerine and even passionfruit, with a long, lingering dry finish. Nice one, Stuart – we salute you (or at least I do)!

Available all year round as an occasional guest at Friends of Ham in Leeds and many other Craft Ale pubs around the country. Magic Rock produce very small batches of beer, so it will be difficult to find any in a bottle. Keep an eye out on beerritz.co.uk for any bottles that might come up.

The Pardoner's Ale, 3.8%, Canterbury Ales, Canterbury, Kent

Initial floral gives way to a sting of grapefruit bitterness and a long, lingering, light, crisp and dry finish. A good example of the classic Golden Ale – the sort of beer that would disappear within moments after a hard day's gardening or putting up a shed!

Available all year round in Kent and in good off-licences in the Kent area.

Golden Hare, 4.4%, Bath Ales, Bristol

When I visited Bath Ales this was the beer that Gerry Condell, head brewer, was tucking into and so I joined him. Very easy drinking, and works well as the social lubricant that beers should be. I find Bath Ales to be about classic beer styles; as Gerry himself says, 'We don't piss about by overloading it with hops. Beer should be about balance and that's what we do at Bath Ales.' He's quite right too, and the butterscotch, caramel and light, refreshing Maris Otter team up nicely with a light touch of traditionally English, earthy herbalness from the hops.

Widely available during the spring in the South West and gone by the summer months. Would recommend the Hare on the Hill in Bristol. Also available in bottles from good bottle shops nationwide.

Black Gold, 4.1%, Kent Brewery, Birling, West Malling, Kent

Some beer drinkers and brewers will get their knickers in a twist about beer styles – everything has to fit into some sort of category. Black Gold is a bit of Y-front noose in this respect: it isn't golden in colour and therefore really shouldn't be classed as a Golden Ale. Yet the brewery calls it a black Golden Ale and I have to say I agree. There is a floral, citrus tangerine tang sitting in a refreshingly roasted malt profile. Too many hops to be a Mild, too dark to be a straightforward Golden Ale and not quite a Bitter. But this beer had to be mentioned, as it really stood out as a firm favourite of the Kent Beer Festival and I wanted to ensure its inclusion. A dark, ruby-coloured Bitter, a wild-flower meadow of hops attuned nicely with some toasted malts.

Available from pubs in the Kent, London and Sussex area, or direct from www.kentbrewery.com. Not currently available in bottles.

Fubar, 4.4%, Tiny Rebel, Newport, Gwent

When I first came across Tiny Rebel in 2012 they were very much in their infancy and had managed to advertise themselves heavily at the Great Welsh Beer and Cider Festival. As soon as you came in there was a brightly coloured bar right in front of you – theirs. Posters were everywhere: when you went to the loo, there they were; they had even infiltrated the currency we were all using, with a big ad on the back of the beer tokens. Had they made rubbish beer this would have been rather embarrassing for everyone involved. Luckily that wasn't the case and I believe this is how a future legend was born, for all of their beers sold out as they struggled to keep up with demand.

The nose was like walking through a wild-flower meadow. Very full, sharp Californian pink grapefruit and a touch of juicy fruit, a touch of almonds, some pine and a little nettle tea, with a dry enough finish to have me gasping for air at times.

Available from various pubs in South Wales, London, Bristol, Brighton, Newcastle, Essex and Manchester. Also available in bottles from good bottle shops.

OTHER NOTABLE GOLDEN ALES

Dorothy Goodbody's Golden Ale, 4.3%, Wye Valley Brewery; Chiron, 5%, Thornbridge; Adam Henson's Rare Breed, 4.2%, Butcombe.

SOME OF THE FINEST BLONDE BEERS

Bitter & Twisted, 4.2%, Harviestoun, Alva, Clackmannanshire

When I was a young(er) man a mark of your 'coolness' was to be into bands that no one else had heard of; as soon as a band made it big enough to be on *Top of the Pops* then they were considered to have 'sold out', regardless of whether or not their music was still any good. It can be similar with beer: get deep into a beer-loving circle and you'll hear murmurs of beers that are not as good as they were when only three pubs served them, or before the brewery was taken over/grew/changed hands. In some cases this is an unfortunate truth, as there is no way a beer can ever be the same after it gets scaled up so far beyond its original recipe. There are, however, a few exceptions and Harviestoun, I believe, is one that is still around 80% as good as it was – and as that was pretty damn good indeed, then it means that they still make very fine beer.

Order a pint of Bitter & Twisted at any beer festival and a beer aficionado will be sure to pop out of the woodwork to tell you that Bitter & Twisted was meant as a tribute to the then brewer Ken Brooker's recently divorced wife.

Marmalade on the nose but grapefruit and acid lemon on the tongue, this beer leaves you with a bitter (lemon) taste in your mouth. A mix of Hersbrucker and Challenger has been used for bittering and a late addition of Styrian Golding is what gives Bitter & Twisted its character.

Widely available across the UK as a guest Ale, and in bottles and direct from the brewery at harviestoun.com.

Trashy Blonde, 4.1%, BrewDog, Ellon, Aberdeenshire

Normally when a brewery is situated in some small town or village that few people have heard of, it too is a fairly small concern. Not so with this behemoth of a brewery making itself known the world over. BrewDog's 'punk' image translates into an almost pathological addiction to the media, manifesting in a constant courting controversy for headlines, whether it's selling beer in bottles mounted in stuffed dead animals, taking potshots at CAMRA or brewing a beer for the 2012 Olympics that was stacked so full of performance-enhancing substances that even Lance Armstrong might think twice before drinking it.

If you can see past what is essentially just inspired marketing, you will see, or rather taste, that they do make some very good beers too. Trashy Blonde is a beer that straddles the gateway between traditional Golden Ales and heavily hopped American craft-brew-inspired beers. The body is light, and a balance of Maris Otter, caramalt and Munich malts means it is bready and crisp, whilst Motueka (Belgian Saaz) and Amarillo hops create a beer with tropical passionfruit aroma and a light, peachy taste.

Widely available in bottles and in cask at BrewDog bars in Aberdeen, Glasgow, Edinburgh, Newcastle, Leeds, Manchester, Nottingham, Birmingham, Bristol, Shoreditch and Camden.

Organic Blonde, 4.5%, Black Isle Brewery, Munlochy, Ross-shire

The Black Isle Brewery started life as a small, five-barrel farmyard brewery surrounded by rare-breed black Hebridean sheep and has subsequently grown into a bigger, thirty-barrel farmyard brewery surrounded by rare-breed black Hebridean sheep. It is a remarkable example of what can be done in terms of creating a local beer. Colin Stronge, the then head brewer, told me that they grow 70% of their own barley, which alas isn't malted on site but, as it only has to take a 14-mile round trip to Bairds Maltings over the water in Inverness, I think they can be forgiven.

The first aroma of this straw-coloured Blonde was grassy and pine. At the first sip I was eating a slice of lemon meringue pie that fizzed into a sherbet dib-dab supported lovingly by a biscuity malt with a slight twang of bananas. I drank this with my mate Max, with whom I've drunk many beers, and this was his favourite of the evening. He exclaimed, 'It's a beer for the people – one to get in at a party. No one is going to not like that.' I have to say I was taken by this beer's charms too and would certainly rate it as my perfect Blonde.

Widely available in bottles all year round and also direct from the brewer at www.blackislebrewery.com. It is also noteworthy that the farm operates under the Woofing scheme (Willing Workers on Organic Farms), which means that you can live on the farm for free as long as you help out and you might assume that you'd at least get a free pint or two if you did!

Hophead, 3.8%, Dark Star, Horsham, West Sussex

During the early 1990s, just as East 17 and Take That were battling in the charts, Dark Star Brewery were setting up in the cellar of the Evening Star

Pub in Brighton, opposite an adult bookshop. Some serious toil followed until they moved to bigger premises in 2001.

Using Cascade hops, Hophead has a floral nose, heady spring scents of sweet perfumed elderflower along with grapefruit – flavours that continue as you drink, with some caramel, grapefruit and bitter lemon. It would be too easy to describe a Hophead as simply 'hoppy'; indeed that is what the label says, but this does have a feel of some of the higher-ABV, heavily hopped IPAs such as Windsor & Eton or The Kernel are making. Especially as the finish is a long and lingering bitter lemon. Exquisite.

Due to the complex nature of distribution channels, breweries don't always know where their beer has gone, so Dark Star have set up an ingenious method of tracking theirs, so for your nearest Dark Star pub see darkstarbrewing.co.uk/beerfinder/. Also available in a 5-litre keg from their site.

Heavenly Blonde, 3.8%, Oldershaw Brewery, Grantham, Lincolnshire

A top-secret recipe made using a blend of First Bold (bittering) and Citra (aroma), as I found out whilst supping it at the Great British Beer Festival (GBBF), unaware that I was standing next to the joint owners Tim and Kathy Britton, the brewer. It was lucky it was a beer I liked! As their website states it is made with a secret recipe, I thought I'd try to find out what is in it, so I quizzed Tim. 'I assume it's Maris Otter malt?' I asked, secure in the knowledge that this is what most were using in the UK. 'No, Maris Otter is a bit like Chablis grapes. If you buy a wine with Chablis grapes you know you are going to get good wine. Quality products mean a quality wine. So with Maris Otter malt you know you are going to get a quality beer. But if you know what to look for in malt, you can get them a lot cheaper. Others would vehemently disagree with me, but that's what I think.' I never did find out what quality malt is cheaper.

Whatever the malt used, it gives Heavenly Blonde a biscuity base on which tropical fruit flavours sit – passionfruit and mango – but there is something very English there too. There's a taste of honey – not overt, but it is there like the first honeycombs robbed from the hive during late summer. All rounded off nicely by a long, dry finish with a suggestion of herbs.

Available as a guest beer in many pubs across Britain during the summer months. At the time of writing, not available in bottles.

BREWING GOLDEN ALES AND BLONDES

MALT

Use pale malt as the base, but this can be Pilsner or Pale Ale malt; for something a little different consider using Golden Promise up to 95% in a Golden Ale. For complexity, also consider making up part with Munich or Vienna malt. An addition of wheat malt for the mouthfeel and the head-retention is useful too – up to 10%. Wheat can really add a 'summer' feel to a pint, I think. Sweetness in a Blonde normally comes from CaraPils, but keep this low – up to 4%.

HOPS

Here the world is literally your oyster: use anything with a bit of flavour. Think citrus and spicy. This means that Noble Hops and New World hops are the order of the day. You can make high alpha acid Golden Ales (as below), but really we are edging into IPA for bitterness levels. Normally, hop levels are kept within a range of 10–24 IBUs, but this is a style to mess about with, tear up the rule book and just enjoy whatever hops you put in.

Consider additions all the way from first wort right through to dry-hopping, but think of the flavours and if they go together. Decide too if one hop might mask another; for instance, a high alpha acid like one of the American 'C' hops (such as Chinook) will overpower a Noble Hop such as Saaz if using both as aroma.

YEAST

For something fruity, try using English Ale strains. Greg from Brew UK recommends 1318 London Ale III yeast smack pack, for example. Safale US-05 could be considered too, and over in Australia many Golden Ales are made using Kölsch yeast strains.

OTHER ADDITIONS

Some herbs can be interesting too – saffron or coriander, for example; the same sort of herbs you might find in a Wheat Beer.

GOLDEN ALES FROM KITS

St Peter's Golden Ale

The St Peter's kits can be a little hit and miss, but the Golden Ale kit is by far one of the best that they make. Unlike a lot of kits, you really don't have to tinker with it to make a decent pint either, although as with most instructions it is still a little optimistic with the time. I'd wait at least a month before drinking it.

The kit contains two tins of extract, which brings it into the premium kit range, but it can often be found on offer and you don't have to buy any extras like spray malt or brewing sugar. The hops provided in a sachet add a smooth, floral spice ideal for a Golden Ale to be quaffed in the summer months. The other bonus of this kit is that the beer it emulates is readily available in bottles, so you can at least try it before you brew it and work out for yourself if it is worth the effort!

Festival Golden Stag Summer Ale

This is at the very high end of the kit market, but it is worth it. The difference here, especially compared with some of the one-tin kits, is immense. Hop pellets are supplied for dry-hopping, along with a hop-straining bag, a bag of dextrose, two bags of liquid malt extract, priming sugar, and the yeast provided is a specially selected strain rather than (as was) a generic and nondescript 'Ale' yeast. The use of Cascade and Columbus hops means that you get a real hit of fruity hoppiness. Expect grapefruit, herbal and earthy flavours to come through.

Coopers Canadian Blonde and Black Rock Pilsner Blonde

Both these Blonde kit beers are worth a brew day, and both are from New Zealand. Each will benefit from an addition of 500g (1¼lb) of spray malt. Blonde being a Belgian style, an addition of some Belgian hops will certainly add something to the final product. In this case I'd suggest a dry-hop addition of 25g (1oz) Saaz after the beer has been fermenting for twelve days – unless your beer is fermenting very slowly, as dry hops shouldn't be added for longer than a week. If using the yeast provided you may have to be patient, as it is known to be sluggish. Swapping it for my go-to yeast, Danstar Nottingham, is a useful idea.

GOLDEN ALE RECIPES

Golden Extract Beer

Here is a relatively easy recipe to follow. The hop additions can be played about with to make many different Golden Ales.

INGREDIENTS
3kg (6lb 10oz) pale dried malt extract
200g (7oz) dried wheat malt extract

Mix the malt extract in 10 litres (17½ pints) of cold water, then bring to the boil. If you have a chiller, make up 25 litres (44 pints) and boil. When boiling starts add the following:

INGREDIENTS
10g (¼oz) Northdown (8.5%) @ 60 minutes
10g (¼oz) Cascade (6%) @ 15 minutes
10g (¼oz) Cascade (6%) @ 0 minutes

Top up with the rest of the water to make 20 litres (35 pints) if you don't have a wort-chiller, and, if you do, chill to 19°C (66°F) and pitch 2 smack packs of Wyeast, 1318 London Ale III. Ferment around 19°C (66°F) if possible.

OG 1.046, FG 1.010, est. ABV 4.7–5%

Trashy Blonde

This is another recipe from Adrian Chapman of Saltaire Brewery. It is his attempt at BrewDog's Trashy Blonde and so, as you might expect, it is rather 'hop-forward'. Adrian says that the Motueka hops are his first experience of pellet hops. The addition of 16g (½oz) of Ahtanum or any aroma hop in the fermenter will give an extra hop hit, if it was needed!

INGREDIENTS

2.47kg (5lb 7oz) pale malt 70%

350g (12oz) caramalt 10%

350g (12oz) Munich malt 10%

350g (12oz) wheat malt 10%

Mash at 68°C (154°F): Adrian says that though he aimed for 69°C (156°F), even after a pre-heat, empty and refill of the mash tun he still lost almost 5°C from 83°C (181.4°F) in the HLT. Mash for a minimum of 60 minutes, then add hops as follows:

INGREDIENTS

8g (¼oz) Ahtanum Whole (FWH) @ 60 minutes

8g (¼oz) Motueka (B Saaz) Pellet (FWH) @ 60 minutes

8g (¼oz) Simcoe Whole (FWH) @ 60 minutes

22g (¾oz) Motueka (B Saaz) Pellet 6.8% @ 10 minutes

22g (¾oz) Simcoe Whole @ 10 minutes

22g (¾oz) Ahtanum Whole @ 10 minutes

16g (½oz) Simcoe Whole @ 0 minutes (80°C/176°F; steep for 20–30 minutes)

16g (½oz) Ahtanum Whole @ 0 minutes (80°C/176°F; steep for 20–30 minutes)

16g (½oz) Motueka (B Saaz) Pellet @ 0 minutes (80°C/176°F; steep for 20–30 minutes)

Ferment with 1 packet Safale US-05.

OG 1.041, FG 1.010, ABV 4%

16

IPAS – INDIA
PALE ALES

T HE LIVELIEST PUB conversations can often have more of a leaning
towards entertainment than truth, and many of us have been known
to embellish a tale to get a laugh or deliver a punchline. It is of little
wonder then that the origins of every beer are surrounded by half-truths,
outright lies and counter-claims. This is perhaps why there has been such
an enduring lie behind the tale of India Pale Ales. The story below is
possibly the one that you have heard.

Towards the end of the eighteenth century, when Britain was flexing its
imperial muscle and stripping the world of resources to feed the increasing
appetites of the emerging elite, she had a large colonial presence in India. The
hot, humid climate and distrust of the water supply gave rise to a thirst for
beer, and for light beers rather than Porters. But the long voyage meant that
most pale beers brewed around that time would spoil over the course of the
journey and be undrinkable upon arrival. In walks a fella called George
Hodgson of the Bow Brewery in London with an answer, or rather a beer, to
solve the problem. He started brewing beers jammed full of hops and ramped
up the ABV, both measures designed to keep beer for longer.

The trouble is, this explanation fits into the half-truth category. It's a
nice story, but the real truth is as murky as a Wheat Beer and dates back
further still.

During the seventeenth century the East India Company moved into India, starting to build factories and deal in fabrics. Many European peoples settled there, and over the next two centuries towns sprang up. The Europeans wanted booze, and at the cheaper end of the scale was the local hooch known as Arak. Like much of the home-made vodka currently being traded around Russia, this hooch was lethal and claimed many lives. A new drink was needed and it came in the form of imported Pale Ales, which were favoured less for their thirst-quenching abilities than because fatal (cheaper) adjuncts were harder to put into them than into other beers. It was essential that these beers were heavily hopped as they were of course cask Ales, and once opened a lower-hopped beer would spoil in days.

But then to say this was the only drink available is certainly a tall tale. By the 1780s cider, Porters and even small beers were all surviving the journey and being sold to the European settlers. The idea that this brewer George Hodgson from London supplied IPA to India is partly true, because his brewery did supply unbranded Pale Ales, but it wasn't until his son Mark took over and adapted the style to suit demands that it really started to take shape. By the 1830s families returning from India wanted the same drink and the term 'East India Pale Ale' was used in newspaper adverts. Thus a name and a style had evolved.

The question of what constitutes an IPA nowadays is another fiercely debated topic. Pete Brown, renowned beer writer and champion of IPA, argues that it is an evolving style. Brewing records from the middle of the twentieth century would have an IPA as a light, refreshing Ale with an ABV of 3.5%. The American craft-brewing revival at the turn of this century would have it as a 7.5%, highly hopped beer. These are very different beers, though the latter might indeed have more than a passing resemblance to the 'East India Pale Ale' of the 1830s, despite being made with hops that could only be dreamed of.

SOME OF THE FINEST IPAS

Jaipur, 5.9%, Thornbridge, Bakewell, Derbyshire

I used to live in a rather dodgy area in inner-city Bristol and a few of the houses in our street were turned into cannabis-growing factories. The air was really pungent outside these houses when the plants were due to be harvested, and Jaipur brought memories of that road flooding back. The taste too will remind many people of their university or teenage years, as it has more than a passing resemblance to skunk spliffs. It's not surprising, really, considering that cannabis and hops are related – part of the reason that hops can have a soporific effect.

Bitterness is carried by carbonation, and in the case of a good IPA it is imperative that the level is just right: not so flat that it misses any flavours and not so overly carbonated that it feels more like you're drinking 7 Up. Jaipur is perfectly carbonated, meaning that, as well as cannabis, grassy and passionfruit flavours are realized.

My perfect IPA.

Available in bottles from good bottle shops and more widely available in many off-licences too.

Hoppiness, 6.5%, Moor Beer, Pitney, Somerset

When I first tried a pint of Hoppiness it was served to me by a young Aussie. 'You might want to try it first,' she said. I muttered that I had tried hoppy beers before, but she was insistent. It did indeed hit me with some hops – grassy rather than creamy, with a dry finish and hints of marmalade like some of the Golden Ales – but this was more robust and the alcohol content made it a heavier beer. A big beer.

The grassy bitter hops filled my mouth and as the taste dissipated I could feel the biscuit-malt finish. Indeed, a very good pint. 'Yes, I'll take that,' I said with delight, looking forward to the next half-hour that we'd be together (myself and the pint, not me and the barmaid). 'As long as you are sure.' I mused that this is what they do in BrewDog bars and, far from denting sales, it might help people think about what they were drinking a bit more, creating a moment of reflection before sitting with a whole pint.

Justin Hawke, head brewer at Moor, is originally from San Francisco and lived there during the American craft-brewing revolution. He then moved to Germany before ending up in the middle of nowhere on the Somerset Levels. He told me that he came here for the 'pubs, people, history, culture, and let's face it – beer!' He bought Moor Beer after seeing it for sale in a CAMRA newsletter. At the time it was not only falling to bits but had a pretty bad reputation. Both of which Justin had to work hard to rectify.

If there is one brewer to point the finger at for subverting the British beer scene, one brewer about whom you could say 'Look, it's him – the bloke that brought us high alpha acids and hop bombs,' then arguably you could well be pointing at Justin. He brought with him his tastebuds and introduced an unsuspecting country to New World hops. Justin and Moor Beer just did what he knew best. 'A lot of what we were doing,' he says, 'was a bit too far ahead of its time – New World hopping, high ABV, global styles, keg conditioning, barrel ageing, naturally hazy unfined beers. But it also put us in a good position to help influence the scene.'

In bottles all year round from good bottle shops and on tap at selected pubs in the West Country.

India Pale Ale Citra, 6.6% (and up to 7.2, depending on batch), The Kernel Brewery, London

An IPA you smell from down the road: citric acid – fake citrus, the kind you get in orange icing on a doughnut, made with so many additives it shouldn't be classed as a foodstuff, but combined with enough pine and the first cuttings of grass in spring to convince you that you will be drinking a beer and not smelling a cake. Perfectly carbonated means that each molecule from the Citra hops hits every tastebud, and they hit with gooseberries, lychees, mango, grapefruit, more cut grass and pepper on the finish. IPAs are supposed to have high IBUs, but the fruit and pepper mean that this doesn't have that lingering marmalade bitterness that so many IPAs can have. A well-chosen hop showcased nicely against a floury baker's bap of malt.

Available on the whim of The Kernel – see thekernelbrewery. com/wheretobuy.html for full details of local stockists.

Conqueror 1075 Black IPA, 7.4%, Windsor & Eton Brewery, Windsor, Berkshire

A few years ago black IPA started to appear on the UK market. Small independent brewers were, of course, in the vanguard. Essentially, black IPAs are just like normal IPAs but with a small percentage of darker grains or coloured with Sinamar, a natural liquid malt colour made from roasted malts. It didn't take long before they became the talk of the town, the drink of choice for the discerning beer drinker. I've yet to have a bad one and so it was tough job whittling down the choice. But then I sipped a Conqueror.

It's not just that Windsor & Eton are one of the better breweries to come out of London in recent years; it's more that they are one of the most exceptional, and Conqueror 1075 is perhaps the most interesting and complex black IPA on the UK market. The nose was like a good Old Ale blended with an IPA – spicy vanilla, rubber (but in a good way), liquorice and plenty of citrus. A full body, the definition of big beer. Mellow fruits, blended with sweet molasses, liquorice and a complexity of malts like sweet-tasting roasted oatcakes. A lingering, warming sensation dissipates as the glass empties to make way for a mellow fruitiness, like walking through a Portuguese lemon grove in late summer.

Available in bottles from good bottle shops and webrew.co.uk/main/shop/category/beers. In cask seasonally at Christmas and New Year around the Thames Valley area and occasionally as a guest beer across the UK.

8 Ball Rye IPA, 6.2%, and Black Betty Black IPA, 7.2%, Beavertown, (East) London

If good beers are just a trend right now, then everything about Beavertown is trendy. They are brewing beers in the hippest part of London, their staff drip trend-setting coolness with ease and each beer they brew is a catwalk model stepping out during Paris Fashion Week, each ingredient an item of clothing designed by the super-chic fashionista. This is written in 2013 and I will bet my right bollock that rye will be one of the ingredients of choice for many brewers over the next ten years. That said, it doesn't take away from the fact they still make remarkably good beer and the 8 Ball Rye is no exception.

Every spring, male pine cones give off a heady scent and as soon as this beer is poured or opened you are transported back to a time when the wind carries huge plumes of yellow pollen through the air. A sensory beer, as a tingle on my tongue builds to a full creamy mouthfeel, as if chewing on a packet of marshmallows that stick to the teeth and release caramel goodness. A murky and rather unassuming amber in the glass, but transforming into a swan in the mouth. It is more like heading into a well-stocked baking section than drinking a beer – cinnamon spice and a touch of earthiness layered upon lychees, raspberries and tropical fruits which interplay with the spicy rye malt and leave with a well-rounded, dried-fruit finish.

Also by Beavertown is Black Betty IPA, a very complex and black IPA that tastes somewhere between a great Porter like Ellands 1872 Porter and the hop-forward taste of Thornbridge's Jaipur. If you haven't tried either, then what I'm trying to say is that the aroma is inviting, full of fresh-cut grass and the floral scent of pine pollen, and the taste is rich and full-bodied. There are tropical fruits at first – pineapple, lychee and mango – but these subside as rich bitter chocolate, coffee and roast flavours take over for a moment before allowing the tropical fruits – which have taken on a slightly stronger and pinier character – back in, and then ending with a very dry and slightly chalky (in a good way) finish. It's the sort of beer that is so great that if you get the slightest whiff after drinking it of anything within its huge canon of flavour or aromas, you'll be reminded of when you drank it. Certainly one of the best black IPAs I've tried.

Both available at Duke's Brew and Que, Hackney, London, and in bottles from all good bottle shops.

BREWING IPAS

MALT

Typically IPAs are made using a pale malt base around 85–100%. The rest can be made up using crystal or caramel malts and this helps add body.

Mash at the lower end of the scale (65–66°C/149–151°F) and for longer than usual – typically a 90-minute mash. This helps to break down the more complex sugar needed to really up the hop flavours.

HOPS

Think bitter and think big for IPAs. High amounts of high alpha acid hops have become the mark that defines the style. Noble Hops will be rather pointless, as their subtleties are lost in the bigness of a bold IPA. American high alpha, like Amarillo, Cascade, Citra, Simcoe and Columbus, are often used both as bittering and aroma. If making something more similar to an English-style IPA, then Fuggles and East Kent Goldings are good choices, as is combining both.

Think about what sort of flavours you are after and perhaps try making a hop tea beforehand, or drinking a beer with the hops you want to try, and this will really give you a better idea of your finished beer.

As IPAs can be one of the best ways really to get to know your hops, I'd also suggest splitting a batch into various secondaries (demijohns will do) and dry-hopping with different degrees and/or different types of hops.

But don't just dry-hop. Multiple additions can and should be put in throughout the boil, but try keeping your hop additions simple. Just because you can add tons of different hops doesn't mean you should. Seven or more different hops will result in an array of jarring flavours rather than a 'hop bomb'. One hop to bitter and one to three varieties for aroma is plenty; indeed, using a single dual hop like Citra for both bittering and aroma is becoming commonplace.

Some brewers are starting to experiment with FWH (first wort hopping) or adding hops to the hot liquor tank/boiler as the sparge water is run into it. If you then leave the hops there throughout the boil, it is said that they impart a less 'harsh' bitterness.

YEAST

Think American for Wyeast 1056 American Ale (or American Ale II). Brewtek CL–50, California Pub Brewery Ale yeast and Safale US-05 are also yeasts with which you can't go wrong.

IPA RECIPES

Extract IPA

This IPA is certainly in the American style with citrus bitterness. To play around with it I'd suggest trying a single-hopped version, perhaps using just Columbus, for example, in 42g (1½oz), 22g (¾oz) and 15g (½oz) additions.

INGREDIENTS

3.5kg (7lb 11oz) light malt extract (6 EBC) 89.7%
400g (14oz) crystal malt (120 EBC) 10.3%

20g (¾oz) Nugget (13%) @ 45 minutes
20g (¾oz) Columbus (14%) @ 45 minutes
20g (¾oz) Willamette (5.5%) @ 45 minutes
10g (¼oz) Nugget @ 10 minutes
10g (¼oz) Columbus @ 10 minutes
10g (¼oz) Willamette @ 10 minutes
10g (¼oz) Nugget @ 0 minutes
10g (¼oz) Columbus @ 0 minutes
10g (¼oz) Willamette @ 0 minutes

Yeast: 2 packets Safale US–05, or starter using Fuller's 1068 ESB
OG 1.068, FG 1.015, ABV 7%, 55.9 IBU

Trashy Black

Another Adrian Chapman recipe. Starting life as Trashy Blonde (see page 253), this shows the progression a brewer can make as he or she applies what they have learned from one beer to the next. A little bit of healthy competition helped to inspire this too, as Adrian has a bit of friendly rivalry with three other home-brewing friends.

INGREDIENTS
4.45kg (9lb 13oz) pale malt 77%
580g (1¼lb) Munich malt 10%
290g (10oz) caramalt 5%
290g (10oz) wheat malt 5%
170g (6oz) Carafa Special III 3%

10g (¼oz) Simcoe (12.2%) @ 60 minutes
10g (¼oz) NZ Cascade (10.2%) @ 60 minutes
10g (¼oz) Motueka (B Saaz;13.8%) @ 60 minutes
21g (¾oz) Simcoe (12.2%) @ 10 minutes
21g (¾oz) NZ Cascade (10.2%) @ 10 minutes
21g (¾oz) Motueka (B Saaz;13.8%) @ 10 minutes
18g (½oz) Simcoe (12.2%) @ 0 minutes
18g (½oz) NZ Cascade (10.2%) @ 0 minutes
18g (½oz) Motueka (B Saaz; 13.8%) @ 0 minutes

20 litres (35 pints), OG 1.064, FG 1.017, ABV 6.2%
Mash at 66°C (151°F) for 60 minutes.
Yeast: Safale US-05

Orfy's Big All-grain IPA

There are a few home-brewers who are talked about in almost hushed tones across internet forums. Orfy (aka Dave Taylor) is one of them. He lives in Cheshire with his wife and two dogs, and it's possibly his lack of television that allows him enough time really to perfect his brewing technique. This will give your mouth a hop tingle.

INGREDIENTS

4kg (9lb) Maris Otter (Thomas Fawcett) 76.2%
1kg (2lb 3oz) CaraPils/Dextrine 9.0%
250g (9oz) crystal malt (60L) 4.8%

30g (1¼oz) Cascade (5.50%) @ 60 minutes (17.1 IBU)
30g (1¼oz) Fuggles (4.50%) @ 60 minutes (14.0 IBU)
30g (1¼oz) Goldings, East Kent (4.00%) @ 60 minutes (13.8 IBU)

30g (1¼oz) Cascade (5.50%) @ 30 minutes (13.1 IBU)
30g (1¼oz) Fuggles (4.50%) @ 30 minutes (10.7 IBU)

28.3g (1oz) Styrian Goldings (5.00%) @ 0 minutes
30g (1¼oz) Fuggles (4.50%) @ 0 minutes

2 teaspoons Irish moss (boil 10 minutes)
60g (2¼oz) Burton Water Salts (mash 60 minutes)

Mash at 68°C (154°F) for 60 minutes.
Boil for 60 minutes.
Yeast: dry English

17

LAGERS

FOR SOME REASON it has only been in relatively recent years that Lager has become the drink of choice over here. There were a few previous attempts at making it popular, most notably by the Scottish brewer Tennant, who in 1888 were brewing Lagers that apparently stood up against 'any foreign article'. But the drink never really won us over, never taking more than a few per cent of the market. Our Brown Ales, Milds and Porters still reigned supreme. But successive wars took the heart out of brewing, with our beers getting weaker not just in ABV but also as products in the marketplace. Things were changing, old institutions were falling and the lines were set for a massive foreign invasion. Irish Guinness launched Harp, Watney teamed up with Dutch Carlsberg and Whitbread brewed Dutch Heineken under licence.

These Lagers were slow to start, but by the 1970s they were sold as 'sexy' new drinks for 'sexy' young men. This was the time when aftershave was replacing soap and men could start buying decent clothes rather than dressing like their dads. Flat caps and string vests were being phased out along with Milds and Brown Ales as the marketing (mostly) men got good at selling us their shit and we ate and drank it by the spoonful. Helped by massive marketing campaigns and the long, hot summer of 1976, Lager took 29% of the market to become a new drink for a new man. (They forgot that women might like a drink too back then, just as some companies do now.) That legacy is only just starting to wane almost forty years on, and in recent years Lager has begun to lose its stranglehold.

It might seem like a funny thing to say in a country whose national beer of choice is Lager, but Britain is behind the rest of Europe by a few hundred years when it comes to brewing it. Yes, we have one or two national Lagers, which in my opinion are nothing to write home about, made for mass consumption and mostly drunk without much regard to what is inside the can or pint glass. Running the risk of sounding like a complete beer snob who will go thirsty at every barbecue I get invited to from now until the end of my life, most mass-produced and consumed Lagers are not proper Lagers at all and are pretty bland, especially when served at colder temperatures. It wasn't until I travelled across the Czech Republic not long after the Wall fell and tasted a heady stream of Lagers and Pilsners that blew what we had away and made me realize how far behind we really were.

Most of Europe makes Lager properly. As mentioned before, 'Lager' is derived from the German word *lagern*, meaning 'to store', and part of the process of making good Lager is to let it mature for weeks or even months on the yeast after fermentation. The reason for doing this is so that unwanted flavour and aromas will disappear, having been taken up and transformed by the yeast. A smell of rotten eggs is not uncommon when making Lager and that's why 'lagering', allowing those sulphurous compounds to be re-absorbed, is so important. Serving at near ice-cold temperatures helps to mask these and other bad flavours.

I am, of course, simplifying things by using the term 'Lager'. It is like saying 'Ale', using a term that describes an anthology of different beers. There are American pale Lagers, Bock beers, Doppelbocks, Dortmunder Exports, Eisbocks, Helles Bocks, Maibocks, Munich Dunkels, Pilsners, Rauchbiers, Schwarzbiers, Vienna Lagers and even Ales such as Kölsch that taste like Lagers – and that is just the tip of the iceberg. Most of them do have German-sounding names, and this is because most Lagers come from Germany; indeed most come from Bavaria. As this century progresses and our Lager improves beyond all recognition, I'm sure that we'll find all of these Lagers being brewed by brewers in this country – most already are!

SOME OF THE FINEST LAGERS

Korev Cornish Lager, 4.8%, St Austell Brewery, St Austell, Cornwall

I treated myself to a pint of Korev after a long brew day. My set-up means I have to lug my hot wort upstairs to cool it in the bath and I always work up a bit of a sweat. Apart from a spot of gardening, it's the closest I get to real work these days and there is nothing like a Lager after some hot manual labour. This hit the spot very well for me – a lovely crisp Lager beginning with a pale Lager malt that reminded me of Mother's Pride (the bread), building to honey and French apples and with a sharp, in both senses of the word, lemon finish.

Available from pubs around Cornwall, Devon, Scilly Isles and Somerset – see www.staustellbrewery.co.uk/pubs for more details. Also available in bottles from many off-licences and bottle shops.

Anarchy, 7%, Anarchy Brew Co., Morpeth, Northumberland

I remember many years ago my local sold two different Lagers. I could never really tell them apart. Both were perfectly well made, but neither really stood out as anything different. I'd often buy friends the one they didn't ask for to see if they noticed and no one ever did. The same could not be said about Anarchy, as there is no way you could mistake it for anything else.

I often struggle to get a decent 'nose' when I first sniff a Lager, but not with Anarchy's flagship beer. A huge alcohol hit reminiscent of vodka made me very curious about what would follow. I have to say I was a little wary, expecting something that might burn as I drank. What I found instead, with my first mouthful, was a big beer that I felt I could chew on; my mouth was alive. A teeth-sticking sweetness followed, leading me towards a load of fruit, with blackcurrant and citrus sitting nicely together as if in a chef's special fruit salad, then building to a lemon sherbet finish and a noticeable warming brandy feel in my chest. A great beer, and certainly a Lager to turn to in the autumn and winter when the mercury goes down and the wind starts to bite.

See anarchybrewco.com/our-beers/ for details of where sold. Also available in bottles widely distributed to many good bottle shops, but might need some hunting out.

Pure Blonde Premium Lager, 5.0%, George Wright Brewery, St Helens, Lancashire

Crisp and dry at first, this Lager then builds, the perfect level of carbonation filling your mouth with bitter Seville marmalade and lemon sherbet. A sticky, candy-sugar sweetness on the finish. A great beer.

Available at the Euston Tap, London, and as an occasional but rare guest beer across the country, and in bottles direct from the brewer or from good bottle shops such as beersofeurope.co.uk.

Essex Lager, 5%, Brentwood Brewing Company, Brentwood, Essex

I found it impossible to resist a beer called Essex Lager for the simple reason that the two words just fit neatly next to each other. Apparently Dave Holmes and Roland Kannor sat in a pub and said to each other, 'This pint's not brilliant, we can do better than this,' and thus, in true Essex fashion, a brewery was born.

A touch of cut grass on the nose and a full creamy mouthfeel with Opal Fruit (Starburst) orange on a bed of malted milk biscuit. Although unmistakably a very easy-drinking Lager, there was more than a hint of the palest of Ales.

Available all year round in bottles from good bottle shops and in selected pubs around London and the South East. See brentwoodbrewing.co.uk/ where-to-buy/outlets/ for more details.

Black Lager, 4.6%, Zerodegrees, London, Bristol, Reading and Cardiff

You have to wonder where Zerodegrees get their wacky names from. I wonder if they just hate having meetings and love beer? 'What's the new beer called?' 'Well, it's a black Lager . . .' 'Yes, great name. Meeting over. Let's all have a Black Lager.' Having sat in many pointless meetings, I wonder if quick decisions such as those would help sort out flagging economies?

A nice smell of haybarn on the nose and the very creamy head don't prepare you for the fresh mouthfeel, similar to a soda-water feel. Chocolate was strong, subsiding to a bit of smoke, walnuts and an earthy bitterness. If you were expecting a traditional German Schwarzbier, this will disappoint: there is too much roasted flavour and not enough clean, crisp, typical Lager notes. It is to be approached as a British take on a German style.

Available at Zerodegrees bars in Blackheath, London, Bristol, Reading and Cardiff during the winter months and occasionally at beer festivals. See zerodegrees.co.uk for exact locations.

Batch 9 Black Lager, 5%, Batch Brew, Winchester, Hampshire

Every Batch Brewed beer and product has a different batch number and according to music-lover Paul Hancock, the head brewer, this idea is loosely based on Factory Records, who assigned a unique sequential number to everything they produced. Batch 9 was the first beer the brewery actually brewed. But perhaps the most interesting thing behind Batch Brew, especially for the home-brewer with an eye on commercial brewing, is that they don't actually have a brewery; they are what is known as a 'cuckoo brewery'. Paul just couldn't afford the initial outlay for equipment and thought the risk too great for an as yet untried product. So he approached his local brewery in Gosport, Oakleaf Brewery, who were happy to 'sublet' their time and expertise to brew some of Paul's recipes.

To a certain extent Batch 9 defies definition. It has too much body to be Lager and yet it is too crisp to be Porter. This doesn't take away from the fact that it is a very tasty beer and so instead it sits in its own little area, nicely in between the two.

Smoky on the nose and with a touch of smoke in the flavour too at first, with dark cooking chocolate and some dark fruits. Yet the most surprising thing I found was how moments after a sip you'd swear you'd had a crisp honeydew melon and not a dark beer.

Available from good bottle shops – see batchbrew.co.uk for stockists.

BREWING LAGERS

MALT

Base malts for a Lager are, surprisingly enough, generally Pilsner/Lager malts, but using a threeway of Vienna, Lager and Munich yields some very interesting results. If using any speciality grains, try CaraPils and light crystal malts.

HOPS

Although some brewers are experimenting with high alpha acid hops in Lagers, this won't give the overall crisp feel that is associated with most Lagers. Saaz and Hallertau make for excellent bittering and aroma additions, as do most of the Noble Hops (see page 178).

YEAST AND FERMENTATION

Favoured strains of yeast are Fermentis Saflager W-34/70, or try the most widely used strain in the world: Wyeast 2124 Bohemian Lager smack pack. But do remember that making a Lager is unlike making an Ale. Fermentation temperatures need to be lower, pitching at a similar level of 18°C (64°F) but fermenting at 7–13°C (45–55°F). In fact, do check your strain of yeast, as some recommend as low as 3°C (37°F) to get those clean, crisp flavours. Higher temperatures will cause fruity and malt flavours which, although they might be tasty, will not be a true Lager. If you want crisp it needs to be fermented cooler.

   If you don't wish to buy a fridge and adapt it for the job, then the next best thing is to find the coolest places in your house. North-facing rooms with no heating during the winter months can be within that range, or houses with no central heating. Check your rooms with a thermometer and take notes before you start brewing, and remember it is just as important not to have widely fluctuating temperatures. Ideally, you'll need to put a stick-on thermometer on your fermenting vessel so you can keep an eye on your temperature, and even move the fermenting vessel if necessary.

Remember to have patience too, as strains of Lager yeast will multiply much more slowly than Ale yeasts.

Pitching rates with Lager are also unlike Ales. If using dry Lager yeast, then pitching the right amount is paramount. In practice this can mean pitching two or more packets of dried yeast in a standard 19-litre (33½-pint) batch, or making a yeast starter (page 209), especially if pitching below 12°C (54°F). It is very important to pitch enough yeast. Fermentation is expected to last around two weeks.

CONDITIONING

In this case we are really talking about 'lagering'. After the initial fermentation a period in a secondary fermenting vessel will set your Lager apart from most of what is sold under the banner of 'Lager'. If possible, keeping the temperature at a steady 4°C (39°F) for a month will make all the difference. Perhaps even try to find a friend with a cool cellar, or consider using a bath or bucket full of ice-cold water, changing the water regularly.

LAGER FROM KITS

Many home-brewers will jump right into brewing Lagers from a kit as one of their first ever brews; and many home-brewers will be somewhat disappointed with the results. I know I was. The real trick is to follow similar practices as you would with an all-grain recipe. If it is impossible to avoid fermenting at higher than ideal temperatures, then a yeast like Safale s-23 will make a good substitute for the one in the pack. If you can control temperatures, then Fermentis Saflager 34/70 is an excellent choice.

Cooper's Australian Lager Beer

There is, of course, an easy way around the whole controlling-temperature thing, and that is to brew a Lager that is actually an Ale (shhh . . . don't tell anyone). The Coopers Lager Beer kit uses an Ale yeast but still ferments to slightly crisper than your average Ale. Messing around with it will always add something else to your brewing and drinking experience. Adding 500g (1¼lb) DME and 500g (1¼lb) Dextrose instead of granulated sugar could be interesting, and you could even dry-hop with a Noble Hop for a bit if feeling adventurous.

Barons Dutch Lager Wort Kit

This is an absolute innovation in kit brewing. If made properly, I'd defy anyone to tell the difference between this and an all-grain brew, because, basically, it is an all-grain brew – albeit one that has been concentrated. It is also very simple to use: add water and yeast and that's it really. But I'd advise brewing it during the colder winter months, unless you have your own cave.

LAGER RECIPES

Extract Lager

If you lager this correctly, it makes a very good, crisp Lager.

INGREDIENTS

3kg (6lb 10oz) pale liquid malt extract (16 EBC; 5.7%)

130g (4½oz) Crystal Malt (40 EBC; 4.3%)

42g (1½oz) Saaz (4%) @ 90 minutes (IBU 20.7)

German Lager yeast WLP830

Dark Lager Extract

Based on a recipe from Shane, the head brewer at Beerd, a very young offshoot of Bath Ales.

INGREDIENTS

3kg (6lb 10oz) pale liquid malt extract

340g (12oz) light crystal malt (88.7 EBC)

200g (7oz) caramel malt (40 EBC)

170g (6oz) Carafa III (1034 EBC)

30g (1¼oz) Spalt (4.75%) @ 60 minutes

13.5g (½oz) Spalt @ 30 minutes

13.5g (½oz) Spalt @ 5 minutes

Yeast: 2 packets Saflager S-189

OG 1.049, FG 1.013, IBU 25, ABV 4.7%

The Malt Miller Lager

INGREDIENTS

4kg (9lb) German Pilsner malt (4 EBC; 96.9%)

130g (4½oz) Melanoiden malt (40 EBC; 3.1%)

42g (1½oz) Saaz (4%) @ 90 minutes

Yeast starter using German Lager WLP830

Mash for 75 minutes at 64°C (147°F).
Boil for 90 minutes.

OG 1.049, FG 1.008, ABV 5.38%, 20.7 IBU

Shane's Dark Lager

This recipe came to Shane from a German brewing student who was studying under him at Bath Ales. It is a tried and tested traditional recipe from a small town in Franconia.

INGREDIENTS

2kg (4½lb) Pilsner malt (3.3 EBC) 47.1%
1.48kg (3lb 4oz) Munich malt (14 EBC) 34.9%
380g (13½oz) light crystal malt (88.7 EBC) 9%
190g (6¾oz) Melanoiden malt (39.4 EBC) 4.5%
190g (6¾oz) Carafa III (1034.4 EBC) 4.5%
30g (1¼oz) Spalt (4.75% AA) @ 60 minutes
13.5g (½oz) Spalt @ 30 minutes
13.5g (½oz) Spalt @ 5 minutes
2 packets Saflager S-189

OG 1.050, FG 1.011, ABV 5.1%, 25 IBU

18

MILDS

ILDS ARE BLACK to dark brown to pale amber in colour and come in a variety of styles, from warming roasty Ales to light refreshing lunchtime thirst-quenchers. Malty and possibly sweet tones dominate the flavour profile, but there may be a light hop flavour or aroma. Slight diacetyl (toffee/butterscotch) flavours are not inappropriate. Alcohol levels are typically low.

CAMRA gives the following specifics for Milds: original gravity – less than 1043; typical ABV – less than 4.3%; final gravity – 1004–1010; bitterness – 14–28 IBU.

When I speak to different brewers or publicans about Milds, they say the same thing: once people actually try a pint of Mild, they often enjoy it and want to come back for more. Mark Arnott-Job from the Two Towers Brewery in Birmingham, brewer of the excellent Mott Street Mild, states that, 'Once people know where they can get a decent Mild they keep coming back for more.' Part of the problem is not that people don't want to buy a pint of Mild, it's just that there aren't many places that sell it. Brewers are reluctant to brew it as it doesn't keep and sells too slowly – perhaps the reason why it makes up only about 3% of the beer at present drunk in this country.

CAMRA are trying to redress this imbalance, and they have dubbed May 'Mild Month', urging drinkers to insist that pubs stock this elusive beer. It seems to be working too, as since the launch of the campaign there are now over 240 Milds being produced, more than twice the number that were made at the start of the century.

It's odd that Milds faced such a decline, as during the nineteenth century a pint of Mild was a highly prized treat, the mainstay of British drinking, the drink of choice. This was perhaps helped by the fact that it was either a pint of Mild or a pint of stale. They were basically the same beer, but one was older than the other – up to a year older – and had gone sour. Milds and sours were often mixed in order to give a beer just the tang the customer was after.

The younger beer, the Mild, simply indicated a beer that was less than two weeks old, meaning that a Porter, Stout or – if the description still stood today – a 10% Pale Ale hopped with (very bitter) Chinook and Apollo hops could all be called Milds as long as they were less than two weeks old. Indeed, many of the commercial Lagers now brewed can be less than two weeks old, so on that basis a Mild might still be one of the most widely drunk drinks in the world!

A style did start to develop beyond this very loose description of a 'fresh' beer. Due to the quick two-week turnaround, brewers found they could use fewer hops: the high levels needed to keep infections at bay were not imperative, as there simply was not enough time for the beer to get infected. For exactly the same reason, Milds did not need to have high levels of alcohol either and thus a style arose which owed more to quick turnaround than to the type of ingredients added.

It is worth noting that, as with any beer style, there are exceptions which deviate from the competition-style description. There are fragrantly hopped versions of Mild, such as Rudgate's double-award-winning Ruby Mild and Iceni's Thetford Forest Mild. There is also a classic Dark Ruby Mild by the Sarah Hughes Brewery in Dudley that is brewed to 6%. On this note, Adrian Tierney-Jones, author of *Great British Pubs*, makes a good point: 'A style category for Mild is imperative but it shouldn't be based on what it was like in the "good old days". A beer style is there as a starting point for innovation and experimentation – you have to learn what something is before disassembling it. Even Tracey Emin probably got an O-Level in art before she started rearranging beds.'

The two world wars saw the rot set in for this much-cherished pint. At the start of the First World War, Milds could still be strong, the average ABV being 4%, but the government wanted people to drink less so that they could work better in munitions factories and keep food production going, so they forced breweries to make a lower-strength Ale. The beer survived this attack and increased again in alcohol during peacetime. Then the Second World War saw Milds turn into weak 'war pints', and the view of a weak, thin beer seemed that it would tarnish the style for ever. This, coupled with the unscrupulous antics of some brewers who simply added caramel to their Pale Ales and produced a rather inferior product, meant that even die-hard Mild fans wouldn't stomach the crap they were being served.

This reputation of a weak, miserable pint has prevailed, and it's easy to be put off Milds. Picture a glum-looking man staring into nowhere, wearing a cloth cap and tatty clothes, with a scrawny dog on a bit of string solemnly curled up under a table in a dimly lit, tobacco-stained pub, nursing his pint all afternoon, and you'll assume he'll be drinking a pint of Mild. If you dare ask for a pint of Mild in company, you have to do it in secret or risk a chorus of 'It's an old man's drink.' Unless of course you are an old man. Then you can just raise your pint and say, 'Cheers,' and mutter to yourself about the youth of today.

Personally, I think Milds are wholly underrated and are a welcome, low-alcohol alternative in a sea of increasingly strong (in ABV) beers. I'm in danger of sounding boring, but one or two pints of Mild a night and you'll get to taste a full-flavoured, satisfying beer that can be drunk with friends; and to top that, not only will you be within the recommended bracket for daily drinking, but you would still be legally able to ride your bike back from the pub (80kg man, over 2 hours, drinking 3 pints of Mild).

A good pint of Mild should mean you can enjoy the full flavour of the malts used. Often this can include nutty, fruit, biscuit or caramel, with little or no hop distraction. Milds are predominantly dark beers and I personally think you can almost get the taste of a Porter or even a Stout without the hops (or indeed the alcohol) distracting from the rich flavours of the malts. But then this is to do Milds an injustice, as they are more than a weaker Porter or Stout – they have their own distinct flavour. A sweet, fruity beer that is as refreshing as it is satisfying, a Mild is indeed a liquid meal. Indeed, this makes it an ideal lunchtime or early-evening drink – that drink that you have when you genuinely only want just one pint.

SOME OF THE FINEST MILDS

During the Victorian era the Black Country, with its steelworks and foundries and smog, needed a beer to keep the workforce happy. Here is where the Mild reigned supreme, known as the 'workers' beer'. Back then Milds were often stronger than they are today and closer to what we now call a Porter.

The Midlands was, and to a certain extent still is, the place to go for a decent pint of Mild. That said, there are many examples across our country.

Dark Mild, 4%, Bank Top Brewery, Bolton, Greater Manchester

The aroma is the first thing that hits you when confronted with a pint of Bank Top's 'jet'-brown Dark Mild. Roasted bitter coffee jumps right out and my first taste took me straight into a field of barley with such fresh-tasting biscuit aromas. But that doesn't prepare you for the complexity of this perfectly woven Mild. Hints of chocolate are in there, as are dark fruits and slightly muted liquorice. The tangy, chalky mouthfeel lingers and the liquorice makes itself known on the farewell; breathing out after a sup, the liquorice stays in your nose! This has to be a contender for perfect Mild.

Available at the Bank Top Brewery Tap, Bolton, and in bottles from good bottle shops. See banktopbrewery.com for more information.

Mild West, 3.6%, Arbor Ales, Bristol

With its name originating from one of Banksy's most famous works, *Mild Mild West*, featuring a teddy bear throwing a petrol bomb at the police, you'd expect Mild West to be a bit anarchic, a bit different – a far cry from flat caps and old men. It doesn't disappoint. It is brewed using five different malts to create complexity that punches well above its low ABV. Luxurious dark chocolate, roasted coffee beans and hazelnut, and even a small hint of liquorice, are all there, perfectly complemented with Bramling Cross hops to give a lingering blackcurrant finish.

Available seasonally at the Three Tuns and the Old Stillage, Bristol, pubs around the Bristol area and in bottles at specialist bottle shops nationwide. See ArborAles.co.uk for more information.

Ilkley Black, 3.7%, Ilkley Brewery, Ilkley, West Yorkshire

Within spitting distance of Ilkley Moor lies the Ilkley Brewery, thought to be on the site of the legendary Timothy Taylor's old brewery and with beer made by enthusiastic brewers Luke Raven and Chris Ives. Ilkley Brewery does exactly what any good brewery should be doing in the twenty-first century: it makes exceptionally good beer by magically blending New World ingredients with Old World recipes.

Their Mild is no exception. It smells like a Mild and even tastes like one: a dark-fruit, spicy-herbal, sweet Mild that lingers. But it's the carbonation that made this beer for me – granted not something you'd hear every day, but the carbon dioxide bubbles dart the sumptuous flavours all round your mouth. It's a lot like drinking a refreshing, full-bodied, alcoholic, malty cherry cola that leaves a vanilla-y and liquorice finish long after you've supped.

Available all year round in and around Ilkley and as a guest Ale nation-wide. Also available in bottles – see ilkleybrewery.co.uk for more information.

Black Dragon Mild, 4.3%, Banks and Taylor (now B&T), Shefford, Bedfordshire

Made with five different malts and lightly hopped with Goldings hops, this Mild has some hedgerow fruit to the nose and the combination of the malts offers liquorice but a slightly unexpected smokiness too.

Find at the Brewery Tap in Shefford and pubs around the Midlands. See banksandtaylor.com for more information.

Dark Munro, 4%, Highland Brewing Company, Orkney

Winner of the Champion Beer of Scotland in 2007. This is a beer to drink in a pub, the ruby reds tinkling in the firelight. Aromas of coffee and a coal-lit fire emanate, enticing you into the glass. Then it's as if you are sipping a fruity, malty hot chocolate. The finish is refreshing and lightly bitter.

I drank this at a beer festival and so it was fairly young; according to the Highland Brewing Company the taste profile changes in the cask, becoming hoppier with age.

Available throughout Scotland and the North East of England. Also available in bottles as alesela.co.uk. See highlandbrewingcompany.co.uk/buy_orkney_beer/for other stockists.

Mildly Rockin', 3.7%, Rockin' Robin, Maidstone, Kent

The beauty of beer is that within each style there are limits and brewers tend to play with them. It being a Kentish beer, you'd expect more hops and that is what you get: a blend of local Fuggles and Goldings give it a dry-hoppy finish. The low carbonation makes it quite quaffable, something to down in two after digging over an allotment or shifting heavy furniture. Perfect for the spring when Milds should be drunk.

Dark roasted malts have been used to give it that burnt-molasses flavour. If you have ever made toffee in a pan and burned it, this is the flavour you get – which might not work as a sweet, but as they have been balanced the sweetness of the other malts comes through.

Smallish brewery so you might have to hunt, but otherwise available all year in and around Kent. No website details.

Mulberry Dark 1944, 3.8%, Conwy Brewery, Conwy, Gwynedd

Wartime beer has a bit of a bad name, but perhaps if it was always brewed to this standard things would be different. The nose is as complex as this oxblood/ruby-red beer itself. Dark fruits, chocolate and coffee are all evident on the nose. Chocolate roasted malt builds, I'm guessing, a hint of rye and dark fruits, which leads to woodsmoke; liquorice and molasses creep around in the background throughout and it finishes with a hint of lemon zest.

Available on cask at various locations in North Wales during CAMRA's Mild May, and from various good online bottle shops. See conwybrewery.co.uk for more details.

Mild, 4%, George Wright Brewery, St Helens, Lancashire

Dark fruits dominate at first in this fruity Mild, predominantly a Morello cherry flavour reminiscent of flat cherry cola. This subsides to burnt molasses with a slight mouth-puckering and a lingering morning-breakfast feel, rather like the smell of hot milk on sugary Weetabix.

Available all year round across the country, often as a guest Ale. See georgewrightbrewing.co.uk for more details.

Vanguard, 3.9%, Ashley Down Brewery, Bristol

There aren't many commercial breweries situated in the back gardens of mid-terrace houses, and there aren't many brewers like Vince Crocker of the Ashley Down Brewery in Bristol. Vince is an inspiration to any home-brewer wishing to start their own brewery. On the basis that the only official body really interested in his set-up was HMRC, Vince established his brewery in his garage after getting some backing from his beer-loving friends. He had a three-year plan to which he kept – and the first year involved learning how to make beer! He's now a well-established brewer and supplies many of the pubs in the St Andrews area of Bristol, transporting kegs using just a handcart!

Vanguard reveals some sweet raisin and a whiff of lightly roasted coffee on the nose, then a lovely balance of roasted barley and a touch of white bread from the malt. Fairly reminiscent of something a bit stronger: the Traquair House Ale (page 322) springs to mind, as there are some similar fruity flavours – damson and dark cherry, but with a touch of soy sauce. In fact, it reminded me of experimenting with putting balsamic vinegar on strawberries and the resulting combination of sweet and umami. The dry finish left that bowl of balsamic strawberries in my mouth, itching for another spoonful.

Available seasonally at the Green Man, Alfred Place, Kingsdown, Bristol, and in bottles from Corks of Cotham and Grape and Grind, both in Bristol.

OTHER NOTABLE DARK MILDS

Colchester's Mild, Timothy Taylor's Dark Mild, Batemans Dark Mild, Great Oakley Brewery's Welland Valley Mild and Wantsum Brewery's Black Prince.

PALE MILDS

Pale Milds are often found next to the rocking-horse shit – that is to say, they are not the easiest drinks to track down. However, I did discover one example on my doorstep:

Cotswold Way, 4.2%, Wickwar Brewing Company, Wickwar, Gloucestershire

There are few pale Milds available these days, but a nice example can be found from Steve Calderbank, the brewer who first made the very popular

Old Speckled Hen. Cotswold Way has many of the flavours associated with a dark Mild – some dark fruit flavours interlaced with roasted caramel and a touch of nuttiness.

Available in many pubs along the Cotswold Way and in bottles across the country from good bottle shops. See wickwarbrewing.co.uk for more details.

BREWING MILD ALES

MALT

Milds are a great beer to experiment with if you really want to get to know the differences between your malts as (despite fine examples to the contrary) this is certainly the style that showcases the grain bill (the grains you are using) above anything else. This includes the yeast, hops or even alcohol level.

A Mild malt should be used as the base malt, but as this is not always very easy to get hold of then the usual Maris Otter, or any pale malt, will certainly make a great substitute. The colour, body and flavour that characterize a Mild are taken from the other malts and adjuncts. Pale Milds are made with a little crystal malt and/or a lightly roasted malt. A standard dark Mild would be 10–15% crystal malt, 2%–3% chocolate malt and 1% black malt. That said, it's still an evolving style that can be slightly subverted; for example, Arbor Ales have also made a one-off Rye Mild West using 25% rye malt, crystal rye and oats. I have even seen Mild made using smoked malts.

The trick really is to keep the grain bill low so that you don't have a beer that is strong in ABV.

HOPS

Crystal malts and other speciality grains contain non-fermentable sugars, meaning that when they are used the beer can be overly sweet if not balanced with a bittering agent (that is, hops; see crystal malt, page 120). Balance is the key word when designing a Mild. The hops should be there to take just enough sweetness away from the malts without imparting too much character. The character should all come from the malts. If the hop character were pronounced, then it would transform the Mild into a Bitter or brown beer. Early additions of hops when boiling (bittering hops) create less hop aroma and flavour characteristics, perfect for a Mild.

A crude rule of thumb to keep the hop profile low and the malt profile high is to stick to Old World hops. American and many New Zealand hops are out, as the strong citrus flavours will survive even the longest boil. This is due to their higher than average alpha acid levels. Old World or the Noble Hops are essentially the same hops that have been used by brewers for centuries to make Milds. That said, like any crude rule of thumb there are some examples of New World hops that will work well – Willamette and Target are two of them.

Bramling Cross hops will give a blackcurrant flavour which works well on dark Milds, as it helps balance the darker malts. Fuggles, Goldings and Northern Brewer are other examples of hops that are good for this style. I think that Fuggles are so widely used in the UK that it gives a real air of authenticity to a Mild.

YEASTS

Just as you'd expect, good results are had by using typically English yeasts. I pitched two yeasts against each other on the same batch of Mild: dry yeast and liquid. The yeasts in question were Danstar Nottingham, which is one of the favourite dry yeasts used by the home-brewer, and White Labs WLP0037, a Yorkshire Square Ale yeast. It would be easy to think that the twice-as-expensive liquid yeast would come up trumps, but in this test (at least) I found the Nottingham made the better Mild.

Other yeasts to consider include White Labs British Ale yeast WLP005, Wyeast Fullers WY1968, or a Safale s-04.

CONDITIONING

Don't! As I've mentioned, Milds were originally beers that were drunk young. Ageing might really transform some beers, but a Mild isn't one of them. If true IPAs and Porters keep for longer due to the higher ABV and hop additions, then the opposite is true for a beer with less of each. Between two and four weeks will be enough time to let the characters develop in the keg or bottle. But again, it depends on preference.

KEG OR BOTTLE

Either as a matter of preference, but Milds are meant for session drinking and the fact that they don't really keep for any great length of time means that a keg would be preferable.

WHEN TO BREW/DRINK

A Mild can be brewed very quickly and it also goes down very quickly too. If you wanted to brew a beer for a Bank Holiday barbecue, for a lunchtime treat or to share over a weekend with friends, then Mild is the drink of choice (although your tastebuds can become muted outside and around smoke). If this were still the session beer of choice, then I suspect that a stag do would be an altogether more refined institution.

What's more, with the low ABV this really is a beer you can drink without feeling the hangover forming with each sip. Think of it as a far more forgiving Porter and you'll not go far wrong.

MILDS FROM KITS

A couple of kits that will give you a decent enough session Mild are Brewer's Choice Black Country Mild from Brew UK and Heart of England Platinum Black Country Mild from Hamstead Brewing Centre (see Homebrew Shops, page 386).Other, cheaper kits are also available.

It might seem daft to play around with a kit, as everything you need is in there, but often the yeast is generic and you are brewing with just one type of malted grain. If this is the case, then a bit of 'pimping' doesn't go amiss (see Turbo-boosting Your Kit, page 86) especially with one-can kits. Adding dark spray malt, which is available from all good home-brew shops, will improve the beer, as will boiling 20g (¾oz) of hops with the extract provided for 20 minutes. Beyond that and you might as well move into proper extract brewing.

MILD ALE RECIPES

Orfy's Mild Mannered Ale

Dave Taylor from Cheshire (aka Orfy) sent me this recipe as a fitting tribute to his granddad, Sam Taylor, who used to love a glass of this classic northern dark Mild. Dave, his dad (Jim) and granddad would nip off down the pub on a Sunday for a few jars before going home to eat the Sunday lunch lovingly prepared by his mother. In many ways you could say this was the beer that Dave was brought up on.

As the years passed, Dave found that fewer and fewer places served a Mild, the drink synonymous with the Taylor family. So when he found he had the skills to create recipes, he wanted to make this beer in honour and remembrance of his granddad and the simple pleasure of three generations sharing a lazy Sunday pint (or two). If you are looking for a classic dark Mild recipe, then this really is the ticket.

INGREDIENTS
2.2kg (4lb 13oz) light extract (8.0 SRM) extract 75.0%
400g (14oz) crystal malt (60L; Thomas Fawcett)
125g (4oz) chocolate malt (508.0 SRM; Thomas Fawcett)
25g (1oz) Fuggles hops (94.50%) @ 45 minutes (15.1 IBU)
25g (1oz) Fuggles hops (4.50%) @ 15 minutes (8.2 IBU)
1 packet Danstar Nottingham Ale Yeast

Original Gravity: 1.034 SG, final gravity: 1.010–1.016

Orfy's All-grain Mild

This is the all-grain version of the above.

Batch size: 23.00 litres (40 pints)
Boil size: 30.50 litres (53½ pints)
Estimated OG: 1.037 SG
Estimated colour: 21.0 SRM
Estimated IBU: 23.3
Brewhouse efficiency: 70.0%
Boil time: 60 minutes

INGREDIENTS

3kg (6lb 10oz) pale malt, Maris Otter (3.0 SRM) (Grain 76.9%)

750g (1lb 10oz) crystal malt (60L; Thomas Fawcett) (60.0 grain 19.2%)

150g (5oz) Chocolate Malt (Thomas Fawcett) (508.0 SRM grain 3.8%)

30g (1¼oz) Fuggles hops (4.50%) @ 45 minutes (15.1 IBU)

30g (1¼oz) Fuggles hops (4.50%) @ 15 minutes (8.2 IBU)

1 packet Nottingham Dry Yeast

Ale mash schedule: single infusion, batch sparge – hot
Total grain weight: 3.9kg (8lb 9oz)
Primary ten days, conditioning two weeks

T'Mild / A Mild Shot

This recipe I've tried with both Nottingham yeast strain and a Yorkshire Square Ale Yeast WLP0037. The Yorkshire attenuated a little further than the Nottingham and took a day or so longer in the fermenter before it stabilized. A slightly different flavour was had by both, which interestingly changed as the beer aged. Drinking the beer very young, at ten days, at first my preference was for the drier, crisper-tasting Nottingham (a Mild Shot); but as the beer was left to age for three weeks the Nottingham started to taste thinner, whereas the over-pronounced chocolate flavours started to mellow and became more like dark fruits in exactly the same way as good Christmas pud ages! Therefore, if you have no patience I'd suggest using the Nottingham yeast, but if you are prepared to wait for a superior beer I'd suggest the Yorkshire strain.

INGREDIENTS

3.35kg (7lb 6oz) pale malt, Maris Otter (5.9 EBC)

250g (9oz) extra dark crystal malt (340 EBC)

200g (7oz) chocolate malt (1000 EBC)

200g (7oz) chocolate rye (500 EBC)
200g (7oz) flaked barley (3.9 EBC)
35g (1¼oz) Fuggles hops (4.50%) @ 60 minutes (16.2 IBU)
1 packet Nottingham dry yeast, or 2 vials Yorkshire Square Ale WLP0037

OG 1.046, FG 1.010 (Nottingham), FG 1.008 (Yorkshire)
Boil time 60 minutes
Primary ten days, conditioning five weeks

Casper's Mild

A pale beer named after the friendly ghost, this is at the stronger end of
the scale for a Mild, coming out at around 3.9%. A slightly nuttier Mild,
with traces of floral hop flavours just edging their way on to your palate.

INGREDIENTS
3kg (6lb 10oz) mild malt (7.9 EBC)
500g (¾lb) pale crystal malt (150 EBC)
200g (7oz) biscuit malt (45 EBC)
250g (9oz) flaked barley (3.9 EBC)
20g (¾oz) East Kent Goldings (5%) @ 60 minutes
20g (¾oz) Fuggles (4.5%) @ 15 minutes
2 vials WLP002 English Ale or 1 packet Windsor dry yeast

OG 1.046, FG 1.016, ABV 3.94%, 16.6 IBU
Boil time 60 minutes
Mash in 75°C (167°F) water to achieve mash temperature of 69°C
(156°F) for 45 minutes.
Primary ten days, conditioning five weeks

19

PORTERS

PORTER HAS BEEN described as 'the first truly global beer', which is highly appropriate considering that the name derives from its popularity with transport porters (and dockers) in eighteenth-century London, as they could drink it and still be able to work. Thomas Pennant, the eighteenth/nineteenth-century travel writer wrote of Porter as 'a wholesome liquor, which enables the London Porter-drinkers to undergo tasks that ten gin drinkers would sink under'.

It has been suggested that this drink originated from the practice of mixing three different beers – one (strong) Old Ale, one Mild or high-quality hopped Ale and one often stale or soured Ale – to create a fourth beer greater than the sum of its parts. The mix could and would differ slightly depending on what the landlord had in stock and, of course, what he wanted to rid himself of. This practice was indeed common during the seventeenth and eighteenth centuries and it meant publicans could mix beers at point of sale to match the requirements of drinkers, as well as perhaps offloading a barrel or two of worthless soured Ale. The drink was known as Three Threads. Eventually brewers started to make beers that tasted like Three Threads and these were known as 'Entires'. However, evidence to back up these claims is lacking. The whole story seems to hinge on a single letter used as evidence by John Feltham in his book *The Picture of London*, published in 1802, regarding a brewer called Ralph

Harwood, who owned a brew house in Shoreditch, East London, in 1722. Harwood grew tired of mixing three pints to serve one and so devised a single beer called 'Entire', which re-created the flavour of Three Threads and became known as 'Porter'. The Entire was aged in and dispensed from a single cask. However, as with all good pub stories, some beer historians are now suggesting that these claims could be false. It's a nice story, but it might just be that.

Other sources suggest the origin was a simple development of the then popular brown beers or Milds on offer. There certainly can be some strong similarities in flavour and colour between some Milds and some Porters, but due to lack of evidence and/or a time machine it is not possible to know for certain. But that won't stop endless Porter-fuelled conversations on the topic.

Even the name Porter is up for debate. At a London Amateur Brewers' meeting another possible etymology for the name was mooted: that the word actually derives from a fourteenth-century Dutch beer known as *poorter*. Another explanation suggests that Harwood would send porters around to people's houses carrying his beer and on arrival they would shout 'Porter', meaning themselves rather than the beer, but the name stuck.

The origin and name of Porter might be in dispute, but what isn't is that these were the most popular beers of the nineteenth century, helped somewhat by their long shelf-life and the cheapness of production. Early London Porters were strong by present-day UK standards at around 6.5% ABV and higher; they were also made entirely using brown malts, which imparted a rather smoky flavour. As you can imagine, this made the beer rather too acrid to drink young, so it would have to be aged for up to eighteen months, over which time the flavour became less pronounced.

Over the years the style of Porter fell foul of a number of factors, of which perhaps the most surprising is that cheap, imported, high-quality glass started to come to Britain. This meant that the beer glass replaced the pewter tankard and so richer people started to drink paler Ales as was the fashion, leaving poorer people to drink dark beers from tankards. Thus a class divide arose over what you were drinking; in this case, as in many others, the rich won out. Over subsequent years – and due in part to wars, from the Napoleonic to the First and Second World Wars – the strength and hop rate were greatly reduced and Porter was not at all the same drink. By the twentieth century, suffering the same fate as Brown Ales and Milds, it fell out of fashion. And the demise of Porter was spectacular, from being the most widely drunk drink ever in the world to going completely out of commercial (UK) production.

Wherever it started and whatever it was, Porter today has evolved to include a number of different styles, including brown, smoked, robust, Baltic/Imperial and London Porter. Porters are always dark beers, and generally made with roasted malts. They are of medium body, especially compared with the much heavier-bodied Stout. It has to be said, though, that most people agree that it can be difficult really to define a strong difference between some Stouts and Porters, as both lend themselves to massive interpretation. Brown Porters can be relatively low in alcohol and full-bodied, like many dry Stouts, but at the other end of the scale Imperial and Baltic Porters can be brewed to be stronger than wines, just like Imperial Stouts.

During my drinking years (1988–present day) I've seen this beer move from being one that I could find only in the enthusiastic, well-read and adventurous home-brewer's shed (my mate Paul's) to become a beer that any brewer worth their salt will brew.

Over in the States, where the home-brewers became commercial brewers, the Porter was one of the very early 'Craft Beers'. Anchor Brewery first bottled their Porter in the year of my birth, 1974. This in part helped its slow rise from relative obscurity, as other breweries both over there and over here slowly started to produce their own. After its relative obscurity, the massive spread that Porter now enjoys really is testament to the power of the home-brewer when it comes to saving old styles.

SOME OF THE FINEST PORTERS

The Famous Taddy Porter, 5%, Samuel Smith, Tadcaster, North Yorkshire

There is a hint of buttery figs and even chocolate cake in the first smell of this Porter, and it pours black, almost like a Guinness. A creamy mouthfeel lends itself to the complex palate of caramel, toast, chocolate (but mildly so) and even almond. If it wasn't so balanced this would be a travesty of a beer and it really isn't! It works very well and would be something a little different to try to turn Guinness fans on to.

Widely available from all good bottle shops (and some bad ones) all year round and from Samuel Smith pubs – see www.jamesgretton.co.uk/samuelsmiths for your nearest.

Black Band Porter, 5.5%, Kirkstall Brewery, Kirkstall, Leeds, West Yorkshire

A recommendation which I first tasted in one of the many city-centre back-street pubs in Leeds, all of which are worth a go. Despite the fact that my trip around them was after a skinful with the Leeds home-brewers, none of whose names I can recall, I did manage to record my thoughts on my trusty voice-recorder and this Porter stood out amidst the alcoholic haze as being good and fairly strong (for UK standards). Seb the home-brewer noted smoky flavours with a sweetish caramel background. It also had a good coffee background, a dry finish and there were hints of liquorice and rich fruit flavours. In all, a good Porter that won't disappoint.

*Available in cask in pubs around Sheffield, Leeds and York, and at The
Beagle, Chorlton, Manchester.*

Porter, 5.4%, Humpty Dumpty, Reedham, Norfolk

John Tuck, author of *The Private Brewer's Guide to the Art of Brewing Ale
and Porter*, wrote in 1822, 'It has been well remarked, that out of the innu-
merable tribe of home-brewers, there is not one that knows any thing of
brewing Porter, and hence they conclude there is some impenetrable
secret.' So when something like Humpty Dumpty's Porter comes along I
really wish I could somehow pass it to John Tuck and ask if this is what he
meant. This really is a Prince among Porters!

A lovely jet-black colour with a smell of rum fudge and burnt coffee.
A very complex yet perfectly balanced beer with dried fruits, cloves, rich
smoky coffee, chocolate and liquorice flavours, all perfectly balanced by
the late addition of earthy Fuggles hops. It has a velvety and full mouthfeel, a beer with so much body you feel like you could chew on it.

*Available all year round in Norfolk/Cambridgeshire area and in bottles
at good bottle shops, including therealaleshop.co.uk/norfolk/.*

1872 Porter, 6.5%, Elland Brewery, Elland, North Yorkshire

Some beers build in character down the glass as you drink and a half pint
just isn't enough really to appreciate them. This Porter is just that sort of
beer. Despite drinking it at a beer festival where variety is the order of the
day, I went back for a full pint.

If you've got to know your dark beers, you will know to expect
molasses, liquorice and sometimes burnt flavours. In this 1872 Porter the

molasses is more of a burnt-toffee flavour and the liquorice dries as you drink, giving way to dark fruits and a chocolate flavour reminiscent of the finest Belgian chocolate fondant.

Martin from Elland also shared a glimpse of the recipe for this Porter, telling me that pale, chocolate, amber and brown malts are used, along with Target and Northdown hops. Mash and boil times are both nearer what was usual for the nineteenth century, at 90 minutes and a massive 120 minutes respectively!

Available all year round at selected locations throughout Yorkshire and as a regular beer at The Paramount, Manchester. Also available in bottles from specialist bottle shops.

Manchester Star Ale, 7.3%, JW Lees, Middleton Junction, Manchester

As a family business that has survived across six generations, the JW Lees brewery is not only a rarity in the brewing industry but a rarity in the business world. I wonder if J. W. Lees, when he first fired up his mash tun back in 1828 to make a Best Bitter, would have dared even imagine that it would still be brewed in the same place almost two hundred years later by his great-great-great-great-grandson. With that many generations having passed through the brewery's gates, it's perhaps no surprise that it is said to be haunted. Spanners have been seen flying across the brewery, cloaked figures walking around and ghostly goings-on in the boardroom. Obviously even the dead like the beer so much that they don't want to leave.

Unlike the dead that haunt the place, the Star Ale, which is re-created from a recipe dating back to 1884, is thankfully full-bodied. There was a certain amount of cedarwood on the nose, along with slightly sweet roasted malts. Poured to what seemed at first to be jet black, but under the light a refraction of ruby reds and pre-war furniture brown came through. A rich and full mouthfeel – dark chocolate clung to figs, dates and black coffee as I almost chewed it down. Yet another deceptively strong beer, it washed down within no time leaving an earthy, liquorice finish.

Available in cask all year round in selected pubs around Manchester and Greater London, from good bottle shops or online at jwlees.co.uk/shop/.

Hazelnut Coffee Porter, 4.6%, Saltaire Brewery, Shipley, West Yorkshire

If I were allowed to drink only beer brewed from one county in the UK, I would choose Yorkshire. Without a shadow of doubt, some of the best beer in the world is brewed in the land between the Peak District and Yorkshire Dales. The Saltaire Brewery is a relatively new addition to the Yorkshire beer legacy, formed in 2005. Their head brewer, Tony Gartland, brings a lifetime of home-brewing experience to this awarding-winning company.

Their Hazelnut Coffee Porter is rather lighter than most would expect of a Porter, being a similar copper colour to a traditional Bitter. It's also a beer to sit and sniff: chocolate, red wine, nuts and coffee, with a light Fuggle aroma, all emanate as soon as the bottle is opened. I opened this beer late on a dark, wet February evening. My bike had been nicked earlier in the day, my local coffee shop was packed so I couldn't get a seat, and my son had not been sleeping and had been crying all day. Needless to say, it had been a shit day. I put him to bed and, with just a sip of this powdery cocoa, fruit, rich, warming Porter, I was immediately relaxed. A perfect beer for a shitty winter's day!

Available in cask around Yorkshire, Greater London and occasionally at the Boat Inn, Ashleworth, Gloucestershire GL19 4HZ, as well as from specialist bottle shops.

Teleporter Ten Malt Porter, 5%, Summer Wine Brewery, Holmfirth, West Yorkshire

There are breweries that can be relied upon to keep consistently making great beers and I believe that the Summer Wine Brewery is one of them.

Sticking your nose in a Teleporter is like sticking it into the pudding bowl of an award-winning Women's Institute member as she puts the final touches to her end-of-year entry in the Best of Britain cake competition: rich, boozy fruits, plus a touch of treacle and caramel, all entice you to your first sip. That first sip is sweet, then it feels as if tiny bubbles full of hop compounds are rebounding off your tongue, where the malt sits, and on to the roof of your mouth in a delightful play of flavours alternating between lemon and biscuit. Rich fruits continue apace, as do molasses, bready malts, a hint of Marmite (not as in the clawing you get on toast, but the zing you can get when you stir a bit into a casserole), a hint of coffee and a touch of chocolate on a finish drier than the bottom of a birdcage left in the dessert.

Available online from shop.summerwinebrewery.co.uk and from good bottle shops.

BREWING PORTERS

MALT

Get passed a Porter at a home-brew club and you're likely to hear that it was just a way of using up all the malts, as indeed Porters are open for interpretation. That said, the base is almost always made up of Pale Ale malt, about 40–70% of the grain bill (more for extract brewers). Brown malt, although by no means a necessity in a Porter, makes for an interesting addition, and in my opinion it gives at least a nod towards the traditional style. If introducing it for the first time, I'd use no more than 7–10% in a recipe, but you can use much more if you intend to age your Porter. Very simple recipes can have the addition of just chocolate malt up to 15%, or the same amount of dark crystal/caramel malts. Up to 10% black malt can be a useful addition for colour, and up to 5% wheat malt for head-retention. Mash temperatures are in the range of 64–67°C (147–153°F).

HOPS

Bitterness levels should hit a range of 20–30 IBUs and if you want to be true to the style then traditional English hops are the key; think Goldings and Fuggles. I'm also a fan of Bramling Cross in darker beers as a later aroma addition.

YEAST

Nottingham comes up trumps again as a decent all-round yeast to brew with, although it will ferment to a lower ABV, meaning a slightly drier Porter. Two other great yeasts are Wyeast 1968 (London ESB) and White Labs WLP002 (English Ale). Robust Porters can be interesting to make using a Scottish yeast such as Wyeast 1728, or even 1084 Irish strain. Ferment at below 22°C (72°F).

WATER

This should be as close as you can get to London water, 160ppm carbonate, 100ppm sodium and 60ppm chloride. In soft-water areas this can just mean a small addition of around 4g gypsum.

OTHER INGREDIENTS

You can almost 'go wild' with other ingredients in a Porter. I've had them tasting like whisky, Christmas pudding, Stout or even hot chocolate. This is perhaps why there are so many different sub-categories to the style: Robust, Imperial/Baltic, Brown, London, smoked. And of course there are many speciality Porters using many different flavour combinations, including chillies and various fruits, such as plums, coconuts or pumpkin.

Other ingredients for flavour and aroma should be added towards the end of the boil.

A NOTE ON ROBUST PORTERS

With an original gravity of 1.045–1.060 (FG 1.012–16) and measuring 5–6.5% ABV, Robust Porters are often brewed to above sessionable strength. Since the hops shouldn't be a predominant feature, you are looking at a bitterness level of 20–40 IBUs, and up to 50 IBUs for some American versions. This is normally obtained by hopping at the start of the boil. That said, an American brewer will disagree and some of their versions can even be dry-hopped. As with all beers, unless entering a competition, interpretation of the style is all part of the fun.

Robust Porters should also be rather dark brown/black or even reddish, so you are looking at around 40+ EBC. This can be achieved by using dark caramel, chocolate malt and black malt. The extract brewer can achieve the colour by steeping speciality grains and adding them (see page 89). There should also be no roast barley flavours and some sweetness.

PORTER FROM KITS

For a complex and moreish Porter, Pride of London Porter by Festival at the high end of the market comes with glowing recommendations, to say the least. Unlike some of the cheaper kits, this needs nothing added to it, and the instructions are clear and easy to understand. Leave it for at least a month (if you can) to allow some conditioning.

If going slightly cheaper, Muntons Gold Docklands Porter is a good, reliable kit and, as a two-can kit, you don't have to think about adding any sugar. However, priming with some sugar and a touch of treacle or molasses would be an interesting experiment, as would boiling the extract and adding some spices. I'd suggest putting small amounts in a muslin bag towards the end of the boil, or even using one of those mulled spice bags. For a stronger beer, use less water. About 2 litres (3½ pints) less will give you a lovely, strong winter beer.

PORTER RECIPES

Partial-grain Extract Porter

This makes 19 litres (33½ pints) and is adapted from Mike Carter's All-grain Running Porter recipe below.

INGREDIENTS
3.54kg (7lb 13oz) pale malt extract (16 EBC) 87.3%
200g (7oz) roasted barley (1200 EBC) 5.1%
310g (11oz) medium crystal malt (120 EBC) 7.6%
35g (1¼oz) Nugget
12g (¼oz) East Kent Goldings

Any strain of English Ale yeast, but you could try for something a bit different and use Wyeast 1056 American Ale or 1084 Irish Ale.

Steep grains for 30 minutes at 68°C (154°F). Boil for 45 minutes, adding the Nugget, then add the 12g (¼oz) East Kent Goldings at the end.

OG 1.057, FG 1.015, est. ABV 5.6%, primary ten days, secondary three weeks

Running Porter

This recipe is originally from Reid's Griffin Brewery in 1877 and is reproduced by kind permission of the Durden Park Beer Circle from *Old British Beers and How to Brew Them* (see Further Reading, page 406).

I tried this Porter along with the Brown Porter below and six other beers at a London Amateur Brewers' meeting. The forty-strong beer-lovers and I were judging beers for a home-brew competition. Four tables of ten beer-lovers voted on their favourites and poor old Mike Carter had his rejected in a high-calibre race with an opposing table, and possibly because it was a little lighter than many Porters. A slightly inebriated master of events overseeing the competition somehow sent the rejected 1877 Porter to our table. A serendipitous mistake, as it transpired. We duly drank and were all very impressed. Lots of roast flavours coming through and an edge of authenticity to it. Having tasted it, I ran over to Mike and asked for the recipe. Here it is. 19-litre (33½-pint) recipe.

INGREDIENTS

4.23kg (9lb 5oz) pale malt (5 EBC) 87.8%

360g (12½oz) brown malt (150 EBC) 7.5%

230g (8oz) roasted barley (1350 EBC) 4.7%

48g (2oz) Nugget @ 90 minutes

12g (¼oz) East Kent Goldings at 0 minutes

OG 1.057–1.058, 70 IBU

Dave Halse's Award-winning Brown Porter _____

There are many home-brew clubs across the country and one of the most successful, in terms of numbers of people in attendance, is held in the capital. London Amateur Brewers (LAB for short) meet in the basement of Draft House, Tower Bridge, on the first Monday of every month. The club is full of brewers from all walks of life and ability, from kit brewers who are just starting out to people with their own micro-breweries. I was invited to one of their sessions in order to help pick what turned out to be the winning entry in the 2013 inter-club Porter competition. It was brewed by Dave Halse, an actuary from New Zealand who came over to the UK in 2001 for a two-year working holiday and is still here.

Dave has a mostly stainless-steel set-up, which can be expensive, but he doesn't put his success as a brewer down to his kit alone. He told me that 'from experience trying member beers through the LAB home-brewers' club, a cheap basic set-up applied correctly can produce perfect beer, and at least as good as any commercial brewery'. Which is certainly reassuring, especially if you don't have money to throw at the hobby.

Please note that many of the recipes in this book are 19 litres (33½ pints), but this is one of the exceptions. However, it can easily be changed using brewing software such as Beersmith. I wanted to stay as true to Dave's recipe as possible and so, apart from adding a mash time and imperial measures, I have not changed anything from the original email that he sent.

Brew length: 23 litres (40 pints)

Water treatment: Treat your water to remove chlorine/chloromines and reduce the alkalinity to acceptable levels.

INGREDIENTS
Maris Otter 4.4kg (9lb 11oz)
Pa crystal 0.25kg (9oz), EBC 50–70
Pa chocolate 0.40kg (14oz), EBC 500–550
Brown malt 0.40kg (14oz), EBC 140–160 (Note that brown malt is traditional and this quantity is apparent and recognizable in the flavour.)

Mash temperature 67°C (153°F) for a fuller body. Mash 60 minutes or until conversion is complete.

Boil: 60 minutes

IBU: 35

Use whatever bittering hops you have that won't impart much (nil, preferably) hop flavour to get to 35 IBU given the following addition: I added 100g (3½oz) of Fuggles 5.17% AA at 5 minutes before flame-out to try to get some English hop flavour. To be honest, I can't really tell in the finished product, but others suspected Fuggles were present. Little hop flavour is to style.

Yeast: Danstar Windsor (dried)

OG 1.055

FG 1.019

ABV ~ 4.7%

Ideally ferment 18–20°C (64–68°F) for one week.

I rack-off to a secondary for one week in the same temperature environment (i.e. in a corny, or Cornelius keg) and then artificially carbonate the corny in my fridge.

Ageing the beer at cold temperatures for several weeks improves it.

20

SAISONS

S AISON IS ORIGINALLY a Belgian beer style which derives from Wallonia, one of the French-speaking areas of the country. The word simply means 'season'. As with Porter, the name of this beer comes from those who favoured it, in this case the seasonal migrant workers who came to help with the harvest. It is also known as a Farmhouse Ale.

It might seem out of place mentioning Saisons in a book that is essentially about British beer. Why not mention Belgian Triples, Lambics or American Pale Ales? This is, of course, a worthy accusation. However, the same question could have been asked a few years ago about Black IPAs, which were considered something of a novelty, but now many brewers have them in their brewing portfolio. Saison could be considered fairly rare here in Britain at the moment, making up only a small percentage of beers drunk, but its entry here reflects what I think is a glimpse into the future of brewing: a beer that will be drunk in great volume in this country in years to come. Mind you, I still think that Northampton Town have a chance at winning the FA Cup in this same future!

Saisons are moderately to lightly hopped beers, ranging in strength from a very sessionable 3% up to around 8%. Unlike many British beers, Saisons are normally bottle-conditioned. Spiced Saisons are common and, due to the yeasts used, a haze is also a common sight. Above all else, Saisons are refreshing!

SOME OF THE FINEST SAISONS

Siberian Rhubarb Saison, 5.9, Ilkley Brewery, Ilkley, West Yorkshire

There is something to be said for allowing beer the proper amount of time that is needed in order for the right flavours to develop. When Luke Raven, the Ilkley brewer, invited me to bottle some Siberian Rhubarb Saison I have to admit to being rather impetuous when it came to trying some. I waited just two weeks after bottling and the beer had a distracting hot feeling. It was not a patch on the same beer that I'd tried from a keg the day before, nor the bottles I've tried since, as this is a great beer.

The idea for this Saison came from a collaboration between the brewers and beer writer Melissa Cole. The reason behind using rhubarb was to make what is essentially a foreign beer (Saison) with local Yorkshire ingredients, and as Yorkshire is home to the famous Rhubarb Triangle, an area where most of the UK's rhubarb is grown, Melissa and Luke figured that you can't get more Yorkshire than that! But why call it Siberian, you may well ask? This is where Melissa and Ilkley are being rather clever, as rhubarb originates from the banks of the River Volga in Siberia.

As for the beer itself, it pours to a murky, pale colour and has a peppery, spiced aroma from the yeast. A fruity, refreshing beer. There is rhubarb in there, but instead of taking over it gives the beer a touch of sourness on the finish which is paired with some vanilla.

Seafood Lovers' Ale, 7.1%, Poppyland, Cromer, Norfolk

One of the whole reasons for creating a Saison chapter in a book about British beer was not just to be thorough, but to mention this beer. I'd headed east, as far east as you can go and still be in Britain, and was exploring Norfolk by train. Unfortunately, the pubs we were finding either sold beer I'd already tried, had closed down, or were shut for refurbishment. We were starting to lose heart as we soberly traipsed the streets of Cromer. Then, on a residential street, we saw a shop window full of beer neatly displayed in baskets along with a note asking passers-by to call a number. I did so and a rather short, red-faced man came bounding across the street with a basket full of beer. He took us to where his beer conditions – a rather dusty-looking room with home-made shelving laden with beer, more shelving in bits waiting to be made, and barrels gurgling away with a secondary fermentation of On the Edge. Martin (the brewer) remarked on the smell. This was the first time I'd smelt Saison actually brewing – a smell that filled the air with the haybarns of Wallonia.

I took the beer away. This time I was forced to wait for it, as not long after this trip my son was born and beer had to take a back seat for a while. When I eventually popped the cork, the room filled again with that haybarn smell.

When I drank it, I was amazed. Had I found my perfect pint? It was not far off, and was certainly the perfect pint of Saison.

Available from 46 West Street, Cromer, NR27 9DS.

Epic Saison, 5%, Wild Beer Co., Evercreech, Somerset

In Brixton there is an amazing indoor market, full of stalls populated by traders selling fruits, meats, fish and spices from every corner of the globe. Each step around this market is a new sensory experience, and this beer and that market have a lot in common. With the first smell you are in a Flemish haybarn unchanged since the eleventh century; with the first sip you are sitting in a tropical paradise eating pineapples. As this mellows, more fruit – this time Mediterranean citrus. Turn a corner and you find yourself on the spice trail – peppercorns from India, cinnamon from Ethiopia, a whisper of Sri Lankan cloves and Madagascan vanilla all packaged in Alpine spring water, minerals bubbling off the tongue to create a beer from the West Country with a global taste.

Available as a guest beer at many 'Craft Ale' bars around Bath and Bristol, and from good bottle shops. But expect it to be much more widely available in the coming years, as Wild Beer plan world domination.

Galaxy Saison, 5.4%, Partizan Brewing, Bermondsey, London

A first hit of Galaxy is entwined with the classic Saison haybarn yeasty aroma along with some wood shavings and vanilla too – an aroma that gets the mouth ready. This gives a full mouthfeel, rather like that of an American Pale Ale to start with, until it takes your whole mouth in a different direction – sour at first, as if crunching on a lemon pip, then puckering to a dry and lime-zest, crisp finish. I'm not sure that many tasters will use this terminology, but I found this one had plenty on the 'burb' too, giving an extra taste long after I'd drunk it, with hints of banana and even sharp rhubarb (ironically, perhaps more so than the Ilkley – see above). A multi-layered Saison that seems to change each and every moment a morsel of it lies in your mouth.

Seasonally available in bottles from many great online and actual bottle shops.

BREWING SAISONS

If IPAs are hop-forward and Milds are malt-forward, it could be said that Saisons are yeast-forward, or at the very least yeast-driven. They should be very dry, with high bitterness from low alpha acid hops; typically these will be European. The ABV normally sits within the range 4.5–6.5%.

Saison stats – original gravity: 1.048–1.065, colour: 9.8–27.6 EBC, final gravity: 1.002–1.012 SG, bitterness: 20.0–35.0 IBUs.

MALT

The simplest part of a Saison design is the malts, as they can be 100% Pilsner malt or Pilsner with a portion of Vienna and/or Munich. Some people will add granulated sugar or honey in order to have a drier Saison with a thinner body. Wheat, spelt and/or oats are not uncommon either, as these help give a more rounded mouthfeel.

HOPS

No need to go too wild with the hops, but use floral hops such as English and Noble. A mix of Hallertau to bitter and perhaps East Kent Goldings would work as an example.

SPICES AND OTHER INGREDIENTS

Spices can be an interesting addition, but think about what will go. Undercutting with some pink peppercorns, black pepper, orange peel, coriander and of course rhubarb makes for a rather interesting Saison.

WATER

If you are in a soft-water area, treat it with a little gypsum, but Saisons are great for those of us in hard-water areas as there is no need to treat; the hard water really accentuates the bitterness.

YEASTS

Yeast really is the key ingredient for a Saison. Even before adding spices, think yeast and what flavours certain strains may offer. A worthwhile experiment would be to seek out a Belgian bottle-conditioned Saison, culture the yeast up and use that. Failing that (and for a much easier option), White Labs WLP565 Belgian Saison I or Wyeast 3724 Belgian Saison is perfect for the job. To obtain the required dryness you may also need to add a yeast to finish – that is, if your wort is hovering around the 1.025–1.020 mark – as you really do need to get it down as low as possible. Something like Safale US-05 will do the job.

SAISON RECIPES

Extract Saison

The idea behind this Saison is just to keep it simple. The trick will be to keep the yeast happy. It will be a little on the pale side, but there will be a pepper flavour coming straight from the yeast that should delight.

INGREDIENTS
4kg (9lb) Bavarian Pilsner liquid malt extract 100%
45g (1¾oz) Hallertau (4.8%) @ 45 minutes
20g (¾oz) Styrian Goldings (5%) @10 minutes
2 vials White Labs WLP565 (Belgian Saison I)

Make a starter the day before using the WLP565.

1. Bring 12 litres (21 pints) of water to the boil and put in the malt extract and Hallertau addition.

2. After 35 minutes add the Styrian Goldings. You can also consider dry-hopping with them (see page 128).

3. Top up to make 20 litres (35 pints) and pitch the yeast starter when the wort is 19°C (66°F).

4. Ferment fairly warm at 22°C (72°F) and above; some people have even brewed at 30°C (86°F)! The trick is to have patience: it's not uncommon to leave Saison fermenting for forty-five days, then to let it condition for up to three months at room temperature before drinking.

OG 1.063, IBU 25.6, ABV 5.9%

The Malt Miller Saison

Here is a standard 19-litre (33½ pint) version of Rob Neal's all-grain Saison.

INGREDIENTS
3.87kg (8lb 8oz) Pilsner malt (3.9 EBC) 85%
230g (8oz) Munich malt (39.4 EBC) 5%
460g (1lb) Candi Sugar (1 EBC) 10%
45g (1¾oz) East Kent Goldings (5% AA) @ 60 minutes
4g (0.14oz) coriander seed @ 5 minutes
2 vials Belgian Saison II Yeast (White Labs WLP566)

Mash at 64°C (147°F) for 75 minutes.
Boil for 60 minutes.

OG 1.054, FG 1.005, ABV 6.4%

SCOTTISH ALES AND WEE HEAVIES

COTLAND HAS A rich beer heritage. It is known that the Vikings had brew houses, but there is evidence to suggest that beer is even older in Scotland and was brewed there more than 5,000 years ago. These would have been Gruit Ales (see page 135), made with herbs rather than hops. But of course what most people know of Scottish beers is the 'Shilling System' – a method of naming beers that was brought in during the nineteenth century. Instead of using a number of Xs, X being the weakest and XXXX the strongest, as was popular with the Sassenach breweries further south on their Milds, the Scots decided that cost would give a better description and so they named their beers after the invoiced cost per barrel. These ranged from 40/– (40 shillings) for Mild beers up to 160/– (160 shillings) for a stronger Ale.

The stronger, heavier Ales were sold as 'wee' nips equivalent to a third of a pint. In time these became known as Wee Heavies.

SOME OF THE FINEST SCOTTISH ALES

Dark Island, 4.6%, Orkney Brewery, Quoyloo, Orkney

Known as the 'Standard-bearer for Traditional Scottish Ales', it was like opening a can of treacle pudding as I got my nose near this beauty, along with a rich, chocolate-sauce-drenched Christmas pudding. It is a very carbonated, dark beer that looks almost identical to a glass of cola. But that is where the cola similarity ends. Here is a full, silky mouthfeel that builds to a tang of strange flavours – initially sour, but there is also something of the sea about it; seaweed and salt spring to mind, washing away to leave a sour edge built around a smoother, dry, malted-milk biscuit flavour and a liquorice/molasses dry, bitter finish. Every moment that even a speck of Dark Island spends in your mouth brings a different flavour. Even a burp after having some brings back a beer that is so complex and refreshing that one isn't enough.

Available in casks from good pubs, often as a guest Ale, and in bottles from most good off-licences and specialist bottle shops.

Orkney Brewery also releases a limited edition, a whisky-barrel-aged 10% ABV bottle version of Dark Island, known as Dark Island Reserve, adding oakwood and whisky to an already complex and magnificent Ale. It has limited release and you should expect to pay around five times the price of a normal bottled Dark Island beer, but it will be worth every penny.

Traquair Jacobite, 8%, Traquair House Brewery, Innerleithen, Peeblesshire

The Traquair House Brewery was rescued from dereliction by the 20th Laird of Traquair in 1965, complete with its 250-year-old coppers which were shortly put back into working order. Originally the brewery was set up to brew beer solely for the house workers, who would pour their Ales directly from the oak barrels in which it was conditioned. The beer was fermented in large wooden fermenters and sparged using well water. Apart from the use of spring water and modern bottles and casks, the 250-year-old process – now managed by the Laird's daughter Catherine, the 21st

Lady of Traquair – hasn't really changed. To drink beer from Traquair House is to drink beer as it was drunk by Bonnie Prince Charlie. It is history in a pint glass.

Their Jacobite Ale is brewed using a recipe that dates back to Jacobean times and it was brewed to celebrate the 250-year anniversary of the Jacobite Rebellion. Far from being a one-off celebratory Ale, it became so celebrated itself, winning the title of World Champion Winter Ale in the World Beer Championships back in 1997, that they continue to brew it today, much to the delight of beer connoisseurs around the globe.

A mixture of dark fruits, and more specifically plums, dominates the first aroma of this rich, dark, rosewood-coloured Ale. A complexity of flavours ebbs and flows in a perfectly choreographed dance around the mouth – molasses, rich dark cherry, plum, raisins, coriander, spice and Black Jack treacle. Then comes a long, lingering, full-on Bertie Basset liquorice finish – indeed so lingering that as I write this the next day I can still taste the fruit-scented liquorice. This is a beer so great that it could cause a rebellion – if not a Jacobite one, a brewing one.

Another Wee Heavy is the Traquair House Ale, brewed to 7.2% ABV. This was the beer that was brewed for the people who worked in the house. I put this in front of me and just kept smelling, and with each sniff the smells changed. The first is very bready, akin to walking through a bakery at 5am when the ovens are filled with the next morning's buns and loaves. The next was brown sugar; then dark fruits, like opening a packet of malt loaf; and finally caramel and liquorice. Flavours followed that same pattern, with some molasses to boot. But this went down far too quickly. I can imagine if this was served every day in Traquair House it must have been quite a fun place to stay in.

On the finish I felt I could taste the oak – or should I say acorns, as it reminded me of acorn coffee with that rich tannin quality. This made it very dry and my mouth almost clamped shut post gulp. Still, it was another alcohol-rich pint that defied the tastebuds and it would be very easy to drink pint after pint and perhaps get into a lot of trouble for doing so!

Scottish Beers

If you want to know about beer in Scotland, ask a brewer who is brewing in Scotland. I did just that, asking Colin Stronge when he was brewing at Black Isle Brewery. (He is currently at Buxton.) Here is what he told me he does when making Scottish Ale.

'For a Scotch Ale, I like to lean on tradition. Going back into the annals of time it is generally believed that Scotch Ales or Scottish beers were strong and malty with a low to medium hop content. There are texts that somewhat decry this and show that, although the Scottish climate does not suit hop-growing, there was a large trade in Scotch Ales being traded for Kentish hops and so most Scottish brewers would have used Goldings or similar varieties to hop their beers. It is considered that the beers would have been a rich ruby colour, made from the darker malts available in the days before Pale Ale malts, etc. But using modern brewing malts we can recreate the colours, and to a certain extent flavours, that would have been present in these beers. The standard things which I think most historians agree on is that the beers would have been sweet, and have caramel notes from long boils in direct-fired coppers, fairly low bitterness and medium hopping overall.'

BREWING SCOTTISH ALES

MALT

As with most British Ales, a good Pale Ale malt (or pale liquid extract for extract brewers) is a great base up to around 90%. Golden Promise is a good Scottish malt and is a likely candidate, but also the not very Scottish Rauchmalt making up some of the base-malt grain bill will give an interesting smoky flavour. As Colin recommends, an addition of peat-smoked malt is rather interesting too, although on a cautionary note this can be overpowering, so go easy if you have never had it before. Try a beer with just 2% and work up, unless you are very partial to a peaty whisky such as Islay; using this malt will give similar flavours. But of course the malts that give most Scottish Ales their character are the caramel flavours from crystal and caramel malts, up to around 10%. For stronger Ales, above around 6% ABV, darker crystal malts are certainly worth using. Higher mash temperatures are usual too: 68–70°C (154–158°F), which will help give the beers more body.

HOPS

Taking Colin's lead, East Kent Goldings, or indeed Styrian Goldings in fairly low levels. Northern Brewer or Nugget could be interesting too, and perhaps Boadicea. IBU levels should be around 10–20 for lower ABV (60/– and below), increasing only to 35 IBU for Wee Heavies and the strongest Scottish Ales.

YEAST

White Labs WLP028 Edinburgh Ale has been specially cultured for use with Scottish Ales and is particularly great with Wee Heavies. Have patience with it, as it can be slow. Wyeast 1728 Scottish Ale is another good one and it copes well at the lower end of the temperature scale. If you can't get hold of Scottish Ale yeast, English Ale yeast will do the job too.

FERMENTATION AND CONDITIONING

Scottish Ales will benefit greatly from a long, slow fermentation at lower temperatures, and also from long, cold conditioning times in the fridge. Remember, these beers originate from a land that sits on the same latitude as Moscow and Denmark. I'd suggest brewing during the winter months.

SCOTTISH ALE FROM KITS

Young's do a fairly cheap one-tin extract kit known as 'Scottish Heavy', which is good but with a bit of tinkering can be excellent. Steep 250g (9oz) dark crystal malt, add some dried malt extract instead of the recommended sugar, or even some DME and brown sugar (50:50), and use a Scottish Ale yeast to improve. I'd also recommend leaving it for at least one month before drinking.

SCOTTISH ALE AND WEE HEAVY RECIPES

Scottish Ale

INGREDIENTS
3.5kg (7lb 11oz) pale liquid extract
170g (6oz) dark crystal malt
80g (3oz) chocolate malt
22.4g (¾oz) East Kent Goldings (5%) @ 90 minutes
22.8g (¾oz) East Kent Goldings @ 10 minutes
40g (1½oz) Bramling Cross (6%) @ 10 minutes

Boil for 90 minutes.

2 smack packs Wyeast 1469 West Yorkshire Ale or 1728 Scottish Ale yeast
OG 1.058, FG 1.013, ABV 6%, 12 IBU

Stronge Scottish Ale

This recipe comes from Colin Stronge, formerly of Black Isle Brewery (see
page 254) and now at Buxton. It has been designed to celebrate his time
in Scotland, but tweaked a little to allow for modern tastes. In order to be
more authentic, Colin has included peated malt. Opinion on whether
these beers would have used peated malt is fairly well divided, so its inclusion is optional, depending on personal tastes.

INGREDIENTS
4.67kg (10lb 5oz) pale malt 80%
790g (1¾lb) peat-smoked malt 13.6%
260g (9¼oz) dark crystal malt 4.4%
120g (4oz) chocolate malt 2%
22.4g (¾oz) East Kent Goldings (5%) @ 90 minutes
22.8g (¾oz) East Kent Goldings @ 5 minutes
40g (1½oz) Bramling Cross (6%) @ 5 minutes

Mash for 75 minutes at 65°C (149°F).

It will help the beer if the chloride:sulphate ratio is about 1:1 or 1:15
so as not to accentuate the hop bitterness too much; this will also help the
sweetness come across without being overpowering.

Boil for 90 minutes. Ferment at 19°C (66°F), raising to 21°C (70°F)
after 48 hours.

Wyeast 1469 West Yorkshire Ale Yeast, or Wyeast 1728 Scottish Ale
Target OG 1.066, target FG 1.014, ABV 6.8%, 12 IBU

This is a simple recipe and process. No real dry-hopping is required
in this traditional beer style, although a delightful variant can be achieved

by adding 0.6g per litre each of Bramling Cross and Chinook for a modern twist at the end of primary fermentation.

Highland Heavy

This recipe comes from Greg Hughes, owner of the online brewing supplier Brew UK. It is an export-strength Highland classic. This is a malt-forward beer with no hop aroma but a very clean, neutral flavour.

Take note: this is for a 23-litre (40-pint) batch rather than 19 litres (33½ pints) like many of the other recipes.

INGREDIENTS
4.4kg (9lb 11oz) pale malt 88.7%
291g (7¾oz) CaraMunich III malt 5.9%
195g (6¾oz) light crystal malt 3.9%
75g (3oz) roasted barley 1.5%

Mash for 1 hour at 70°C (158°F).

29g (1¼oz) First Gold (8%) @ 70 minutes
1 teaspoon Protofloc @ 15 minutes

WLP028 Edinburgh Ale yeast
Ferment at 18°C (64°F). Condition for six weeks at 12°C (54°F).
OG 1.050, FG 1.013, colour: 30.7 EBC, est. ABV 4.9%

22

WINTER WARMERS AND OLD ALES

O LD ALES ARE beers that were brewed before the Industrial Revolution of the mid-eighteenth century, when Milds and Old Ales were the only beers on offer. They were referred to as 'Old', 'Stock', 'Stale', 'Strong' or 'Keeping' Ales, or when brewed during the winter months, often with a higher ABV and some spice, they could become 'Winter Warmers'.

These beers were brewed to last and would be served when they were old – months, sometimes years, old, having spent that time ageing in a barrel, picking up tannin flavours from the wood and a touch of sourness from the wild yeasts.

SOME OF THE FINEST OLD ALES AND WINTER WARMERS

Dark & Handsome, 5%, Box Steam Brewery, Holt, Bradford on Avon, Wiltshire

Box Steam Brewery, like many breweries, is tucked away on an industrial estate. Which fits with the whole industrial Brunel theme to their labelling and marketing. Head brewer Tom Downes is one of those sort of understated, quiet blokes who just get on with stuff. The stuff that he gets on with at Box Steam is making great and perhaps understated beer.

Dark & Handsome is one of those great beers: a full, creamy mouth-feel with cherry and blackcurrant and coffee on the nose. Then spiced Christmas chocolate, damsons and a balance of woody and smoked malts, with a long, warming chocolate finish.

A seasonal beer, available during the winter months at the Cross Guns, Avoncliff, The Inn at Freshford, and in bottles nationwide from many good bottle shops, and direct from the brewery at www.boxsteambrewery.co.uk.

Hocus Pocus Old Ale, 5%, Loddon Brewery, Dunsden Green, Oxfordshire

Every good Old Ale should give a complex nose that entices you in, and this is no exception: rich damsons drenched in wine and treacle begin to describe to your nose what is waiting in the glass. A full and tingly mouth-feel, burnt toffee and hazelnut sticking to the mouth, with some damson continuing to chocolate – drinking chocolate which doesn't let its presence be known immediately, but once you know it's there it blankets everything else. Then a very small hint of floral hops smiling in the background, waving its hand and reminding you that this beer is made using English hops. If you want to learn how a beer can build from flavour to flavour, then this will certainly send you along the right track.

Available at freehouses throughout the Thames Valley, direct from the brewery at loddonbrewery.com and with limited availability from some bottle shops.

Old Peculiar, 5.6%, Theakston, Ripon, North Yorkshire

Just as when you live in a town you never go and see the tourist attractions, so I've ignored Old Peculiar, allowing unfair prejudice to dismiss it as some mass-produced, tasteless offering from a massive brewery. As with every prejudice I have – with beers, foods or even people – once I get over them I realize what I've been missing out on. This really is the black pudding or the properly cooked tripe of my beer world.

An autumn hedgerow on the nose – plenty of damson and rich elder-berries, with rich, sticky fruit-pudding malt aromas. A lovely ox-blood red/black colour in the glass, and dark fruits continue with the first sip, as do a rich sweetness and some molasses, but not overtly – certainly not as a signature, as with many darker beers. I also felt there was some oak in there too, but it kept flowing back up towards sweetness balanced with earthy hops, carried by the perfect carbonation. Putting the beer down for a few minutes and coming back to it (same temperature), I found some bitter coffee jumping out. One of those beers that could be given to a room full of people and each one in turn could offer a new flavour that everyone would be able to pick out. A beer taster's beer.

The taste continues long after the last sip, with a surprising touch of sour which gradually leads back to some sweetness and a touch of cherry cola and over-ripe bananas. A rich beer, and perhaps a reminder that some-times you shouldn't judge a beer by its label.

Available in bottles all year round in most corner shops and off-licences up and down the country. Also available in many pubs nationwide, including Shepherd and Flock, Farnham, Surrey, and Weavers Answer, Shaw, Oldham, Lancashire.

Winter Ale, 6.5%, St Peter's Brewery, Bungay, Suffolk

The people at St Peter's Brewery are certainly not without a sense of humour. After the 2013 Budget, when the chancellor single-handedly saved the British brewing industry by offering a massive 1p cut in duty off every pint, one of the St Peter's pubs, the Jerusalem Tavern in Farringdon, left a bowl on the bar offering a 'Free penny with every pint of beer, courtesy of Mr Osborne.'

With their very distinctive bottle shape, like an old medicine bottle, St Peter's beers are known to most beer drinkers across our country. What is less well known is that they make a wide range of beers, including twelve seasonal beers. The Winter Ale is one of them, pouring as a dark Stasi brown, and with an aroma of roasted chocolate malts, dark stone fruits, caramel, molasses and rich winter spices. I certainly tasted some liquorice, with a hint of salt, a soft mouthfeel and some soy sauce and coffee coming through the longer it stays in the mouth. Lovely and complex, just as you want from a Winter Warmer.

Available during winter months (although it was still available in May) direct from St Peter's Brewery at stpetersbrewery.co.uk. Also from the Jerusalem Tavern in Farringdon, London, and with limited availability from some bottle shops.

BREWING OLD ALES AND WINTER WARMERS

MALT

The bulk of an Old Ale is not too dissimilar to many British beers, in that it is made up of mostly pale malt or Golden Promise. A good pale extract for extract brewers would be an excellent choice, between 70 and 100%, although most people will use roasted and caramel malts to make up the rest of the grain bill. Crystal malt is a given, and using darker crystal malts will add a more pronounced caramel sweetness and some burnt flavours; darker crystal malts lend themselves for use in stronger beers. Chocolate, roasted barley, black malt (but not if you are already using chocolate malt) and even a small addition of wheat or even brown malt would not be uncommon either. Experimenting by adding some extra malt in the form of malt extract would be quite common too, especially when increasing the ABV.

Although you can go stronger, up to 9%, especially when making a Winter Warmer, the typical ABV for an Old Ale will range from around 4% up to about 6.5%. Also, to get more pronounced flavours from the malts, a higher mash temperature is advisable – around 68–70°C (154–158°F).

HOPS

As the hop profile is fairly unpronounced, this is not a beer to lob hops at. The character comes from the grain bill, yeast and ageing. That said, you still want some hops – think earthy English, Fuggles and East Kent Goldings, or Challenger would be an excellent choice. Or, as they are often cheap, some Willamette. IBUs must match the strength in order to make a balanced beer. Beers around the 1.040 OG mark should aim for around 25 IBUs, increasing to 45 for 1.090.

Dry-hopping is not uncommon either, but still with English strains, at a rate of up to 75g (3oz) in a 19-litre (33½-pint) batch.

YEAST

A good British Ale yeast is typical for making an Old Ale: White Labs WLP002, Wyeast 1968 London ESB, or even White Labs WLP004 Irish Ale made into a starter. If you are feeling experimental, try using a *Brettanomyces* strain, either on its own or after initial primary fermentation, and ageing your beer for over a year. This will be especially interesting if you have access to an oak barrel, as this soured beer would be similar to the beers that were used in Three Threads (see page 299) and you could even consider making your own.

High-gravity Old Ales and Winter Warmers need to be aged. The flavours need to rest and develop. Three months is the least amount of time you will need, and longer for beers that will be above 6%.

OTHER FLAVOURS

Old Peculiar uses flaked corn and sugar, added to increase the ABV and to reduce the nitrogen level.

I've known brewers make Winter Warmers by adding mulling spices to their Porters with good effect. Stroud Brewery's Ding Dong is a successful example. Mulling spices can include cloves, cinnamon, allspice, orange peel and ginger, and they are generally added to the last 10–15 minutes of the boil. You might also consider 'dry-spicing' – adding spices during secondary fermentation. I like using wood avens (see page 142), which give a subtle clove-like aroma.

OLD ALES AND WINTER WARMERS FROM KITS

For a kit that is a little different, then an all dry-malt extract by Hambleton Bard Old English Ale is a decent enough option. I'd recommend whisking together the extract in some water that has been boiled and then cooled to prevent clumping. I'd also suggest this kit as a basis for some experimentation using spices, for example. Instead of adding sugar as directed, I'd add a bag of dark spray malt – it will give a greater depth of flavours.

For a Winter Warmer kit, Muntons Santa's Winter Warmer comes highly recommended. As is usual with kits, don't use the amount of sugar suggested; instead use a mix of dark muscavado at a 50:50 ratio with some dark spray malt for a slightly more complex beer.

Both kits will benefit from ageing.

OLD ALE RECIPES

Any Old Ale

INGREDIENTS

3.88kg (8lb 9oz) pale liquid extract

430g (15oz) Carafoam

240g (8oz) light crystal malt (88 EBC)

240g (8oz) wheat liquid extract

150g (5oz) extra dark crystal malt (236 EBC)

90g (3¼oz) molasses

50g (2oz) chocolate malt (1240 EBC)

44.3g (1½oz) Challenger (7.5%) @ 60 minutes

2 smack packs Wyeast 1968 London ESB Ale, followed by 2 vials White Labs WIP645 *Brettanomyces claussenii* added when ESB slows down after four–seven days.

Boil for 60 minutes.

OG 1.069, FG 1.020, ABV 6.5%, 32 IBU

Dobson's Old Ale

This is a recipe given to me by Tom Dobson, a music teacher and barman from Brighton. He tells me, 'I'm intrigued by beers that require long ageing. The idea of adding *Brettanomyces* to the initial recipe was down to the fact that such beers would have traditionally been subjected to extended ageing in wood, which would have undoubtedly harboured wild yeast. It was just an attempt to recreate an old style from various texts. *Brettanomyces claussenii* is said to be the strain which was isolated from old British beer barrels so it seemed appropriate.'

INGREDIENTS

5kg (11lb) crisp pale malt 81%

310g (11oz) light crystal malt 5%

250g (9oz) flaked wheat 4%

250g (9oz) flaked oats 4%

190g (6¾oz) Special B 3%

120g (4oz) molasses 2%

60g (2¼oz) chocolate malt 1%

44.3g (1½oz) Challenger (7.5%) @ 60 minutes

2 smack packs Wyeast 1968 London Ale ESB, followed by 2 vials White Labs WIP645

Brettanomyces claussenii added when a 1.016 reading is achieved by the WY1968

Mash for 90 minutes at 67°C (152°F).

Boil for 60 minutes.

OG 1.068, FG 1.014, ABV 7.2%, 32 IBU

Nutcracker

Another *cracking* recipe from Salisbury's finest, Greg Hughes from online home-brew suppliers Brew UK. It's a complex, warming winter beer which can also be spiced for a festive twist.

Unlike most of the other recipes, this makes a 23-litre (40-pint) batch.

INGREDIENTS

5kg (11lb) pale malt 90.9%

200g (7oz) Special B malt 3.7%

100g (3½oz) wheat malt 1.9%

100g (3½oz) chocolate malt 1.9%

Mash for 60 minutes at 65°C (149°F).
Boil for 70 minutes.

INGREDIENTS
21g (¾oz) First Gold (8.0%) @ 70 minutes
8g (¼oz) Challenger (7%) @ 10 minutes
500g (1¼lb) Honey @ 5 minutes
10g (¼oz) Target (10.5%) @ 0 minutes
2 smack packs Wyeast 1187 Ringwood Ale

Ferment at 20°C (68°F), condition for six weeks at 12°C (54°F).
OG 1.060, FG 1.014, ABV 6.1%

23

STOUTS

THERE IS OFTEN debate as to what makes the difference between a Stout and a Porter. Most will agree that Stouts are typified by the use of roasted grains. However, writing in 1889, John Bickerdyke in his book *Curiosities of Ale and Beer* suggests, 'The name Stout was used originally to signify strong or Stout beer. This excellent brown beer only differs from Porter in being brewed of greater strength and with a greater proportion of hops.' Indeed there is evidence of these 'Brown Stouts' made by various brewers, including Whitbread, and with 50% brown malts and 50% pale, and generally brewed to a third stronger than Porters.

Before Bickerdyke's day, back in Georgian times, the term 'Stout' was more popularly used to describe 'Stout Porters'; then as Porters fell out of fashion so the word 'Porter' was dropped. In fact, Guinness made one of the first Stouts: it was known as Guinness Extra Stout Porter, which became known as Guinness Extra Stout and it is pretty much the same drink now as it was then.

Using the term 'Stout' is almost like using the term 'wine', as there are many variations on the theme – the most popular, of course, being a certain dry Irish Stout heavily marketed on St Patrick's Day. Yes, Guinness is a Stout, but not all Stouts are Guinness, and if you don't like a pint of the black stuff try branching out, as there are many other styles available, each with its own charm and character. It's also a style that has huge parameters, from the rather weak (by comparison) 4% ABV dry Stouts to full-bodied and strong 9% Imperial Stouts, sweet Milk Stouts and Stouts made with oysters.

SOME OF THE FINEST STOUTS

Blackberry Stout, 3.8%, Waen Brewery, Llanidloes, Powys

It's hard to imagine that a beer of 3.8% could be called Stout, but this gives a great, full, silky mouthfeel despite the low ABV. At first smoky, the blackberry is very subtle – a tang more than a fruitiness. Having tasted some fruit beers, it can be difficult to get the balance right, but the background flavour works well, adding credence to the lightly roasted flavour of the malts and chocolate. A great dry, lingering finish to round off this unusual and very quaffable Stout.

Available all year round in selected pubs in Wales, the Midlands and the South West. Often to be seen at beer festivals and occasionally at good bottle shops. Also available direct from the brewery at thewaenbrewery.co.uk.

Heartless Chocolate Stout, 4.9%, Red Willow, Macclesfield, Cheshire

If you have ever had a really decent peaty whisky, you'll know that medicinal flavour – a flavour that is just like sticking plasters – and this Stout has much of that flavour in it. This might sound like a bad thing to those who have never tried a peaty whisky: sticking plasters – how can that possibly be good? Well, it is, I assure you, and in dark beers I think it works very well if not overdone. Here the smoky balance is just right. It sets off this Stout, which is so full-bodied you could confuse it for oil. Yet there is a rich, fruity sweetness, the flavour of Christmas pudding batter, completing with a dry finish.

Available seasonally around the North East and occasionally found in bottles nationwide from good bottle shops. Or use the Heartless beerfinder – redwillowbrewery.com/beer-finder.

Oyster Stout, 4.6%, Arbor Ales, Bristol

Jon at Arbor Ales is one of those people who just doesn't stop – a trait that shows in his beer, or at least in his array of beers, as every Friday he produces a new one. It's great news for us drinkers in Bristol, as it means there is always a new Arbor Ales beer to try. It also means for Jon that the bestsellers can be brewed again and so the drinkers decide what stays and what goes. It can be frustrating at times, as great one-off brews might never resurface, but it keeps us on our toes. The Oyster Stout, however, is one that Jon brews regularly (for him), meaning that it can often be found.

Generally speaking, all beer is boiled for at least 45 minutes (see page 91). Hops added at the start of the boil will impart bitterness and hops added at the end will impart aroma and flavours. It is towards the end of the boil, too, that cloves, bay and other spices can be added. Jon argues that a true Oyster Stout should be made with, rather than served with, oysters. So, in the case of Arbor's Oyster Stout, whole oysters have been added towards the end of the boil! A rather brave move from one of the leading experimental brewers in the UK.

What he has created is a rich, smooth Stout with something odd lurking in the background – not as of the sea as in something like the Orkney Dark Island Old Ale, but a touch of sourness and seaweed. It's a taste that wouldn't work on its own, but with roasted malts, pepper, caramel and molasses to balance it there is more than enough going on in this, another of Jon's lovely Stouts.

Also look out for Jon's Port Stout, which has a hint of smoke, port and Ethiopian coffee; his Breakfast Stout, made with locally roasted coffee; and his Impy Stout, full of earthy chicory and fortified caramel.

Jon's beers rotate at the Three Tuns and Old Stillage pubs in Bristol and are also available in bottles across the British Isles in all good bottle shops.

Titanic Stout, 4.5%, Titanic Brewery, Stoke-on-Trent, Staffordshire

Beers can sometimes be like people: they can seem great straight away, really exciting, but after a while you realize there is little depth to them. This Stout is more like that quiet bloke who sits a few seats away from you at work. There is nothing remarkable about him at all, but if you gave yourself some time and got to know him a little better you'd find that he is a complex character and it will be a pleasure to spend time with him.

That is to say, Titanic Stout develops, each sip building around the dark roasted malts. Molasses teams up with tart Morello cherry, coffee sits with chocolate, and the whole thing builds to the sort of vinerous (wine-like) flavours one might attribute to beer that is not only older but has a much higher ABV.

Available during the winter months as a guest Ale from limited good Real Ale pubs such as the Bull's Head in Stoke-on-Trent; also in bottles nationwide from good bottle shops and direct from titanicbrewery.co.uk

Polar Eclipse, 4.8%, Beartown, Congleton, Cheshire

As red as autumn twilight with a nostril full of chocolate and pepper. This crisp, dry Stout builds from cocoa to a caramel – the reverse of eating a Cadbury's chocolate éclair – carried to a very subtle, almost indistinguishable, tang of citrus peel and a dry coffee finish. What Ian Burns, head brewer, has created is a Stout that could happily sit alongside Lagers and Golden Ales during the hot summer months, a dry, thirst-quenching Stout.

Available from the Beartown Tap, Congleton, Cheshire, and in bottles direct from the brewery at beartownbrewery.co.uk, or from specialist bottle shops.

Double Stout, 4.8%, Hook Norton Brewery, Hook Norton, Oxfordshire

A beer that took an eighty-year holiday! It is thought to have been first brewed at some point in the nineteenth century, but then, a casualty of war, brewing ceased from 1917, not to be picked up again until 1996.

Sweet raisin is on the nose of this reddish Stout, with a nice, creamy, full mouthfeel. The sweetness continues, but all the time it sits arm in arm with a rather intense, tart, bitter, pithy citrus and some liquorice, all balanced nicely by some slightly singed (rather than burnt) toast.

A long finish that starts bone dry then lifts to include some resinous hop bitterness and a hint of bitter coffee beans.

Good availability during the winter months in bottles.

Export Stout London 1890, 7.2%, The Kernel, London

Rich coffee on the nose with a hint of chocolate and oak. It pours like engine oil – thick, tar-like and very black. Bitter dark 90% cacao chocolate dominates; it's akin to chewing on raw cacao and drinking a cup of coffee through it, but as these initial strong flavours subside they give way to a symphony of roasted malts and a hint of thick Bovril, yet still leave room for the most delicate of floral aromas from the hop, roses gently lifting the medley of stronger flavours. The alcohol, despite being far above a sessionable strength, doesn't show itself at all and this is a Stout which is smoother than Isaac Hayes or Huey Morgan. Very dry, clean and slightly vinerous/rum finish.

Available in bottles all year round from good bottle shops; see thekernelbrewery.com/wheretobuy.html for full details of local stockists.

SOME OF THE FINEST IMPERIAL STOUTS

Imperial Stouts were regular Stouts brewed to a higher ABV for the Russian Imperial Court, who liked their beer strong!

Bearded Lady, Imperial Brown Stout, 10.5%, Magic Rock, Huddersfield, West Yorkshire

You have to get a personal licence in order to run a licensed premises. It's basically a multiple-choice exam full of questions on the legal side of running one. It doesn't cover basic arithmetic, knowing who is next at the bar or what temperature a beer is to be served at. The seasoned punter can weather the first two with a bit of humour (hopefully); however, the latter can completely alter what you are drinking and is reason enough to bring back hanging (or at least a very British loud tut and a passive-aggressive boycott of the premises). Sitting in a Craft Ale pub, excitedly surveying the range, I didn't expect to be served an Imperial Stout at Lager temperature. Jagged flavours of strong, cheap Co-op whisky, bitter chocolate and discombobulated dandelion leaf competed for dominance rather than gently subsiding to give way to each other. It still wasn't a terrible pint, but it needed some TLC.

Over the next hour I read, ate some food and slowly sipped at this beer; after half an hour I was starting to get it a bit more. The assault on my tastebuds was subsiding to a peaceful protest, strong whisky was mellowing to a bourbon, and the dandelion leaf was disappearing altogether. After a full hour the beer had warmed to room temperature. I was now drinking a wondrous love-in: rich Christmas pudding fruits which were hitherto incognito, a delicate touch of coconut and pine, wrapped up in comfortable coffee chocolate biscuit and finished with lingering, warming bourbon.

Occasionally available as a guest Ale nationwide, often at Craft Ale bars rather than pubs; more likely around the Yorkshire area. Also available in bottles in good bottle shops with limited to good availability, or direct from the brewery at magicrockbrewing.com.

Gorlovka Imperial Stout, 6%, Acorn, Barnsley, South Yorkshire

Imperial Stouts are also known as Russian Imperial Stouts, and Gorlovka is a city in Ukraine.

I drank this beer rather late in the day at the Great Welsh Beer and Cider Festival and as such my notes had a much more ethereal quality than usual. I have scrawled, 'You can imagine a Soviet-style steam train serving this as you are whisked across the frozen tundra of Siberia.' There is an engine-oil quality to it and a creaminess that is evident as you pour. A tinge of molasses, coffee and liquorice, but there is a slight twist in the drinking as it is not as rich and full bodied as many Stouts or even Porters can be – not a negative criticism, as it means this is easy drinking rather than a sipping Stout.

Nicely finished with a dry, smoky, bittersweet flavour. Marked by my drinking partner, James, as 'a contender for best Stout'.

Available seasonally direct from the brewery in polypin (or cask to trade) www.acorn-brewery.co.uk or from mybrewerytap.com.

STOUTS ARE NOT WHITE, ARE THEY?

Think Stouts and I know most will be thinking of one style. In fact, 90% of people I questioned (in a survey of ten friends) said Guinness when I asked, 'What sort of beer do you think of when someone says Stout?' I would not have minded if I hadn't served three of them with a White Stout just days before! My White Stout was brewed by Durham Brewery using just pale malt and to a strength of 7.2%. Believe it or not, this beer is closer to the original meaning of Stout than the darker Guinness, or any other dark Stouts for that matter. Back in Georgian times Stouts were named as such from the adjective 'stout' meaning 'strong'. They could be 'white' (pale), brown or even dark.

White Stout, 7.2%, Durham Breweries, Durham

The White Stout did not have the traditional flavours associated with the modern-day Stout style. Instead this beer is full of fruit flavours: coarse, acid-drop citrus from the Columbus hops, but with a damson flavour too. You can tell it is a strong beer as there is an alcoholic bite, but not one that suggests anything above 6%. This Stout certainly has body and I'd casually describe it as a mealy IPA.

Available around Durham and Newcastle, and limited availability in bottles from good bottle shops. Also available direct from the brewery at durhambrewery.co.uk.

BREWING STOUTS

MALT

One of the characteristics that can set a Stout apart from a Porter is the addition of roasted barley. Using as little as 2% in total will be noticeable, but you can go up to about 10%, though your beer will need longer conditioning time. Though that said, it is certainly not necessary and Stout is one of those styles with a lot of scope; many brewers will opt for black malt instead.

Pale malts should be used as a base at around 80% or so, and here too some experimentation can take place. Adding a portion of Munich and/or Vienna malt can give interesting results, while a touch of sweetness can be given by crystal/caramel malts up to around 15%. Although not essential, chocolate malt is also another great addition.

Flaked barley or oats can be used to add extra body and aid head-retention.

Mash at temperatures of 66–68°C (151–154°F) for extra body.

HOPS

To help bring out some of the roasted flavours, it is a good idea to keep aroma hops to a minimum in Stouts: just one bittering addition (early in the boil) of Northern Brewer, Fuggles, East Kent Goldings, Target or Willamette. For Imperial Stouts aroma hops do add something extra. Stuart Ross of Magic Rock uses Target, but Willamette and Fuggles would both be up for the job too.

YEAST

If using a dry yeast, Nottingham will of course work, but Stuart from Magic Rock recommends California Ale yeast (US-05). He also suggests any English Ale yeast, and good results can be obtained in all but dry Stouts by using Wyeast 1084 Irish Ale yeast or White Labs WLP004.

STOUT KITS

One of the best Stout kits on the market happens also to be one of the easiest to get hold of and the cheapest. The Australian Coopers Stout comes highly recommended by an army of kit brewers. It can be made as per instructions, but to improve it hugely use 500g (1¼lb) dark spray malt in place of the sugar, and just for an extra bit of ABV and flavour add a 454g (1lb) tin of treacle too. Another little trick many kit brewers have is to add less water than is recommended, in this case anything from 18 to 21 litres (31½ to 37 pints) instead of 23 (40) will give you a thicker and more flavoursome Stout. Also, if you can force yourself to leave even just a few bottles to condition over a couple of months, that will make all the difference to the flavour

Of the other notable kits on the market, the Edme Superbrew Irish Stout also stands out. This too is readily available online (see Home-brew Suppliers, page 381) and from good home-brew shops. It makes a rather smoky, liquorice Stout and, like all kits, it lends itself to a bit of experimentation. Adding spray malt, treacle and/or molasses will improve the flavour, as will using less sugar and more of the kit.

STOUT RECIPES

Extract Oatmeal Stout _____

INGREDIENTS
3.27kg (7lb 3oz) light dry extract
20g (¾oz) wheat liquid extract
110g (3¾oz) Carafoam
60g (2¼oz) crystal malt
30g (1¼oz) black malt
30g (1¼oz) chocolate malt
20g (¾oz) Chinook (13%) @ 60 minutes
10g (¼oz) Fuggles (4.5%) @ 5 minutes

Nottingham dry yeast or any English or Irish Ale yeast
Boil for 60 minutes.

All-grain Stout _____

This recipe came to me from Stuart Ross of Magic Rock. If you see him
out and about in Leeds, the chances are he'll be out with beer writer Zak
Avery. Since Zak introduced me to Stuart, I recommend buying them both
a pint to say thanks.

INGREDIENTS
5kg (11lb) pale malt 75%
550g (1¼lb) brown malt 8.3%
55g (2oz) black malt 8.3%
270g (9½oz) amber malt 4.1%

Stuart recommends experimenting with 1–1.5kg (2lb 3oz–3lb 5oz) of different sugars near the end of the boil. Start with brown sugar and work your way through.

INGREDIENTS
44g (1½oz) Admiral (14%) @ 90 minutes
30g (1½oz) Target (11%) @ 5 minutes
Fermentis California Ale US-05, or any English Ale yeast

Ferment at 21°C (70°F).
OG 1.090–1.100, FG 1.020–1.025, ABV 9.2%-10.5%, 78 IBU

Oatmeal Stout

If you ever find yourself in Frome, the home town of Formula 1's Jenson Button and author Charlie Higson, then I'd highly recommend a visit to the Griffin Inn, a great, old-fashioned pub with a brewery in the back yard. This is the Milk Street Brewery, home of Funky Monkey (see page 225), and you might find Rik working or enjoying one of his Ales. He kindly gave me the recipe below, so buy him a pint to say thanks! Incidentally, you can use shop-bought oats for this recipe.

INGREDIENTS
5.08kg (11lb 3oz) pale malt 95.5%
50g (2oz) oats 1%
50g (2oz) crystal malt 1%
50g (2oz) flaked barley 1%
30g (1¼oz) torrified (heat-treated) wheat 0.5%
30g (1¼oz) chocolate malt 0.5%
30g (1¼oz) black malt 0.5%

20g (¾oz) Chinook @ 60 minutes
10g (¼oz) Fuggles @ 5 minutes

Mash at 66°C (151°F) for 75 minutes.
Boil for 60 minutes.

OG 1.064, FG 1.014, ABV 6.6%, 29.5 IBU

24

SPECIALITY BEERS

SPECIALITY BEERS ARE everything else. These are the beers that don't fit within any style guidelines. Brewers will often make special beer to mark an anniversary or an event; in 2012 the Queen's Diamond Jubilee and the London Olympics saw a glut of them. Many will disappear without trace, but some will create such a buzz for the brewer that it would be silly for them not to brew again. They can be beers that fit existing styles but are brewed with unusual ingredients, such as rice, oats, potatoes, maple syrup, juniper, chillies, plums, or they might be beers brewed without using hops.

SOME OF THE FINEST SPECIALITY BEERS

Chilli Plum Porter, 6.1%, Waen Brewery, Caersws, Llandinam, Powys

The beer world can often be divided on many things, clarity being one of them. Sue Hayward, the expert brewer at the Waen (pronounced Wine – it's Welsh), is unapologetic about her Porter being cloudy, as this is due to the high pectin level in the fruit. It would be difficult to have a clear pint of Chilli Plum Porter. I asked Sue about this and she said, 'Our Porter looks like mud. You may get it to clear, but it will look like mud. But it's a great pint as long as you look past that.' In some competitions she would be marked down for this, which is a real shame as there are lots of things in life to get anal about but beer shouldn't be one of them.

This is certainly not a clear beer; it does pour to a muddy brown/black. As you can imagine, there is some dark fruit on the nose – I think this is really where you get the plums, which combine with roasted notes and a touch of oak. It has a pleasant, full, creamy mouthfeel and a dance of coffee and dark fruit – if pushed I'd say Victoria plum – subsiding to sweet malt and roasted grains. The chilli just gives it that little nudge around the edges of the mouth to carry and complement the roasted grains which build to sweet milk chocolate. A nice, long, dry 'Stouty' finish, with an appearance again from the chillies urging you to take another sip.

Available in casks in pubs around Mid/South Wales, the West Midlands and on tap at the Waen Brewery, Caersws, Llandinam, which is well worth a visit. Also available in bottles and polypins from www.thewaenbrewery.co.uk and good bottle shops.

Treacle Stout, 5%, Ossett Brewery, Ossett, West Yorkshire

This is a rich, mahogany-coloured Stout with a first aroma of wood shavings followed by treacle and chocolate. It is hard to taste much past an intense treacle flavour at first, but this then ebbs to create a perfect bed for the double burst of bitterness from chocolate malt and a background of marmalade. This richly bodied Stout lasts beyond the full mouthfeel, as a long, lingering, sticky molasses clings to your cockles and warms you right down to your toes after each sip. This is a perfect antidote to a cold, cold day and I can quite imagine keeping a bottle in a first-aid box to drink only after I've been soaked to the skin.

Limited availability in bottles from good bottle shops nationwide; or online (and in store) at beerritz.co.uk, and direct from Ossett Brewery (see ossett-brewery.co.uk for more details).

Kelpie Seaweed Ale, 4.4%, Williams Brothers Brewing, Alloa, Clackmannanshire

Most famous for their Fraoch Heather Ale, Bruce and Scott Williams also make a whole range of speciality beers. The Fraoch is a good beer, but it is very different from much that precedes it. The Kelpie, on the other hand, drinks like a regular Scottish Ale; indeed, it would be easy to fool many drinkers into thinking that they were drinking a regular low-hopped Scottish Ale. Which is what essentially this is. It reminds me very much of a mixture between two other Scottish beers: Orkney's Dark Island (page 320) and Traquair House Jacobite (page 321). Malt is very sweet, like glacé cherries on top of an iced bun – a good, full, creamy mouthfeel; a sticky molasses too that coats your teeth as if you have drunk a few spoonfuls of treacle in some hot water. The seaweed flavours do not hit you at first; instead they come after a few mouthfuls, perhaps because it is an unexpected flavour. Once you are aware of it, it stays, and it took me back to childhood beach holidays. One of the most unusual things about this beer is the salty aftertaste. No matter how much you wash seaweed there will always be some sea water and for some reason salt works in a sweet Scottish Ale.

Widely available in bottles from most good bottle shops; to find a stockist near you try their beerfinder at williamsbrosbrew.com.

SPECIALITY BEER RECIPES

Quetzalcoatl Xocolatl Imperial Stout – all grain _____

This recipe is for a Mexican hot-chocolate-inspired Imperial Stout, estimating 10% ABV with a bitterness level of 56 IBUs. The recipe came from Chad and Jess Mckinney, my American home-brewing friends living in Brighton. They tend to brew 'big' beers, which are Jess's favourite, and then they might split a beer every evening. I found this one very interesting. It's not one that you'd want to drink on a session – the high ABV puts paid to that. But it is one of the nicest beers I've tried that I didn't want to drink a whole pint of!

INGREDIENTS
3.72kg (8lb 3oz) pale malt (Maris Otter) 45%
3.14kg (6lb 15oz) Munich malt 38%
660g (1lb 7oz) chocolate malt 8%
410g (14½oz) roasted barley 5%
330g (11½oz) brown malt 4%

Mash at 65°C (149°F) for 90 minutes.
Boil for 120 minutes.

32g (1¼oz) Target (11%) @ 120 minutes
100g (3½oz) cocoa powder @ 30 minutes
20g (¾oz) Target @ 25 minutes
20g (¾oz) Target @ 15 minutes
20g (¾oz) Target @ 5 minutes

White Labs California Ale yeast (WLP001). Make sure to stir and aerate thoroughly. This is the only time you want to oxygenate the beer.

After primary fermentation, about seven–ten days, siphon into a secondary fermenting vessel, adding:

1 vanilla pod (sanitized with vodka)
120g (4oz) cocoa nibs (sanitized with vodka)
2 large dried ancho chillies, de-seeded
2 large dried pasilla chillies, de-seeded

To prepare the vanilla pod, split it lengthwise and scrape out the seeds. Put the pod and seeds into a bowl with the cocoa nibs and pour some vodka in, just enough so that everything gets sterilized, and let it sit for 30 minutes or so. Then put all of that in the fermenter, vodka included, as it will have extracted some flavour.

To prepare the chillies, split them lengthwise and remove the seeds. Place them in a pan and cover them with water. Bring to a simmer and cook for about 15 minutes, or until the chillies are fairly rehydrated and the water is reduced and looks dark. You don't want too much extra liquid. Let it cool a bit and then add it to the fermenter.

Leave in the secondary for two–four weeks, then take a final gravity reading; the target is 1.021. Bottle using 160g (5½oz) of dried malt extract or 94g (3¼oz) of normal granulated sugar.

To make an extract version, substitute the grains for 6kg (13¼lb) of pale malt extract and steep 310g (11oz) crystal malt, 400g (14oz) roasted barley, 630g (1lb 6oz) chocolate malt.

Rob's Belgian Cross ESB

Another great recipe gifted to me from Rob (the Malt Miller) Neale and, as he rightfully states, 'This one's a cracker!' Rob is the owner of online brewing supplier the Malt Miller and the first ever recipe he made was one of mine he found online.

INGREDIENTS

3.78kg (8lb 5oz) pale malt (6 EBC) 82%

440g (15½oz) biscuit malt (45 EBC) 9.6%

220g (7¾oz) Caravienne malt (43 EBC) 4.8%

170g (6oz) acid malt (6 EBC) 3.6%

48.6g (1¾oz) East Kent Goldings (5% AA) @ 60 minutes

½ teaspoon Irish moss @ 10 minutes

21g (¾oz) East Kent Goldings @ 5 minutes

15g (½oz) Fuggles @ 5 minutes

13g (½oz) East Kent Goldings @ 0 minutes

3 packets Yorkshire Square Ale yeast (WLP037), or yeast starter

35g (1¼oz) East Kent Goldings – dry-hop for the last 5 days of fermentation

17g (½oz) Fuggles – dry-hop for the last 5 days of fermentation

Mash for 75 minutes @ 66°C (151°F).

Boil for 60 minutes.

OG 1.052, FG 1.017, ABV 4.6%

For an extract version, steep 10g (¼oz) Caravienne malt, 20g (¾oz) light crystal malt, use 3.28kg (7¼lb) pale liquid malt extract and the same hop schedule.

Barley Wine & Milk Stout _____

This recipe was given to me by Michael Hopart from Top Out Brewery in Edinburgh. It uses a mashing style called 'parti-gyle', where two beers are made at once. Parti-gyle is a traditional method of British brewing and one still employed by some brewers. Stronger beer is made with the first runnings and up to two more beers can be made with the run-off. Since the wort will get successively weaker, this means so will the beers, and traditionally a Barley Wine would be made first and a small beer last. The resulting beers are often fuller and smoother than those using modern-day methods.

This recipe will make around 10 litres (17½ pints) of Barley Wine and 19 litres (33½ pints) of Milk Stout, and this is Michael's account of how he makes them.

INGREDIENTS
6kg (13¼lb) Maris Otter pale malt
400g (14oz) crystal malt
500g (1¼lb) oat or rice hulls (for easier run-off – it's a lot of malt for your small mash tun)
25g (1oz) Admiral or other neutral bittering hop – aim for 45 IBU
25g (1oz) East Kent Goldings for 10 minutes
1 packet dry British Ale yeast

This is a pretty simple recipe really, but you'll be surprised how much complexity you'll get from the high alcohol content. I used a double infusion mash with rests at 63°C and 71°C (145°F and 160°F). The trick now is to collect only the first run-off so you end up with a gravity of 1110 or so. Boil with the hops as normal.

The remaining malt in your mash tun is still full of sugars but is lacking a certain oomph. To compensate for that I added a few speciality grains and topped up with hot water to bring it back to 70°C (158°F). Since Maris Otter is already converted, you don't need to run a full mash again, just let it infuse to get the flavour, colour and body from the added grains. Sparge and boil as normal.

INGREDIENTS
250g (9oz) crystal malt
350g (12oz) chocolate malt
300g (11oz) black malt
250g (9oz) roasted barley

I also added 500g (1¼lb) of lactose towards the end of the boil, but feel free to leave it out or use something else.

For the fermentation of the Barley Wine it is crucial that you use an alcohol-tolerant yeast. Mine was WLP005, which actually took it all the way from 1.128 to 1.042 with a strength of 11.6% alc./vol.

Quite sweet, but fairly typical for a Barley Wine. Make sure you aerate the chilled wort well; your yeast is going to need all the help it can get.

Mature the Barley Wine for at least six months, but remember it will keep for up to three years or more, improving with time.

PART SIX

Directory

THE YEAR IN BEER FESTIVALS

J UST AS EVERY beer is different, so each beer festival differs and there is no one standard set-up. They range in size from small ones held in a pub, with perhaps just five or six extra beers on tap, to huge extravagant affairs like the Great British Beer Festival held every year at Olympia, with over 800 beers on offer. There are festivals held outdoors with magnificent natural backdrops or set by a tranquil river; others take place inside church halls, social clubs, pubs, clubs, tents and sports clubs. Each will have all walks of life rubbing shoulders with one another in a sweaty, entangled appreciation of beer. They are all (generally) pretty friendly, and if you are a fairly gregarious creature like myself you'll end up chatting to plenty of folk and perhaps even make some beer-loving friends – especially if you get there once everyone has had a few.

DO YOUR HOMEWORK

I love to attend beer festivals, no matter what size, and I go for two reasons only: to try new beers and to have a good time. Most festivals will release a beer list beforehand, so with a bit of homework you can suss out beers that you really want to try. It is always worth making the list longer than you are capable of drinking, as sod's law will dictate that many of the beers you want will not have arrived or will have been drunk before you get there. I remember running up for a pint of Elland's 1872 Porter only to be told by a small Elvin-looking bloke that 'There has been an exodus.' No further explanation was offered and he just stared crazily into the distance!

If you do want to make a list, then there are many ways to research beer. This book is, of course, a start and you might also want to look in the Further Reading section (page 405) for other beer books. Beer bloggers too are a great source of information: again, have a look at the back of this book (page 407). But seriously, fun is the order of the day and getting recommendations from your new friends, the bar staff or taking pot luck by randomly picking anything can be interesting ways of finding new beers.

However, don't just go with what others say. Try to remember which breweries you like and which styles. Don't forget, too, that at a festival it can be easy to be persuaded by silly names and this is not always the best way to get good beer.

FOOD AND WATER

Some supplies can be a good idea. I sat at a festival in Wales where a fella seemed to have brought his own weight in food and water. Food can be pretty basic at some of the provincial festivals and I've seen 'Menu – Burgers £1.50, Cheese Burgers £1.75' at one festival; obviously vegetarians were a rare breed in that part of Scotland. At some of the bigger festivals food can be overpriced and often water isn't on offer at all. I don't need to tell you that food helps soak up alcohol and a few snacks mean you can not only try more beers but you will be better in the morning for a few Scotch eggs. As you will be too for necking a few pints of water.

DON'T BE LATE

Get there early. Latecomers miss out on luxuries like seats, somewhere to put their beer, sometimes food, sanitary toilets and, in the very worst-case scenarios, the best beers will have gone like lightning. Arrive late on the last day of a beer festival and you might well be drinking the dregs of the least popular beers.

KEEP RECORDS

You'll often see blokes with notebooks marking off various beers – a great idea. That way you'll always try something new at each festival. If you are a little self-conscious about doing the same, then there are plenty of online sites that you can use to keep tabs. Two of the most popular are untapped.com and ratebeer.com.

THE YEAR

This list is by no means exhaustive, but if you live anywhere but the most remote parts of the UK I'd be very surprised if you didn't find a festival just a bus ride, or hopefully within staggering distance, from your house. See also www.aletalk.co.uk/events/eventlist.php.

JANUARY

Beamish Hall Beer and Music Festival, Beamish Hall, nr Stanley, Co. Durham

Burton Beer Festival, Town Hall, Burton upon Trent, Staffordshire

Cambridge Winter Ale Festival, University Social Club, Mill Lane, Cambridge

Colchester Winter Ale Festival, Colchester Arts Centre, Church Street, Colchester, Essex

Elysian Beer Festival, The Maltings, Ship Lane, Ely, Cambridgeshire

Exeter & East Devon Beer Festival, Exeter City FC, St James Park, Stadium Way, Exeter

Frodsham Winter Ales Festival, Parish Church Hall, Church Street, Frodsham, Cheshire

Heronsgate Land of Liberty Beer Festival, Land of Liberty, Peace and Plenty Pub, Long Lane, Heronsgate, Hertfordshire

London: Snooty Fox Ale Festival, The Snooty Fox, 75 Grosvenor Avenue, London N5

Manchester: National Winter Ales Festival, Sheridan Suite, The Venue, Oldham Road, Manchester

Salisbury Winterfest, Castle Street Social Club, Scots Lane, Salisbury, Wiltshire

St Neots Winter Beer Festival, Pig 'n' Falcon, New Street, St Neots, Cambridgeshire

FEBRUARY

Atherton: Bent & Bongs Beer Bash, The Formby Hall, Alder Street, Atherton, Manchester

Battersea Beer Festival, Battersea Arts Centre, Lavender Hill, London

Chelmsford Winter Beer & Cider Festival, King Edward VI Grammar School, Broomfield Road, Chelmsford, Essex

Chesterfield CAMRA Beer Festival, Winding Wheel, Holywell Street, Chesterfield, Derbyshire

Derby Winter Beer Festival, The Roundhouse, Roundhouse Road, Pride Park, Derby

Dorchester Beerex, Corn Exchange, Dorchester, Dorset

Dover: White Cliffs Festival of Winter Ales, Town Hall, Biggin Street, Dover, Kent

Fleetwood Beer & Cider Festival, Marine Hall, The Esplanade, Fleetwood, Lancashire

Gosport Winterfest, Thorngate Halls, Alverstoke, Gosport, Hampshire

Liverpool Beer Festival, Metropolitan Catholic Cathedral Crypt, Brownlow Hill, Liverpool

Luton Beer & Cider Festival, Hightown Community Sports & Arts Centre, Concorde Street, Luton, Bedfordshire

Pendle Beer Festival, Colne Municipal Hall, 61 Albert Road, Colne, Lancashire

Redditch Winter Ale Festival, The Rocklands Social Club, 59 Birchfield Road, Redditch, Worcestershire

Stockton Ale & Arty Beer Festival, ARC, 60 Dovecot Street, Stockton-on-Tees

Tewkesbury Winter Ale Fest, George Watson Memorial Hall, Barton Street, Tewkesbury, Gloucestershire

MARCH

Bradford CAMRA Beer Festival, Victoria Hall, Victoria Road, Saltaire, West Yorkshire

Bristol Beer Festival, Brunel's Old Station, Temple Meads, Bristol

Burton Beer & Cider Festival, The Town Hall, Burton upon Trent, Staffordshire

Leeds: Horsforth Beer & Cider Festival, St Margarets Hall, Church Road, Horsforth, West Yorkshire

London: Drinker Beer & Cider Festival, Camden Centre, Bidborough Street, London

Loughborough Beer Festival, The Polish Club, True Lovers Walk, Loughborough, Leicestershire

St Neots 'Booze on the Ouse' Beer & Cider Festival, Priory Centre, Priory Lane, St Neots, Cambridgeshire

Sheffield: Beer X, Ponds Forge International Sports Centre, Sheaf Street, Sheffield, South Yorkshire

Sussex Beer & Cider Festival, Hove Town Hall, Norton Road, Hove, East Sussex

Wigan Beer Festival, Robin Park Indoor Sports Centre, Loire Drive, Wigan, Greater Manchester

APRIL

Bexley Beer Festival, Dartfordians' RFC, War Memorial Clubhouse, Bourne Road, Bexley, Kent

Boxmoor Social Club Ale & Cider Fest, Boxmoor Social Club, 81 Horsecroft Road, Boxmoor, Hemel Hempstead, Hertfordshire

Bury St Edmunds: East Anglian Beer Festival, The Apex, 1 Charter Square, Bury St Edmunds, Suffolk

Chippenham Beer Festival, The Olympiad Leisure Centre, Sadlers Mead, Monkton Park, Chippenham, Wiltshire

Coventry Beer Festival, Butts Park Arena, Spoon End, Coventry, Warwickshire

Doncaster Beer Festival, Doncaster College, The Hub, Chappell Drive, Doncaster, South Yorkshire

Farnham Beerex, Farnham Maltings, Bridge Square, Farnham, Surrey

Maldon Beer Festival, Town Hall, Market Hill, Maldon, Essex

Mansfield: Rufford Mini-Festival, Rufford Arms, 335 Chesterfield Road, Mansfield, Nottinghamshire

Newcastle Beer & Cider Festival, Northumbria Students' Union, 2 Sandyford Road, Newcastle upon Tyne

Paisley Beer Festival, Paisley Town Hall, Abbey Close, Paisley, Renfrewshire

Stourbridge Beer Festival, Stourbridge Town Hall, Crown Centre, Crown Lane, Stourbridge, West Midlands

Thanet: CAMRA Planet Thanet Beer Festival, Winter Gardens, Fort Crescent, Margate, Kent

MAY

Alloa Beer Festival, Alloa Town Hall, Marshill, Alloa, Clackmannanshire

Banbury Beer Festival, Territorial Army, Oxford Road, Banbury, Oxfordshire

Bolsover: Derbyshire Food & Drink Festival, Elvaston Castle Country Park, Borrowash Road, Elvaston, Derby

Cambridge Beer Festival, Jesus Green, Cambridge

Chester Charity Beer Festival, Chester RUFC, Hare Lane, Littleton, Chester, Cheshire

Chesterfield: Real Ale Festival, Barrow Hill Roundhouse, Campbell Drive, Chesterfield, Derbyshire

Colchester Real Ale & Cider Festival, Colchester Arts Centre, Church Street, Colchester, Essex

Glenrothes: Kingdom of Fife Real Ale, Cider & Perry Festival, Rothes Hall, Rothes Square, Glenrothes, Fife

Halifax Mayfest, The Square Chapel, 10 Square Road, Halifax, West Yorkshire

Kingston Beer & Cider Festival, Kingston Workmen's Club and Institute, Old London Road, Kingston upon Thames, London

Lincoln Beer Festival, Lincoln Drill Hall, Free School Lane, Lincoln

Macclesfield Beer Festival, Macclesfield Rugby Club, Priory Park, Priory Lane, Macclesfield, Cheshire

Newark Beer Festival, Riverside Park, Newark, Nottinghamshire

Newark & Nottinghamshire County Show, Newark Showground, Lincoln Road, Newark, Nottinghamshire

Newport: Tredegar House Folk Festival, Tredegar House and Country Park, Newport, Gwent

Northampton Beer Festival, Delapré Abbey, London Road, Northampton

Poole: Parkstone Beer Festival, 66 North Road, Poole, Dorset

Reading Beer & Cider Festival, Kings Meadow Recreation Ground, Napier Road, Reading, Berkshire

Skipton Beer Festival, Town Hall, High Street, Skipton, North Yorkshire

Stockport Beer & Cider Festival, Edgeley Park, Hardcastle Road, Stockport, Cheshire

Wolverhampton Beer Festival, Wulfrun Hall, Mitre Fold, North Street, Wolverhampton, West Midlands

Yapton Beerex, Yapton and Ford Village Hall, Main Road, Yapton, Sussex

JUNE

Aberdeen & North East Beer Festival, Pittodrie Stadium, Pittodrie Street, Aberdeen

Braintree Real Ale Festival, The Bocking Arts Theatre, 15 Bocking End, Braintree, Essex

Cardiff: Great Welsh Beer & Cider Festival, Motorpoint Arena, Mary Ann Street, Cardiff

Edinburgh: Scottish Real Ale Festival, Edinburgh Corn Exchange, 10 New Market Road, Edinburgh

Lewes: South Downs Beer & Cider Festival, Lewes Town Hall, High Street, Lewes, East Sussex

Rugby Beer & Cider Festival, Thornfield Indoor Bowls Club, Bruce Williams Way, Rugby, Warwickshire

St Ives Beer Festival, St Ives Guildhall, Street-An-Pol, St Ives, Cornwall

Salisbury Beerex, Salisbury Arts Centre, Bedwin Street, Salisbury, Wiltshire

Southampton Beer Festival, Southampton Guildhall, West Marlands Road, Southampton, Hampshire

Stratford-upon-Avon Beer & Cider Festival, Stratford-upon-Avon Racecourse, Luddington Road, Stratford-upon-Avon, Warwickshire

Thurrock Beer Festival, Thurrock Civic Hall, Blackshots Lane, Grays, Thurrock, Essex

JULY

Ardingly Beer Festival within Ardingly Vintage & Classic Vehicle Show, South of England Showground, Ardingly, West Sussex

Bromsgrove Beer & Cider Festival, Bromsgrove Rugby Football Club, Finstall Park, Finstall, Bromsgrove, Worcestershire

Canterbury: Kent Beer Festival, Barn at Merton Farm, Merton Lane, Canterbury, Kent

Chelmsford Summer Beer & Cider Festival, Admirals Park, Rainsford Road, Chelmsford, Essex

Derby Summer Beer Festival, Assembly Rooms, Market Place, Derby

Devizes Beer Festival, 9 Walden Lodge Close, Devizes, Wiltshire

Ealing Beer Festival, Walpole Park, Ealing, London

Hereford: Beer on the Wye, Hereford Beer & Cider Festival, Hereford Rowing Club, 37 Greyfriars Avenue, Hereford

Plymouth Beer Festival, Plymouth Pavilions, Millbay Road, Plymouth, Devon

Winchcombe: Cotswold Beer Festival, Tithe Barn, Postlip Hall, Winchcombe, Cheltenham, Gloucestershire

Woodcote Steam & Vintage Transport Rally, north of Reading, RG8 0QY

AUGUST

Barnstaple: North Devon Beer Festival, The Pannier Market, Barnstaple, Devon

Clacton-on-Sea Real Ale & Cider Festival, St James's Hall, Tower Road, Clacton-on-Sea, Essex

Durham Beer Festival, Dunelm House, New Elvet, Durham, County Durham

Grantham Beer Festival, Railway Club, off Huntingtower Road, Grantham, Lincolnshire

Harbury Beer Festival, Village Hall, Harbury, Warwickshire

Ipswich Beer Festival, Ipswich Waterfront, Ipswich, Suffolk

London: Great British Beer Festival, Olympia, Hammersmith Road, London

Peterborough Beer Festival, The Embankment, Bishops Road, Peterborough, Cambridgeshire

Stafford Beer Festival, Blessed William Howard School, Rowley Avenue, Stafford

Swansea Bay Beer & Cider Festival, Brangwyn Hall, Swansea

Worcester Beer, Cider & Perry Festival, Worcester Racecourse, Grand Stand Road, Worcester

SEPTEMBER

Barnsley Beer Festival, Milton Hall, Fitzwilliam Street, Barnsley, South Yorkshire

Bridgnorth Beer Festival, Bridgnorth Station, Hollybush Road, Bridgnorth, Shropshire

Chappel Beer Festival, East Anglian Railway Museum, Station Road, Wakes Colne, Essex

Faversham Hop Festival, Town Centre, Faversham, Kent

Hinckley Beer Festival, The Atkins Building, Lower Bond Street, Hinckley, Leicestershire

Jersey Beer & Cider Festival, People's Park, St Helier, Jersey

Keighley Beer Festival, Central Hall, Alice Street, Keighley, West Yorkshire

Letchworth Beer & Cider Festival, Letchworth Green House, The Green House Market, Station Road, Letchworth Garden City, Hertfordshire

Maidstone: Hops n Harvest Beer Festival, Kent Life, Lock Lane, Sandling, Maidstone, Kent

Melton Mowbray Beer Festival, Melton Mowbray Market Banqueting Suite, Scalford Road, Melton Mowbray, Leicestershire

Nantwich Beer Festival, Nantwich Cricket Club, Whitehouse Lane, Nantwich, Cheshire

Northwich Beer Festival, Winnington Park Recreation Club, Park Road, Winnington, Northwich, Cheshire

Redcar Beer Festival at Redcar Rocks Festival, Turned In, Majuba Road, Redcar, North Yorkshire

St Albans Beer & Cider Festival, Alban Arena, Civic Centre, St Albans, Hertfordshire

St Ives: 'Booze on the Ouse' Beer & Cider Festival, Burgess Hall, St Ivo Recreation Centre, Westwood Road, St Ives, Cambridgeshire

Saltaire Beer Festival, Saltaire Brewery, County Workshops, Dockfield Road, Shipley, West Yorkshire

Southport & West Lancs Beer Festival, St Johns Hall, Liverpool Road, Ainsdale, Southport, Lancashire

Tamworth Beer Festival, Assembly Rooms, Corporation Street, Tamworth, Staffordshire

York Beer & Cider Festival, York Knavesmire, York

OCTOBER

Ascot Beer Festival, Ascot Racecourse, High Street, Ascot, Berkshire

Ayrshire Real Ale Festival, Troon Concert Hall, South Beach Ayr Street, Troon, South Ayrshire

Basingstoke: Hampshire's Octoberfest, Milestones Museum, West Ham Leisure Park, Churchill Way West, Basingstoke, Hampshire

Bath: Wessex Beer Festival, The Court Hotel, Chilcompton, Somerset

Birmingham Beer & Cider Festival, Second City Suite, 100 Sherlock Street, Birmingham, West Midlands

Huddersfield Oktoberfest Beer & Cider Festival, Sikh Leisure Centre, Prospect Street, Springfield, Huddersfield, West Yorkshire

Milton Keynes: Concrete Pint Beer Festival, The Buszy, 401 Elder Gate, Central Milton Keynes, Buckinghamshire

Norwich Beer Festival, St Andrews Hall, St Andrews Plain, Norwich, Norfolk

Nottingham Robin Hood Beer & Cider Festival, Nottingham Castle, Nottingham

Redhill Beer Festival, Merstham Village Hall, Station Road North, Merstham, Surrey

Richmond Ale Festival, Richmond Market Hall, Richmond, North Yorkshire

Sheffield: Steel City Beer & Cider Festival, Ponds Forge, Sheaf Street, Sheffield, South Yorkshire

Solihull Beer Festival, Solihull Royal British Legion, Union Road, Solihull, West Midlands

Stoke Beer & Cider Festival, Fenton Manor Sports Complex, City Road, Stoke-on-Trent, Staffordshire

Twickenham Beer & Cider Festival, York House, Richmond Road, Twickenham, London

Wallington: Croydon & Sutton Beer & Cider Festival, Wallington Hall, 3A Stafford Road, Wallington, Surrey

Weymouth Octoberfest, Weymouth Pavilion, The Esplanade, Weymouth, Dorset

Worthing Beer Festival, St Pauls Centre, Chapel Road, Worthing, West Sussex

NOVEMBER

Dudley Winter Ales Fayre, Dudley Town Hall, St James's Road, Dudley, West Midlands

Heathrow Beer Festival, Concorde Club, Crane Lodge Road, Cranford, Middlesex

Rochford Beer & Cider Festival, Freight House, Bradley Way, Rochford, Essex

Shrewsbury Beer Festival, Morris Hall, Bellstone, Shrewsbury, Shropshire

Watford Beer Festival, West Herts Sports Club, 8 Park Avenue, Watford, Hertfordshire

Whitchurch Beer Festival, Whitchurch Longmeadow Sports & Social Club, Winchester Road, Whitchurch, Hampshire

Woking Beer Festival, Woking Leisure Centre, Kingfield Road, Woking, Surrey

DECEMBER

Harwich & Dovercourt Bay Winter Ale Festival, Kingsway Hall, Dovercourt, Essex

London: Pig's Ear Beer Festival, The Round Chapel, Powerscroft Road, Hackney, London

SPECIALIST BOTTLE AND ALE SHOPS

* internet/mail order delivery available across the UK
** mail order available only locally

SOUTH WEST AND WEST COUNTRY

Best Cellars
42 The Square
Chagford
Devon TQ13 8AH
01647 432262

Brewers Droop
36 Gloucester Road
Bristol BS7 8AR
0117 9427923

Coombe Bissett Stores and Post Office
Homington Road
Coombe Bissett
Wiltshire SP5 4LR
01722 718852
shop@coombebissettstores.co.uk

Corks of Cotham
54 Cotham Hill
Bristol BS6 6JX
0117 9731 620

Gardiner Haskins
Straight Street
Bristol BS2 0JP
0117 929 2288

Grape and Grind
101 Gloucester Road
Bristol BS7 8AT
01179248718

Independent Spirit of Bath
7 Terrace Walk
Bath BA1 1LN
01225 340636
www.independentspiritofbath.co.uk

Kernow Harvest
Eddystone Road
Wadebridge
Cornwall PL27 7AL
01208 816123

Open Bottles
131 Taunton Road
Bridgwater
Somerset TA6 6BD
01278 459666

Phoenix Wines
51 Station Road
Swanage
Dorset BH19 1AD
01929 423006

Shaftesbury Wines
57 High Street
Shaftesbury
Dorset SP7 8JE
01747 850 059

Supersave Wine
99 Poole Road
Westbourne
Bournemouth
Dorset BH4 9BB
01202 767 190

Teign Cellars*
3 Union St
Newton Abbot
Devon TQ12 2JX
01626 332991
www.teigncellars.co.uk

The Bottle Bank*
2 Tidemill House
Discovery Quay
Falmouth TR11 3XP
www.bottlebankwine.co.uk

Trumps of Sidmouth
36 Fore St
Sidmouth
Devon EX10 8AQ
01395 512446

Tuckers Maltings
Brewery Meadow
Stonepark
Ashburton
Devon TQ13 7DG
01364 652403
www.edwintucker.com

Wadebridge Wines*
Eddystone Road
Wadebridge
Cornwall PL27 7AL
01208 812692
www.wadebridgewines.co.uk

West Country Ales*
The Cliffs
Cheddar Gorge
Cheddar
Somerset BS27 3QA
01934 742435
www.westcountryales.co.uk

Whistle Wines
2 Central Station Buildings
Queen Street
Exeter EX4 3SB
01392 421363;
(mob) 07753 743 921

LONDON AND SOUTH EAST

Ales by Mail*
Image House
34 Radford Way
Billericay
Essex CM12 0DX
01277 523003
www.alesbymail.co.uk

Beer Boutique*
134 Upper Richmond Road
Putney
London SW15 2SP
020 8780 3168
www.thebeerboutique.co.uk

The Bitter End
139 Masons Hill
Bromley
Kent BR2 9HW
020 8466 6083
www.thebitterend.biz

The Bottled Ale Company Limited*
Newcourt House
Pretoria Road
Halstead
Essex CO9 2EG
adam@bottled-ale.co.uk
www.bottled-ale.co.uk

The Bottle Shop
The Goods Shed
Station Road West
Canterbury
Kent CT2 8AN
07515 398 685
www.bottle-shop.co.uk

Kris Wines
394 York Way
London N7 9LW
020 7607 487
www.kriswines.com

Mr Lawrence Wine Merchant*
391 Brockley Road
London SE4 2PH
0208 692 1550
www.mrlawrencewinemerchant.co.uk

Onlyfinebeer
The Vineyard
Crix Green
Felsted
Essex CM6 3JT
01245 362950
www.onlyfinebeer.co.uk

Real Ale Ltd**
371 Richmond Road
Twickenham
Middlesex TW1 2EF
020 8892 3710
www.realale.com

Utobeer
Borough Market
Southwark Street
London SE1 1TL
020 7378 9461
www.utobeer.co.uk

REST OF THE SOUTH

Trafalgar Wines
23 Trafalgar Street
Brighton and Hove
East Sussex BN1 4EQ
01273 683325

EAST OF ENGLAND

Bacchanalia
79 Victoria Road
Cambridge CB4 3BS
01223 576292
www.winegod.co.uk

Beautiful Beers
1 St John's Street
Bury St Edmunds
Suffolk IP33 1SQ
01284 767205
www.beautifulbeers.co.uk

Beers of Europe
Garage Lane
Setchey
Kings Lynn
Norfolk PE33 0BE
01553 812000

The Little Beer Shop
(smallest off-licence in the world)
58 Yarmouth Road
Blofield
Norwich NR13 4LQ
01603 717197
www.littlebeershop.co.uk

MIDLANDS

Alexander Wines
112 Berkeley Road South
Earlsdon
Coventry CV5 6EE
020 7667 3474
@Alexanderwines

Stirchley Wines & Spirits
1535/1537 Pershore Road
Birmingham B30 2JH
0121 459 9936
www.stirchleywines.co.uk

The Offie*
142 Clarendon Park Road
Leicester LE2 3AE
01509 413970 (day);
0116 2701553 (evening)
www.the-offie.co.uk

NORTH OF ENGLAND

Ake & Humphris
32 Leeds Road
Harrogate
North Yorkshire HG2 8BQ
01423566009
www.wineways.co.uk

Archer Road Beer Stop
57 Archer Road
Sheffield

South Yorkshire S8 0JT
0114 2551356

Beer-Ritz*
14 Weetwood Lane
Leeds LS16 5LX
0113 275 3464
www.beeritz.co.uk

Crafty Pint
59/60 Market Hall
Darlington
Co. Durham DL1 5PZ
07804 305175
www.thecraftypint.co.uk

The Dram Shop
21 Commonside
Walkley
Sheffield S10 1GA
0800 048 8469
www.offlicencesheffield.com

DrinksWell
34 Old Market Place
Ripon
North Yorkshire HG4 1BZ
01765 607766
info@drinkswell.co.uk

Gluggles
9 Goodramgate
York YO1 7LW
01904 675027
www.gluggles.co.uk

Grassington Wine Shop**
13 Main Street
Grassington
Skipton
North Yorkshire BD23 5AD
01756 754468

The Red Shed
(on-premises drinking/members only
– beers change daily)
Wakefield Labour Club
18 Vicarage Street South
Wakefield
West Yorkshire WF1 1QX
01924 215626
www.theredshed.org.uk

Roberts & Speight
40 Norwood
Town Centre
Beverley
East Yorkshire HU17 9EY
01482 870717
www.hamperbox.co.uk

Trembling Madness Ltd
48 Stonegate
York YO1 8AS
01904 640009; (mob) 7751 851143
info@tremblingmadness.co.uk

York Beer and Wine Shop
28 Sandringham Street
Fishergate
York YO1O 4BA

01904 647136
www.yorkbeerandwineshop.co.uk

WALES

Discount Supermarket
97–99 Whitchurch Road
Cardiff CF14 3JP
02920 619049
sales@discountsupermarketcardiff.c
o.uk

SCOTLAND

The Scottish Real Ale Shop
The Lade Inn
Kilmahog
Callander
Perthshire FK17 8DN
01877 330152
www.scottishrealAles.com
info@theladeinn.com

ONLINE ONLY

www.beerbarrels2u.co.uk/
www.beersofeurope.co.uk
www.beermerchants.com
www.drinkfinder.co.uk

WHOLESALE

Cave Direct Ltd
Unit B10, Larkfield Trading Estate
New Hythe Lane
Larkfield
Kent ME20 6SW
01622 710 339
info@cavedirect.com
www.cavedirect.com

Beer Paradise
Unit 20, Centre Park,
Marston Moor Business Park,
Tockwith
York YO26 7QF
01423 359533
01423 359534 (fax)
www.beerparadise.co.uk

Utobeer Ltd
14 Winchester Walk
London SE1 9AG
020 7378 9461
www.utobeer.co.uk

HOME-BREW SUPPLIES

HOME-BREW SHOPS

UK

Abbey Beer & Winemaking Supplies
205 Lockwood Road
Huddersfield
West Yorkshire HD1 3TG
01484 430691

Abbey Home Brew
Wren Lane
Church Hill
Selby
North Yorkshire
01757 210752

Abbey Home Brew
8 Commercial Road
Kirkstall
Leeds LS5 3AQ
0113 278 2459

Aberdeen Home Brew
122 King Street
Aberdeen AB2 3BB
01224 634425

Abertawe Homebrew
306 Llangyfelach Road
Swansea SA5 9LG
01792 650388

Allan's Home Brew Corner
6 Beaumont Road
Middlesbrough
Cleveland TS3 6NL
01642 247990

The Ark
11 Quay Street
Haverfordwest
Pembrokeshire SA61 1BG
01437 767499
info@thearkhaverfordwest.co.uk

Arkwrights
114 The Dormers
Highworth
Swindon
Wiltshire SN6 7PE
01793 765071

Art of Brewing
D8 Barwell Business Park
Leatherhead Road
Chessington
Surrey KT9 2NY
020 8397 2111

B & J Homebrew
8 Gloucester Street
Stroud
Gloucestershire GL5 1QG
01453 757282

Barr's Homebrew
Stall F145
Birkenhead Market
Birkenhead
Merseyside
0151 334 5393

Beercraft
72a High Street
Frodsham
Cheshire WA6 7HE
07807 444628
beercraft@hotmail.co.uk
www.beercraft.co.uk

Beers Unlimited
500 London Road
Westcliff-on-Sea
Essex SS0 9LD
01702 345474

Betterbrew
8 Corporation Street
Rotherham
South Yorkshire S60 1NG
01709 369278

Bilston Homebrew
5 High Street
Bilston
West Midlands WV14 0EH
01902 490803
www.bilstonhomebrew.co.uk

Birkenhead Health Shop
34 Oxton Road
Birkenhead
Merseyside CH41 2QJ
0151 652 1927

Bolton Homebrew
9K Longcauseway
Bolton
Lancashire BL4 9BS
07969 842923

Brew2Bottle
75 London Road
Northwich
Cheshire CW9 5HQ

01606 359137
www.brew2bottle.co.uk

Brew Barn
Abbeypark Steading
Templehall
Eyemouth
Berwickshire TD14 5QA
018907 71794
www.thebrewbarn.co.uk

Brewer Bill
111 Retail Market
Queen Victoria Road
Coventry
West Midlands CV1 3HT
024 7655 0876

Brewers Droop
36a Gloucester Road
Bristol BS7 8AR
0117 942 7923

BrewGenie
46 Wellington Market
Market Street
Wellington
Telford
Shropshire TF1 1HG
01952 605594
www.brewgenie.com

Brew In
Watermill Studio
Tonge Mill

Church Road
Sittingbourne
Kent ME9 9AP
01795 421911

Brewing is Us
Birch Farm
Birts Street
Birtsmorton
Malvern
Worcestershire WR13 6AW
07879 853811

Brewing Supplies
48 Buxton Road
Stockport SK2 6NB
0161 480 4880
websales@thebrewshop.com
www.thebrewshop.com

Brew King
910 Leeds Road
Bradford
West Yorkshire BD3 8EZ
01274 669577

Brewmart
2 Abbey Lane
Sheffield S8 0BL
0117 274 6850
www.thebrewmart.com

Brew Shop
2 Riverside Cottages
Watten

Wick
Caithness KW1 5UQ
01955 621941

The Brewstore
61 South Clerk Street
Edinburgh EH8 9PP
0131 667 1296
shop@brewstore.co.uk
www.brewstore.co.uk

Brew UK
Unit 11, Portway Business Centre
Salisbury
Wiltshire SP4 6QX
0844 736 2672
greg@brewuk.co.uk
www.brewuk.co.uk

Brewtopia
20 Silver Street
Bury
Lancashire BL9 0EX
0161 7977698

Burghley Homebrew
Calamity Gulch
Bridge Hill Road
Newborough
Peterborough PE6 7SA
01733 810259
lesrands@freenetname.co.uk
www.burghley-homebrew.com

**Butterworths Health Food &
Herbs**
9 The Traverse
Bury St Edmunds
Suffolk IP33 1BJ
01284 755410
www.butterworths-healthfoods.co.uk

Colchester Home Brew
Unit C4, The Seedbed Centre
Wyncolls Road
Colchester
Essex CO4 9HT
01206 854457
andy@colchesterhomebrew.co.uk
www.colchesterhomebrew.co.uk

Charles Faram & Co. Ltd
The Hopstore
Monksfield Lane
Newland
Nr Malvern
Worcester
WR13 5BB
01905 830734
www.charlesfaram.co.uk

Cheers Home Brew
26 Derby Rd
Nottingham NG10 1PD
0115 972 6716

Cheers Wine Online
19a Newbottle Street
Haughton-le-Spring

Tyne & Wear DH4 4AP
0191 584 5055
wine-on-line@hotmail.co.uk
www.wine-on-line.com

Creative Wine Making
77 Sitwell Street
Derby DE21 7FH
01332 280094

Dixons Shopping Centre Home Brew
The Dixon Centre
157–159 Reepham Road
Norwich
Norfolk NR6 5PA
01603 429186
www.houseproudshop.co.uk

Dorset Homebrew
Wimborne Market Riverside
Industrial Park
Wimborne
Dorset BH21 1QU
07858 294815
www.dorsethomebrew.co.uk/shop

Eastgate Homebrew
48 Eastgate Street
Stafford ST16 2LY
01342 836457
mail@eastgatehomebrew.co.uk
www.eastgatehomebrew.co.uk

East Grinstead Home Brew
Unit 3, 1–11 East Grinstead Road
Lingfield
Surrey RH7 6EP
01342 836457
info@eastgrinsteadhomebrew.co.uk
www.eastgrinsteadhomebrew.co.uk

Easy Homebrew
Unit 19, Connect 10 Business Park
Foster Road
Ashford
Kent TN24 0SH
01233 503222
sales@easyhomebrew.co.uk
www.easyhomebrew.co.uk

Elderberry
28 Station Road
Whitley Bay
Tyne and Wear NE26 2RD
0191 251 3907
algough@blueyonder.co.uk

Flagon & Cask Homebrew Centre
202 Main Street
Nottingham NG6 8EH
0115 8220431

Geoff's Homebrew Centre
47a Cross Street
Camborne
Cornwall TR14 8ET
01209 715708

Goodlife Homebrew Centre
3 Barrow Close
Sweetbriar Industrial Estate
Norwich NR3 2AT
01508 489 584
sales@goodlifehomebrew.com
www.goodlifehomebrew.com

Hamstead Brewing Centre
37 Newton Road
Birmingham
West Midlands B43 6AD
0121 358 6800
www.hamstead-brewing-centre.co.uk

The Happy Brewer
15 Union Street
Bedford
MK40 2SF
01234 353856
contactus@thehappybrewer.com
www.thehappybrewer.com

Headington Homewares
The Parade
Windmill Road
Headington
Oxford OX3 7BL
01865 763258
www.headingtonhomewares.co.uk

The Home Brew Centre
250 Freeman Street
Grimsby
Lincolnshire DN32 9DR

01472 343435
homebrew.centre@ntlworld.com
www.homebrewcentregy.com

Homebrew and Hardware
2 O'Connell Walk
Wednesbury
West Midlands WS10 7BF
0121 270 9023

Homebrew Crew
141 Donald Street
Cardiff CF24 4TN
029 20496547
info@homebrewcrew.co.uk
homebrewcrew.co.uk

Home Brewing Centre
35 High Street
Keynsham
Bristol BS30 1DS
0117 986 8568
info@homebrewcentre.co.uk
www.homebrewcentre.co.uk

Home Brew Kits
329 Oldham Road
Middleton
Manchester M24 2DN
0161 287 0987
diane.lewis@ntlbusiness.com
www.homebrewkits.co.uk

The Home Brew Shop
Unit 2, Blackwater Trading Estate

Blackwater Way
Aldershot
Hampshire GU12 4DJ
01252 540386
homebrewshop@btconnect.co.uk
www.the-home-brew-shop.co.uk

The Home Brew Shop
4–6 Frinton Road
Holland-on-Sea
Essex CO15 5UL
0845 8738076
homebrewshop1@btconnect.com
www.homebrew2u.co.uk

Hop & Grape
117–119 North Road
Darlington
Co. Durham DL1 2PS
01325 380780
enquiries@hopandgrape.co.uk
www.hopandgrape.co.uk

Hop Inn
Basingstoke Road
Reading
Berkshire RG7 1AP
0118 988 5155
www.hopinnofflicence.co.uk
(Real Ale off-licence too)

The Hoppy Brewer
17 Clos Pencarreg
(Aberaeron Craft Centre)
Aberaeron

Ceredigion SA46 0DX
01545 574944

Hops and Vines
38 Corn Street
Witney
Oxfordshire OX28 6BS
01993 708112
info@hopsandvineshomebrew.co.uk

Hop Shop
22 Dale Road
Mutley
Plymouth
Devon PL4 6PE
01752 660382
sales@hopshopuk.com
www.hopshopuk.com

Inn House Brewery
718 Dumbarton Road
Partick
Glasgow G11 6RB
0141 339 3479
glenbrew@btconnect.com
www.innhousebrewery.co.uk

JASS Brewing Supplies
Scarborough Market Hall
St Helens Square
Scarborough YO11 1EU
07920 485711
mfd@live.co.uk

Johnson Homewine Supplies Ltd
2 Gratwicke Road
Worthing
West Sussex BN11 4BH
01903 233832
info@brewathome.co.uk
www.brewathome.co.uk

Jolly Brewer
1 The Avenue
Kidsgrove
Stoke-on-Trent ST7 1AD
01782 776655
info@thejollybrewersot.co.uk
www.thejollybrewersot.co.uk

JP Homebrew
83 Newport Road
New Bradwell
Milton Keynes MK13 0AJ
01908 223328
jphomebrew@aol.com
www.jphomebrew-store.co.uk

Lance Lane Pharmacy
99 Woolton Road
Liverpool L15 6TB
0151 7221920
lancelane@trihealthpharmacy.co.uk
www.comparethebeerkit.com

Leominster Home Brews
99 Woolton Road
Liverpool L15 6TB
0151 7221920
leominster@brewingathome.co.uk

www.brewingathome.co.uk/
leominster.htm

Leyland Home Brew
15 Chapel Brow
Leyland
Lancashire PR25 3NH
01772 431030
Fax: 01772 451928
joe@leylandhomebrew.com
www.leylandhomebrew.com/

Liquid Assets
183 High Street
Honiton
Devon EX14 8LQ
01404 43280

Love to Brew
7 Brislington Hill
Bristol BS4 5BE
0117 9710925
www.lovetobrew.co.uk

Maidstone Winemaking Centre
53 Hardy Street
Maidstone
Kent ME14 2SJ
01622 677619

Matchless Home Brewing
48 Belvoir Road
Coalville
Leicestershire LE67 3PP
01530 813800

Mattock Lane Pharmacy
8 St Johns Parade
Mattock Lane
Ealing
London W13 9LL
020 8567 9153

May & Brett
23 High Street
Dunmow
Essex CM6 1AD
08712 227805
beer-wine@mayandbrett.co.uk
www.brewingshop.co.uk

Millfield Home Brew
115 Millfield Lane
York YO1 3AP
01904 415569
yorkhomebrew@btconnect.com

Modern Grates Co.
4 Barn Street
Liskeard
Cornwall PL14 4BJ
01579 342050
www.moderngratesco-cornwall.co.uk

Morley Home Brew Centre
47a Queen Street
Morley
Leeds LS27 8EE
01132 537688
info@morleyhomebrewcentre.com
www.morleyhomebrewcentre.com

Murphy & Sons
Alpine Street
Nottingham NG6 0HQ
0115 9785494

North Devon Homebrews
50 Bear Street
Barnstaple
Devon EX32 7DB
01271 342549
orders@bearstreetpharmacy.co.uk
www.brewingathome.co.uk

Overt Locke
West Street
Somerton
Somerset TA11 7PS
01458 556434
www.beer-kits.co.uk

Pops Homebrew
10 Grosvenor Street
Cheltenham
Gloucestershire GL52 2SG
01242 232426
mat@popshomebrew.com
www.popshomebrew.com

Quay Side Easy Brew
Londis on The Quay
The Quay
Exeter
Devon EX2 4AB
01392 202251
www.quaysidehomebrew.co.uk

Redcar Home Brew
2a Redcar Lane
Redcar
Cleveland TS10 3JF
01642 484928

Shop 4 Homebrew
42 Zoar Street
Lower Gornal
Dudley
West Midlands DY3 2PA
01384 253073
info@shop4homebrew.co.uk
www.shop4homebrew.co.uk

Simply Natural
26 Poulton Street
Preston
Lancashire PR4 2AB
01772 671489
www.simplynatural.org.uk

Specialist Homebrew Supplies
105–106 High Street
Swansea SA4 4BP
01792 899449/07976 269848
www.specialisthomebrew.co.uk

Spitting Feathers
198 Tonge Moor Road
Bolton BL2 2HN
01204 535217
admin@spitting-feathers.co.uk
www.spitting-feathers.co.uk

Spitting Feathers
50 Gidlow Lane
Wigan
Greater Manchester WN6 0J2
(contact as above)

Stonehelm
The Croft
Marsh Baldon
Oxford OX44 9LN
01865 343275
01865 343394 (fax)
info@stonehelm.co.uk
www.stonehelm.co.uk

Stroud Homebrew
8 Gloucester Street
Stroud
Gloucester GL5 1QG
01453 757282
info@Stroudhomebrew.co.uk
www.stroudhomebrew.co.uk

Sunlit Chemist
Unit 16, Town Square
Syston
Leicestershire LE7 1GZ
0116 260 2695

Sylken Homebrew
153 Bells Road
Gorleston
Great Yarmouth
Norfolk NR31 6AN
01453 757282

sales@norfolkhomebrew.co.uk
www.norfolkhomebrew.co.uk

Taylors Homebrew Supplies
287 Tong Street
Bradford
West Yorkshire BS4 9QJ
01274 918249

Things To Brew
Unit 21, Kershaws Garden Centre
Halifax Road
Brighouse
West Yorkshire HD6 2QD
01484 401423
info@thingstobrew.co.uk
www.thingstobrew.co.uk

Wellingborough and Kettering Health Foods
22 Silver Street
Wellingborough
Northants NN8 1AY
01604 552696

Worcester Hop Shop
Hillside
Withybed Lane
Inkberrow
Worcestershire WR7 4JL
01386 792407
www.worcesterhopshop.co.uk

ONLINE ONLY

Balihoo: www.balliihoo.co.uk
The Malt Miller: themaltmiller.co.uk – highly recommended
Whytes Home Wine Equipment: whyteshomewineequipment.co.uk

IRELAND

Glengarrif Homebrew Centre
Lough Avaul Farm
Glengarriff
Co. Cork
00 352 276 3444

The Homebrew Company
20 Brockview
Mountmellick
Co. Laoise
087 236 9598
sales@thehomebrewcompany.ie
www.thehomebrewcompany.ie

AUSTRALIA

Country Brewer
1/148 Toongabbie Road
Girraween
New South Wales 2145
02 98961366
girraween@countrybrewer.com.au
www.countrybrewer.com.au

Malthouse Brew Supplies
45 Welshpool Road
Welshpool
Western Australia 6106
+618 9361 6424
www.malthouse.com.au

NEW ZEALAND

Aqua-Vitae
268 Lincoln Road
Addington
Christchurch
www.aquavitae.co.nz

Brewcraft
19 Mount Eden Road
Mount Eden
Auckland
www.brewcraft.co.nz

USA

Home Sweet Homebrew
2008 Sansom Street
Philadelphia
PA 19103
info@homesweethomebrew.com
www.homesweethomebrew.com

HomeBrew USA – Norfolk
(The Shops at JANAF)
5802 E. Virginia Beach Blvd. #115
Norfolk

VA 23502
+1 757 459-BREW
brewshop@homebrewusa.com
www.homebrewusa.com

HomeBrew USA – Hampton
96 West Mercury Blvd
Hampton
VA 23669
+1 757 788 8001
brewshop@homebrewusa.com
www.homebrewusa.com

Karp's Homebrew Shop
2 Larkfield Road
East Northport
NY 11731
+1 631 261 1235
sales@homebrewshop.com
www.homebrewshop.com

The Weekend Brewer
4205 West Hundred Road
Chester
VA 23831
+1 804 796 9760
orders@weekendbrewer.com
www.weekendbrewer.com

BREWERIES

This is not an extensive list of all the UK's breweries. For that you can visit the excellent site www.quaffale.org.uk, home of a regularly updated database of every brewery in the country, along with a map to help you find them. Instead, this is a guide to all the breweries I have mentioned.

AllGates
The Old Brewery
Brewery Yard
Off Wallgate
Wigan
Greater Manchester WN1 1JU
01942 234976
www.allgatesbrewery.com
@allgatesbrewery

Anarchy Brew Co.
Unit 5, Whitehouse Farm Centre
Stannington
Morpeth
Northumberland NE61 6AW
01670 789755
@AnarchyBrewCo

Arbor Ales
Unit 4

Lawrence Hill Industrial Park
Croydon Street
Bristol BS5 0EB
0117 329 2711
www.arborales.co.uk
@arborales

Ashley Down Brewery
15 Wathen Road
Bristol BS6 5BY
0117 983 6567

B&T
(formerly **Banks and Taylor**)
The Brewery
Shefford
Bedfordshire
SG17 5DZ
01462 815080/816789
www.banksandtaylor.com

Bank Top Brewery
The Pavillion
Ashworth Lane
Bolton
Greater Manchester BL1 8RA
01204 595800
www.banktopbrewery.com

Batch Brew
17 Sussex Street
Winchester
Hampshire SO23 8TG
07917 035625
batchbrew.co.uk

Bath Ales
Units 3–7, Caxton Industrial Estate
Crown Way
Warmley
Bristol BS30 8XJ
0117 947 4797
www.bathales.com
@bathales

Beartown Brewery
Bromley House
Spindle Street
Congleton
Cheshire CW12 1QN
01260 299964
www.beartownbrewery.co.uk
@beartownbrewery

Beavertown
Unit 4, Stour Road

Fish Island
London E3 2NT
02030060794
www.beavertownbrewery.co.uk
@BeavertownBeer

Black Isle Brewery Co.
Old Allangrange
Munlochy
Ross-shire IV8 8NZ
01463 811871
www.blackislebrewery.com
@BlackIsleBeer

Black Sheep Brewery
Wellgarth
Crosshills
Masham
Ripon
North Yorkshire HG4 4EN
01765 689227
www.blacksheepbrewery.co.uk
@blacksheepbeer

Box Steam Brewery
Box Brewery Ltd
The Midlands
Holt
Trowbridge
Wiltshire BA14 6RU
01225 782700
www.boxsteambrewery.com

Brentwood Brewing Co.
Frieze Hall Farm

Coxtie Green Road
South Weald
Brentwood
Essex CM14 5RE
01277 375577
www.brentwoodbrewing.co.uk
@BrentwoodBrewCo

BrewDog
Balmacassie
Industrial Estate
Ellon
Aberdeenshire AB41 8BX
01358 724 924
www.brewdog.com
@brewdog

Butcombe Brewery
Havyat Road Trading Estate
Havyat Road
Wrington
Bristol BS40 5PA
01934 863963
www.butcombe.com
@butcombebrewery

The Canterbury Ales
Canterbrew Ltd
Unit 7, Stour Valley Business Park
Ashford Road
Chartham
Canterbury
Kent CT4 7HF
01227 732541
www.canterbury-ales.co.uk

Dark Star Brewing Co.
Unit 22, Star Road Trading Estate
Star Road
Partridge Green
Horsham
West Sussex RH13 8RA
01403 713085
www.darkstarbrewing.co.uk
@darkstarbrewco

Exmoor Ales
The Brewery
Golden Hill
Wiveliscombe
Taunton
TA4 2NY
01984 623798
www.exmoorales.co.uk

Fuller, Smith and Turner
Griffin Brewery
Chiswick Lane South
London W4 2QB
020 8996 2000
www.fullers.co.uk

George Wright Brewery
11 Diamond Business Park
Sandwash Close
Rainford Industrial Estate
Rainford
St Helens
Lancashire WA11 8LU
08444 145886
www.georgewrightbrewing.co.uk
www.quaffale.org.uk/php/menu/h

Grain Brewery
South Farm
Alburgh
Harleston
Norfolk IP20 0BS
01986 788884
www.grainbrewery.co.uk
@grainbrewery

Great Oakley Brewery
Ark Farm
High Street South
Tiffield
Northamptonshire NN12 8AB
01327 351759
www.greatoakleybrewery.co.uk

Harviestoun Brewery Ltd
Hillfoots Business Village
Alva Industrial Estate
Alva
Clackmannanshire FK12 5DQ
01259 769100
www.harviestoun.com
@harviestounbrew

Highland Brewing Co.
Swannay Brewery
by Evie
Orkney
KW17 2NP
01856 721 700
www.highlandbrewingcompany.co.uk
@HighlandBrewCo

Hop Back Brewery
Units 22–24, Batten Road Industrial
Estate
Downton
Salisbury
Wiltshire SP5 3HU
01725 510 986
www.hopback.co.uk
@HopBackBrewery

Humpty Dumpty Brewery
Church Road
Reedham
Norwich NR13 3TZ
01493 701818
www.humptydumptybrewery.co.uk
@hdbrewery

Ilkley Brewery Company
The New Brewery
40 Ashlands Road
Ilkley
North Yorkshire LS29 8JT
01943 604604
www.ikleybrewery.co.uk
@Ilkleybrewery

JW Lees
Greengate Brewery
Middleton Junction
Manchester M24 2AX
0161 643 2487
www.jwlees.co.uk
@ JWLeesBrewery

Kelham Island Brewery
23 Alma Street
Sheffield S3 8SA
0114 249 4804
www.kelhambrewery.co.uk
@KelhamBrewery

The Kernel Brewery
Arch 11, Dockley Road Industrial
Estate
Dockley Road
London SE16 3SF
www.thekernelbrewery.com
@kernelbrewery

Kirkstall Brewery
Unit 6, Canal Wharf
Wyther Lane
Leeds LS5 3BT
0113 345 8835
www.kirkstallbrewerycompany.com/
@kirkstallbrew

Loddon Brewery
Dunsden Green Farm
Church Lane
Dunsden
Oxfordshire RG4 9QD
0118 948 1111
www.loddonbrewery.com
@ loddonbrewery

Lymestone Brewery
The Old Brewery
Mount Road

Stone
Staffordshire ST15 8LL
01785 817796
www.lymestonebrewery.co.uk
@lymestonebrewer

Magic Rock Brewing Co.
The Bed Factory
Quarmby Mills
Tanyard Road
Oakes
Huddersfield
West Yorkshire HD3 4YP
01484 649823
@magicrockbrewco

Marston's
Marston's House
Brewery Road
Wolverhampton
West Midlands WV1 4JT
01902 711811
www.marstons.co.uk
@MarstonsBeers

Moor Beer
Chapel Court
Pitney
Somerset TA10 9AE
07887 556 521
www.moorbeer.co.uk
@drinkmoorbeer

Mordue
D1/D2, Narvik Way
Tyne Tunnel Trading Estate
North Shields
Tyne & Wear NE29 7XJ
0191 296 1879
www.morduebrewery.com
@Morduebrewery

Oakham Ales
2 Maxwell Road
City of Peterborough
Peterborough
Cambridgeshire PE2 7JB
01733 370500
www.oakhamales.com
@OakhamAles

Oakleaf Brewing Company
Unit 7/9, Clarence Wharf Industrial
Estate
Mumby Road
Gosport
Hampshire PO12 1AJ
023 9251 3222
www.oakleafbrewing.co.uk

Oldershaw Brewery
Heath Lane
Barkston Heath
Grantham
Lincolnshire G32 2DE
01476 572 135
www.oldershawbrewery.com
@oldbrew

Orkney Brewery
Sinclair Breweries Ltd
Cawdor
Nairnshire IV12 5XP
01667 404 555
www.sinclairbreweries.co.uk
@Orkneybrewery

Ossett Brewery
Kings Yard
Low Mill Road
Ossett
West Yorkshire WF5 8ND
01924 237160
www.ossett-brewery.co.uk
@ossettbrewery

Poppyland
Chesterfield Lodge
West Street
Cromer
Norfolk NR27 9DT
01263 513992
www.poppylandbeer.com
@cliff_bunny

Red Willow
Unit 5, Artillery House
Gunco Lane
Macclesfield
Cheshire SK11 7JL
01625 502315
www.redwillowbrewery.com
@tobymckenzie

Revolutions Brewing Co.
Unit B7,
Whitwood Enterprise Park
Speedwell Road
Whitwood
Castleford
West Yorkshire WF10 5PX
01977 552649
www.revolutionsbrewing.co.uk
@revolutionsbrew

Rockin' Robin
6 Pickering Street
Maidstone
Kent ME15 9RS
077 7998 6087

Rudgate Brewery
Unit 2, Centre Park
Marston Moor Business Park
Tockwith
York YO26 7QF
01423 358382
www.rudgatebrewery.co.uk
@rudgatebrewery

St Peter's Brewery
St Peter's Hall
Bungay
Suffolk NR35 1NQ
01986 782322
www.stpetersbrewery.co.uk
@StPetersBrewer

Saltaire Brewery Limited
The Brewery
County Works
Dockfield Road
Shipley
West Yorkshire BD17 7AR
01274 594959
www.saltairebrewery.co.uk
@SaltaireBrewery

Samuel Smith
High Street
Tadcaster
North Yorkshire LS24 9SB
01937 832225
www.samuelsmithsbrewery.co.uk

Sarah Hughes Brewery
Beacon Hotel
129 Bilston Street
Dudley
West Midlands DY3 1JE
01902 883381
www.sarahhughesbrewery.co.uk

Tap East
7 International Square
Westfield Stratford City
Montfichet Road
Olympic Park
London E20 1EE
0208 555 4467
@TapEast

Theakston Brewery
T&R Theakston Ltd
The Brewery
Masham
Ripon
North Yorkshire HG4 4YD
01765 680 000
www.theakstons.co.uk
@theakston1827

Thornbridge
Riverside Brewery
Buxton Road
Bakewell
Derbyshire DE45 1GS
01629 641000
www.thornbridgebrewery.co.uk
@thornbridge

Timothy Taylor & Co.
Knowle Spring Brewery
Keighley
West Yorkshire BD21 1AW
01535 603139
www.timothy-taylor.co.uk
@TimothyTaylors

Tiny Rebel
Unit 12A, Maesglas Industrial
Estate
Newport
Gwent NP20 2NN
01633 547378
www.tinyrebel.co.uk
@tinyRebelbrewco

Titanic Brewery Co.
Unit 5, Callender Place
Stoke-on-Trent
Staffordshire ST6 1JL
01782 823447
www.titanicbrewery.co.uk
@Titanic_Brewers

Traquair House Brewery
Traquair House
Innerleithen
Peeblesshire EH44 6PW
01896 830323
www.traquair.co.uk

Waen Brewery
Unit 7, Maesyllan Industrial
Estate
Llanidloes
Powys SY18 6YU
01686 627042
www.thewaenbrewery.co.uk
@TheWaenBrewery

The Wild Beer Co.
Lower Westcombe Farm
Evercreech
Somerset BA4 6ER
01749 838742
www.wildbeerco.com
@wildbeerco

Williams Bros Brewing Co.
New Alloa Brewery
Kelliebank

Alloa
Clackmannanshire FK10 1NU
01259 725511
www.williamsbrosbrew.com
@Williamsbrewery

Windsor & Eton
1 Vansittart Estate
Windsor
Berkshire SL4 1SE
01753 854075
www.webrew.co.uk
@WindsorEtonBrew

Wye Valley
Stoke Lacy
Herefordshire HR7 4HG
01885 490505
www.wyevalleybrewery.co.uk
@ WyeValleyBrew

WATER COMPANIES

Affinity Water Limited
(formerly Veolia Water East)
Mill Hill
Manningtree
Essex CO11 2AZ
0845 148 9288
Fax: 01206 399 210
www.affinitywater.co.uk

Albion Water Limited
Customer Services
Harpenden Hall
Southdown Road
Harpenden
Hertfordshire AL5 1TE
0845 604 2355
(customer helpline)
www.albionwater.co.uk

Anglian Water Services Ltd
(Anglian Water Group)
Anglian House
Ambury Road
Huntingdon
Cambridgeshire PE29 3NZ
01480 323 000

01480 323 115 (fax)
www.anglianwater.co.uk

Bristol Water plc
PO Box 218
Bridgwater Road
Bristol BS99 7AU
0117 966 5881
0117 963 3755 (fax)
www.bristolwater.co.uk

Cambridge Water plc
90 Fulbourn Road
Cambridge CB1 9JN
01223 706 050
www.cambridge-water.co.uk

**Cholderton & District Water
Company**
Estate Office
Cholderton
Salisbury
Wiltshire SP4 0DR
01980 629 203
01980 629 307 (fax)

Dee Valley Water plc
Packsaddle
Wrexham Road
Rhostyllen
Wrexham LL14 4EH
01978 846 946
01978 846 888 (fax)
www.deevalleywater.co.uk

Dwr Cymru Welsh Water
Pentwyn Road
Nelson,
Treharris
Mid Glamorgan CF46 6LY
0800 052 0145
www.dwrcymru.co.uk

Essex & Suffolk Water
(part of Northumbrian Water Ltd)
Sandon Valley House
Canon Barns Road
East Hanningfield
Essex CM3 8BD
01268 664 399
01268 664 397 (fax)
www.eswater.co.uk

Island Water Authorities
(Guernsey Water, Jersey Water,
Council of the Isles of Scilly & Isle
of Man Water Authority)
Mulcaster House
Westmount Road
St Helier
Jersey JE1 1DG

01534 707300
www.jerseywater.je

Northern Ireland Water
PO Box 1026
Belfast BT1 9DJ
08457 440088.
www.niwater.com

Portsmouth Water Ltd
PO Box 8
West Street
Havant
Hampshire PO9 1LG
02392 499 888
02392 453 632 (fax)
www.portsmouthwater.co.uk

Scottish Water
Castle House
6 Castle Drive
Carnegie Campus
Dunfermline
Fife KY11 8GG
0845 601 8855
www.scottishwater.co.uk

Sembcorp Bournemouth Water Ltd
George Jessel House
Francis Avenue
Bournemouth
Dorset BH11 8NX
01202 591 111
01202 597 022 (fax)
www.bwhwater.co.uk

Severn Trent Water Limited
Severn Trent Centre
PO Box 5309
Coventry CV3 9FH
024 7771 5000
www.severntrent.com

South East Water Ltd
Rocfort Road
Snodland
Kent ME6 5AH
0845 223 5111
01634 242 764 (fax)
www.southeastwater.co.uk

South Staffordshire Water plc
Green Lane
Walsall
West Midlands WS2 7PD
01922 638 282
01922 621 968 (fax)
www.south-staffs-water.co.uk

South West Water
PO Box 4762
Worthing
East Sussex BN11 9NT
0800 169 1144
www.southwestwater.co.uk

Sutton and East Surrey Water plc
London Road
Redhill
Surrey RH1 1LY
01737 772 000

01737 766 807 (fax)
www.waterplc.com

Thames Water
PO Box 286
Swindon
Wiltshire SN38 2RA
0845 9200 800
www.thameswater.co.uk

United Utilities
Haweswater House
Lingley Mere Business Park
Lingley Green Avenue
Great Sankey
Warrington WA5 3LP
01925 237 000
01925 237 066 (fax)
www.unitedutilities.com

Wessex Water
1 Clevedon Walk
Nailsea
Bristol BS48 1WA
0845 600 3 600
www.wessexwater.co.uk

Yorkshire Water
Western House
Halifax Road
Bradford BD6 2SZ
01274 692515
www.yorkshirewater.com

FURTHER READING

These are the books that have entertained, educated and influenced me and I hope that they do the same for you.

BOOKS

GENERAL

Avery, Zak, *500 Beers*, London: Apple Press, 2010

Beaumont, Steve, and Webb, Tim, *World Atlas of Beer*, London: Mitchell Beazley, 2012

Brown, Pete, *Hops and Glory: One Man's Search for the Beer that Built the British Empire*, London: Macmillan, 2009

Brown, Pete, *Man Walks Into a Pub: A Sociable History of Beer*, London: Macmillan, 2003

Campbell, Andrew, *The Book of Beer*, London: Dennis Dobson, 1956

Cole, Melissa, *Let Me Tell You About Beer*, London: Pavilion, 2011

Cornell, Martyn, *Amber Black and Gold: The History of Britain's Great Beers*, Stroud: The History Press, 2010

Cornell, Martyn, *Beer: The Story of the Pint*, London: Headline, 2002

Evans, Jeff, *The Book of Beer Knowledge: Essential Wisdom for the Discerning Drinker*, St Albans: CAMRA Books, 2011

Jackson, Michael, *Beer*, London/New York: DK Publishing, 2007

Oliver, Garrett, *The Oxford Companion to Beer*, New York: Oxford University Press, 2012

Tierney-Jones, Adrian, *1001 Beers to Try Before You Die*, London: Cassell, 2010

BREWING

Alexander, John, *A Guide to Craft Brewing*, Marlborough: The Crowood Press, 2006

Daniels, Ray, *Designing Great Beers: The Ultimate Guide to Brewing Classic Beer Styles*, Boulder, CO: Brewers Publications, 1996

Hamilton, Andy, *Booze for Free: The Definitive Guide to Beer*, London: Eden Project Books, 2011

Harrison, Dr John (and the members of the Durden Park Beer Circle), *Old British Beers and How to Make Them*, Durden Park: Durden Park Beer Circle, 2003

Hieronymus, Stan, *For the Love of Hops: The Practical Guide to Aroma, Bitterness and the Culture of Hops*, Boulder, CO: Brewers Publications, 2012

Line, David, *Brewing British-Style Beers: More Than 100 Thirst-Quenching Pub Recipes to Brew at Home*, East Petersburgh, PA: Fox Chapel Publishing, 2012

Mosher, Randy, *Radical Brewing: Recipes, Ales and World-Altering Meditations in a Glass*, Boulder, CO: Brewers Publications, 2004

Noonan, Gregory J., *New Brewing Lager Beer: The Most Comprehensive Book for Home and Microbrewers*, Boulder, CO: Brewers Publications, 1986

Palmer, John J., *How to Brew: Everything You Need to Know to Brew Beer Right First Time*, Boulder, CO: Brewers Publications, 2006

Sparrow, Jeff, *Wild Brews: Beer Beyond the Influence of Brewer's Yeast*, Boulder, CO: Brewers Publications, 2005

Strong, Gordon, *Brewing Better Beer: Master Lessons for Advanced Home Brewers*, Boulder, CO: Brewers Publications, 2011

White, Chris, and Zainasheff, Jamil, *Yeast: The Practical Guide to Beer Fermentation*, Boulder, CO: Brewers Publications, 2010

Woodske, Dan, *Hop Variety Handbook: Learn More about Hops, Craft Better Beer*, Beaver Falls, PA: Dan Woodske, 2012

Zainasheff, Jamil, and Palmer, John J., *Brewing Classic Styles: 80 Winning Recipes Anyone Can Brew*, Boulder, CO: Brewers Publications, 2007

ONLINE

As with all information, the most up to date can often be found online. Below are a few of my favourite websites, blogs and web forums. At the time of writing these were my go-to websites for the most up-to-date information about beer.

GENERAL BEER BLOGS AND WEBSITES

beerbrewer.blogspot.co.uk – organizer of Great Welsh Beer and Cider Festival.

beer-pages.com – online beer magazine.

beersay.wordpress.com

beertalk.wordpress.com – well-written blog from Cambridgeshire from 'a girl's point of view'.

bloodstoutandtears.blogspot.co.uk – beer blogging from South Wales. Photos and reviews of beers, all types, new and old.

www.camra.org.uk – official CAMRA site.

ghostdrinker.blogspot.co.uk – 'it's not all about the beer, I also have a degree in woodwork too, so I could probably make some casks for you'.

hopzine.com – enthusiastic beer blogger from up north.

maltworms.blogspot.co.uk – beer blog from the author of *1001 Beers to Try Before You Die* and good bloke Adrian Tierney-Jones.

pencilandspoon.com – Mark Dredge, beer blogger of the year.

pubdiaries.com – read and be inspired.

tandlemanbeerblog.blogspot.co.uk – a CAMRA veteran speaks his mind.

thebeerboy.blogspot.co.uk – Zak Avery, the man, the legend.

theotherandyhamilton.com – me, and I tend to write about foraging and other stuff as well as beer.

HOME-BREWING

andrewdrinks.blogspot.co.uk – a blog about beer, home-brewing and drinking.

beersmith.com/blog – US-based podcasts, brewiki, recipes from the makers of the most widely used brewing software.

broadfordbrewer.wordpress.com – Leeds-based home-brewer.

joshthebrewmaster.wordpress.com – experiments in home-brewing.

leedsbrew.wordpress.com – a useful and straightforward brewing blog.

pdtnc.wordpress.com – an excellent account of everything this home-brewer has brewed since 2009.

BEER REVIEWS

beeradvocate.com – multi-user reviews.

beerreviews.co.uk – more than just a beer-review site.

ratebeer.com – beer reviews with more of an international focus.

theormskirkbaron.com – podcast reviews.

real-ale-reviews.com – individual beers.

BEER HISTORY

breweryhistory.com – the Brewery History Society's site, 'for all who are interested in the history of beer and brewing'.

zythophile.wordpress.com – Martyn Cornell's meticulously researched site.

BEER-TASTING EVENTS

letmetellyouaboutbeer.co.uk – Melissa Cole, entertaining and informative for London and the South East.

school-of-booze.com – beer-tasting in London.

thebeerboy.blogspot.co.uk – Zak Avery, Leeds and the North.

theotherandyhamilton.com – me, Bristol and South West.

BEER WRITERS

The British Guild of Beer Writers – www.beerwriters.co.uk – a Who's Who in beer writing.

WEB FORUMS

brewuk.co.uk – web forum from the home-brew supplier making it easy to chat about the ingredients you buy.

homebrewtalk.com – once you realize that they are speaking their own version not just of English but of brewing terminology, this site becomes an invaluable resource.

jimsbeerkit.co.uk – very active and friendly forum.

thehomebrewforum.co.uk – another active UK web forum, great for the beginner.

HOME-BREWING CLUBS AND GROUPS

www.bristolbrewers.co.uk – BBC (Bristol Brewing Circle) and Bristol
   Craft Brewers
craftbrewing.org.uk – the Craft Brewing Association
communigate.co.uk/ne/dtbg/ – Darlington Shed Brewers
midlandscraftbrewing.org.uk – Midland Craft Brewers
northhantsbrewers.org.uk – North Hampshire Brewers
northerncraftbrewers.co.uk – Northern Craft Brewers
walesandwest.org.uk – Wales and West Federation of Wine and Beer
   Makers
craftbrewing.org.uk/index.php/joinaclub

ACKNOWLEDGEMENTS

First and foremost I have to thank Emma Wright for being there in whatever capacity I needed her to be whenever I needed it.

Chad and Jess McKinney and family, who made my first visit a joy, and of course for sharing their beer and recipes. Zak Avery for his advice on beer of the North and for putting up with some fairly consistent pestering. Louise Hanzlik for introducing me to the beers of East Anglia, for being someone I could turn to for advice and information and for being an old friend. Speaking of East Anglia, thanks too go to Tony, Angie and Albert Fletton for putting me up and Tony for fucking up the train.

Vince Crocker of Ashley Down Brewery for being the only brewer who gave me lunch and for sharing his simple, straightforward, yet amazing brewing knowledge. Sue Hayward from Waen Brewery for plying me with some of my favourite beer, and not forgetting her husband John and right-hand man Paul Reynolds for being excellent drinking partners at the GBBF. John and Garth for being very patient whilst I took out my notebook or recorded them every time we had any of numerous beers together over a year and a half. Indeed to all my drinking partners: Matt Ogbourne, Will Milner, Justin and Caroline Telkins, Frag Ginbey, Sarah Jean-Baptise, Amit Dutta, John Randal, Dan Cameron, Sam Riley, Arne Geshkie (via Skype, proving that 10,000 miles doesn't have to get in the way of sharing a pint). Sarah Eagle just for being a strong supportive force and of course occasional taxi driver. Max Drake for helping me through the Scottish Ale. Kevin Quigley for being sober in Leeds and Seb for not being.

Will, Billy Boy, Bolton deserves a special mention too as on more than one occasion he managed to get us both home safely despite our best efforts to have ourselves destroyed by alcohol. Chris Scullion from Independent Spirit of Bath for his contact and ceaseless commitment to ensure I have them!

To the poor family I accosted at Paddington Station during the Olympics who patiently gave me an interview despite my inability to stand, let alone talk. Iain Houten for his company whilst Megabus decided to turn a six-hour journey into an eight-hour ordeal by taking a shortcut. Francene for putting me up and making a great breakfast after the Kent Beer Festival and for listening to my and the other Andy's shite at 3am, and of course to the other Andy himself for being excellent company and for his joy of beer. Harry Man for being a great mate and drinking buddy too. James and Jo Wilson for their hospitality and for being drinking buddies, and Rich Owen the Barry Island Massive. Russell Bradshaw for Midlands beer knowledge. Brian and Natalie at the Tynllidiart Arms for being great company (don't worry, I kept the secret).

Leo and Max Townsend, Dina, Mark, Flossie and Lima at the Duchess of Totterdown Café for their support, coffee, salt beef bagels and general sanity.

All the members of LAB (London Amateur Brewers), especially Mike Carter and David Halse for their Porter recipes, Paul Spearman for inviting me down, Dan Percy Hughes for the Porter. Colin Stronge for his speedy responses, Scottish Beer knowledge and recipe. Tom Dobson for his recipes.

Shane O'Beirne and Gerry Condell from Bath Ales for allowing me to drink more than I should from their barrels on more than one occasion, and a big thanks to Shane for his recipes too. Box Steam Brewery for showing me around. Tom Raven at Ilkley for giving me an afternoon of good chat and info, despite the fact that I was desperately trying to keep from fainting from the night before's excess. Greg Pilney from Stroud Brewery for showing me about and imparting some knowledge. Robert the Malt Miller Neale and Greg from Brew UK for their recipes – cheers, fellas! Dave 'Orfy' Taylor and Adrian PDTNC Chapman and Tom Evans for their fantastic recipes. Ali Capper from British Hops, Durden Park Beer Circle, Martin from Elland Brewery and Graeme Coates for sending me rare hops.

Tom Spencer and Jane Peyton for tasting advice. Actually, TOM SPENCER, as you pestered me so much for a mention you'll get another one too for being a good drinking buddy. Cheers, Tom Spencer.

Obviously this book would never have got anywhere without my agent Araminta Whitley, but her assistant Sophie Hughes deserves a special mention too, as does my editor Susanna Wadeson, who gave me just the right amount of pressure and support as any good editor should and managed to do it without ever being anything but good-humoured. Speaking of good humour, thanks to my copy-editor Brenda Updegraff, who made the often painful copy-editing process as close to a dream as possible (well, she was good anyway). Thanks too to Claire Gatzen for her help with the festivals section, to Kate Samano and Bella Whittington and all. The wonderful art and design department who made the book shine: that's Sarah Whittaker, Phil Lord and Patrick Mulrey. Not forgetting either the jobs that are very important but rarely get a thanks due to the fact that they happen post-publication, so thanks to Katie Green, Suzanne Ripley and Alun Owen from publicity and sales.

Also a big thanks to anyone I have forgotten. I hope you are not sitting there seething that I've even thanked a fella I got a Megabus with and not your good self. Don't take it to heart. Remember the words of Nelson Mandela: 'It is better to lead from behind and to put others in front, especially when you celebrate victory when nice things occur.' And if that doesn't pacify you, just let me buy you a pint next time we meet!

Finally, I'd like to thank you – yes, you sitting there with a pint in your hand reading this book. Thanks to you I got to drink and make so much great beer, and got away with calling it work.

INDEX

Andy Hamilton lives with his family on top of a hill that overlooks Bristol. He runs brewing workshops at his local home-brew shop and the occasional tasting session, too. He is also a member of the British Guild of Beer Writers and CAMRA. He grows ingredients for beer in his vertical hilltop garden and forages for ingredients for various alcoholic drinks in and around the parks and waste grounds of Bristol.

Andy is often called upon to contribute to various TV and radio shows on subjects from survival and foraging to home-brewing and gardening. Highlights include telling Radio 2's Simon Mayo how to make the perfect elderflower champagne and nearly taking the *Autumnwatch* cast's teeth out with his toffee apples.

He is the author of the award-winning and bestselling foraging/home-brewing book *Booze for Free*, which has made him the biggest-selling home-brew author in the UK for 2011–2012. He regularly blogs about home-brewing, beer, foraging and gardening on his website, www.theotherandyhamilton.com.

When not tasting new and wonderful beers in pubs and at festivals around the country, Andy works as a trustee for Homestart Bristol, a charity that offers support for struggling families in Bristol and South Gloucestershire.